Race and Education
PRIMER

PETER LANG
New York • Washington, D.C./Baltimore • Bern
Frankfurt am Main • Berlin • Brussels • Vienna • Oxford

Aaron David Gresson III

Race and Education PRIMER

PETER LANG
New York • Washington, D.C./Baltimore • Bern
Frankfurt am Main • Berlin • Brussels • Vienna • Oxford

Library of Congress Cataloging-in-Publication Data

Gresson, Aaron David.
Race and education primer / Aaron David Gresson III.
p. cm.— (Peter Lang primers)
Includes bibliographical references and index.
1. African Americans—Education. 2. Minorities—Education—United States—History.
3. Discrimination in education—United States—History. I. Title.
LC2717.G74 371.829'96073—dc22 2008033859
ISBN 978-1-4331-0049-9 (hardcover)
ISBN 978-0-8204-8803-5 (paperback)

Bibliographic information published by **Die Deutsche Bibliothek**.
Die Deutsche Bibliothek lists this publication in the "Deutsche
Nationalbibliografie"; detailed bibliographic data is available
on the Internet at http://dnb.ddb.de/.

Cover design by Clear Point Designs

The paper in this book meets the guidelines for permanence and durability
of the Committee on Production Guidelines for Book Longevity
of the Council of Library Resources.

© 2008 Peter Lang Publishing, Inc., New York
29 Broadway, 18th floor, New York, NY 10006
www.peterlang.com

Printed in the United States of America

Acknowledgments

I owe a special thanks to several people who have made this primer possible. To Derrick Alridge for many constructive insights and clues to important resources; to Pat Fortson for her continuing support and love; and especially to Robert E. Haskell for his brotherly concern and critical comments over several drafts of this book. And to Joe Kincheloe and Shirley Steinberg, who continue to be loyal friends and inspirational colleagues. And my greatest thanks to the libraries and resources at The Pennsylvania State University and Notre Dame and Loyola Colleges in Baltimore.

Finally, I dedicate this volume to the memory of Rhett and Alegra Jones, two inspirational and beautiful souls; and to the memory of Asa Hilliard, princely warrior in the study and practice of "race and education."

Contents

CHAPTER ONE

Introduction

The Meanings of "Race and Education"

> . . . it is good for us to gain clarity, first, about the meaning of the topic race and education and then about the nature of the problem in education that is related to it.
>
> —*Asa Hilliard (2001, 12)*

In 1964, a young African American male transferred from the all Black Frederick Douglass High School in West Baltimore, Maryland, to Calvert Hall College High School in predominately White Towson, Maryland. One of three African Americans attending this 150-year-old preparatory academy of over one thousand students, he had been recruited to integrate the student body and help bring the Catholic Church of Baltimore into the Civil Rights Era (1954–1971).

His schooling had shifted from the **colonial education model** taught for generations at minority schools in the South, East, and North, to the private education model traditionally reserved for the sons of the privileged. At Calvert Hall, this youth gained the benefits of studying in the 300-year-old order of teaching brothers of St. John Baptiste de la Salle. He also got to learn about White

---

Colonial Education Model

Colonialism is essentially the subjugation of a people or group in order to exploit their resources, including labor. People living under colonialism exist for the pleasure and profit of the ruling elite. Thus, the American colonies existed for the British Empire.

people as students and learners. He saw smart and not so smart, industrious and lazy White males in the classroom; he ate lunch with sensitive and outgoing people as well as with shallow, selfish, and, sometimes, unkind youths such as those he had known at Frederick Douglass High School. He also related to a wide cast of White male teachers, remarkably diverse in their thinking, concerns, and characters. And, he overcame those agonizing thoughts of inferiority: that his brain was smaller than Whites'; that he spoke some alien tongue and would not be understood; and that he would shame or fail his "race."

I was the young man who attended both Frederick Douglass and Calvert Hall in the 1960s. This brief reflection on my own educational biography contains clues to the historical and contemporary importance of race and education in the United States. In particular, the existence of two distinct models of education—colonial and elite—points to the central or core **ideology** that traditionally fueled "race and education." This ideology says that humans differ *essentially* in their "nature," capabilities, and calling. From this view, some are superior to others and called to rule, exploit, and "take care of" others. Those who happen to be "inferior" must be submissive, content, and grateful to their "betters."

I belonged to the "racially inferior" group. Accordingly, when I began school in the 1950s, I had no great expectations with respect to high school graduation, college education, a career, owning a home and a car, and a long life. To be sure, there were minority families whose backgrounds did include visions of a "good education" and success. Nonetheless, most of us Blacks, especially in the South, lived in a segregated world.

I went to a segregated school. Although poorly funded in comparison to White schools in Virginia, I had good teachers and felt both well-nurtured and safe. Still, as a poor, African American male living in the pre-1960s South, my expectations out of life were shaped by segregation. Members of the African American community, especially my parents, were my models of the real and the possible.

My father, like most of the Black men in my neighborhood, labored in construction or some other physical work. My mother earned $18.75 a week plus carfare. For this, she cooked, cleaned, babysat, and whatever else was required of her by the White families for whom she worked. I was

---

Ideology

This is defined as set of ideas or beliefs that are accepted at face value. It is what guides a group or society's understanding and interpretation of a wide range of issues, events, circumstances, or relations. Ideologies are thus values that imply what people believe is right, correct, and even necessary.

destined for something more or less similar to them. This was my lived experience.

Fortunately, the 1960s changed the traditional meaning of race and education in dramatic ways. Through activities associated with the Civil Rights Movement and the so-called Radical Sixties, many important changes took place in race relations. These included government initiatives such as the "War on Poverty" (the **Civil Rights Act of 1964**), Head Start, and the recruitment of youngsters like me from poor minorities to elite schools such as Calvert Hall.

As a result of going to Calvert Hall, I discovered a vastly enlarged and different world than my parents knew. In this way, I have shared in the great **American Dream** of bettering myself through opportunities provided by my country and the support, inspiration, and guidance of my family and community. In this, I am truly one among many. And my relative success has seemingly undercut the implicit significance and strength of the ideology underpinning race and education. But my achievements have not been sufficiently replicated and surpassed by others traditionally defined as "racially" inferior (Fryer, 2006). Millions of minority students are failing to realize their potential and achieve high levels in our schools. This condition has given rise to a new concern in race and education.

The dominant concern in contemporary race and education is the so-called **Education Gap**. This achievement gap between certain minorities and the White majority has become *the* race and education challenge not only in the United States, but in other countries as well (Lloyd, Mete, & Grant, 2007; Lloyd, Grant, & Ritchie, 2008). Canada, England, Australia, and continental Europe are notable countries attempting to address the gap (Arora, 2005). The gap has been identified as part of what education scholar James Banks (1991) has identified as the "demographic imperative":

- An increasingly diverse student body;
- A mostly white teaching profession; and
- An education gap characterized by disparities in opportunities, resources, and achievement across class, language, cultural, and racial groups.

A clear understanding of the role of race in education is crucial to the attainment of respect for the place of diverse cultural backgrounds in preparing teachers to

---

Civil Rights Act of 1964

Signed into law on July 2, 1964 by President Lyndon Baines Johnson, this was the most important Civil Rights legislation passed since the nineteenth century. The Act prohibited discrimination in public places. Employment discrimination became illegal and integration of schools and other public places became possible.

The American Dream

A term coined in the 1930s by James Truslow Adams in *The Epic of America*, to indicate the belief or hope in the United States as a land where life could be better for everyone, where opportunities abounded and one could achieve according to one's efforts.

Education Gap

The differences in achievement test scores or outcomes among different groups are called an achievement or education gap.

more fully address the education gap in contemporary schooling. More precisely, "race" in education is intimately related to the education gap that generations of teachers, administrators, researchers, parents, and community leaders have been trying to eliminate. A clearer understanding of this relationship between "race" and "education" is a link in the effort to promote **cultural competence** among teachers and other human service professionals (Diller & Moule, 2005).

The Primer

Cultural Competence

This term refers to both a perspective and a range of remedial efforts aimed at preparing primarily nonminority teachers and human service personnel to adequately understand the diverse cultural backgrounds of their students or clients. The rationale is that more effective teaching or client advocacy can obtain where there is a respectful recognition of how different backgrounds, values, and norms impact choices, perspectives, and behaviors.

In the opening epigraph, the late Asa Hilliard, psychologist and African Studies professor at Georgia State University, suggests that the term "race and education" is related to a problem within education as an enterprise. It is this problematic relationship between "race" and "education" that sets the tone and organizes the material of this primer. But why do the student teacher and the teacher educator need to consider these issues in any systematic or sustained manner?

Peter S. Kowalczewski (1982, 151) has written that classroom teachers "are beset by contradictions and ambiguities at five levels in relation to race and education." According to him, these are:

- Terminology and research on performance and assessment of minority achievement;
- Teacher response to accusations of racism and discrimination;
- Inadequate administrative or central office guidance and support in addressing race-related issues in the classroom and school;
- Weak and conflictive guidance from the scholarly literature on working with race-related issues; and
- The unresolved dilemma of knowing what teachers' roles and abilities are regarding the combating of racism and discrimination both within school and society.

Two important ideas are contained in these five challenges for prospective and practicing teachers of children from diverse backgrounds. The first pertains to the conflictive research on minority abilities and learning, and the second to society's failure to provide consistent guidelines and support for teachers with respect to limiting the influence of racism on minority schooling.

The first of these challenges centers on the massive amount of material on minority student abilities and performance that does not yield a single, conclusive answer regarding what is causing minority underachievement or how teachers figure in it. This is a very real challenge for teachers because they can often find respected scholars saying two very different things about minority ability and performance.

For instance, in their very popular book *The Bell Curve: Intelligence and Class Structure in American Life,* Herrnstein and Murray (1995) essentially argued that intelligence test research proves that African Americans and some other minorities are inferior in critical ways. For them, the education gap is a matter of nature, rather than nurture. That is, innate abilities rather than environmental influences are presumed to account for the observed differences.

However, the edited volume *Measured Lies: The Bell Curve Examined* (Kincheloe, Steinberg and Gresson, 1996) argues against both much of the data used by Herrnstein and Murray, and their interpretations and recommendations. Instead, these scholars argue that **scientific racism** is at the root of repeated efforts to link minority ability and achievement to "racial inferiority." These disagreements among scholars about what is being measured in various assessments and how findings should be interpreted is what Kowalczewski sees as confusing and unhelpful to prospective and practicing teachers.

This type of scholarly debate contributes, moreover, to the other important issue implicit in Kowalczewski: differences in attitudes within society regarding minorities in general and their education in particular contribute to a range of **societal contradictions**. For instance, society has largely failed to provide the wide range of resources needed, especially in urban and rural areas, for children of color to graduate rather than drop out. It has been argued that dropouts are bored and disengaged and given cues or signals that they are not expected to achieve (Milliken, 2007). The dropout's failure to persist, from this view, is largely due to contradictions within society itself.

Teacher educators have also noted the role of societal contradictions in the education and preparation of contemporary teachers (Berlak & Berlak, 1983; Ginsburg, 1988). The general consensus among these scholars is that colleges of teacher education are not providing what is needed: stu-

---

Scientific Racism

This term refers historically to the effort to use scientific concepts and theories to prove biologically based differences in intelligence. Efforts to legitimize White supremacy and racism through science continue unto the present, even though it has been largely discredited by many.

Societal Contradictions

A contradiction is an idea, action, or position that goes in two opposite directions. A societal contradiction is one that is seen as emanating from society itself.

Criticality

We all understand. But to see beyond what we have inherited or been taught to believe calls for the ability to apply ideas that are often against what we initially learned. Ideas—including notions such as "gender," "race," and "class"—can help us to see things from a broader perspective. Also implied in this term is seeing ourselves as part of what we seek to understand, explain, or interpret.

Empowerment

This term has various definitions, but *power* is central to them, as is the idea that power relations can change and expand. The expansion of resources and assets to include minorities or those traditionally denied access to these is the overriding idea in our use of the term. To empower thus means to help people recognize their own abilities, potentials, and interests and the opportunities available for pursuing them.

dents that are cognitively sophisticated. That is, students ought to be capable of **critically** analyzing and assessing their position in the school in order to meet the various challenges to social justice and democratic education.

Today's student teachers need to know the relation between race and education in order to escape the quagmire identified by these teacher educators. They need to understand why the five conditions in race and education scholarship identified by Kowalczewski seem to continue unchanged. Only through attaining this critical understanding can they help **empower** both themselves and their students (Pinderhughes, 1983).

Toward this end, the chapters to follow will explore different aspects of race and education. They are not designed to be a comprehensive treatment of every idea, topic, or scholar associated with the field of race and education. Rather, they represent my own sense of the challenging issues that have contributed to the field as policy and practice. In Chapter Two, focus is on the ideas that have fueled the field. These include beliefs that progress and race were related—beliefs that the highest form of humanity were achieved and exemplified in White American Protestant males. In Chapter Three, the achievement gap between minorities and other groups is examined. In Chapter Four, focus is on the study of "race" in education. Chapter Five examines the relation of pedagogy and education. Chapter Six goes beyond traditional education and racial concepts to consider the influence of globalization.

In the remainder of this chapter, we consider several basic questions. What is race and education? What does it mean to you as a prospective teacher to be aware of the different aspects of race and education? What do you gain? What skills, attitudes, and understandings are involved in pursuing the deeper knowledge of the field?

What Is "Race and Education"?

What is race and education? One search engine on the Internet returned over 200,000,000 "hits" for this term. Eliminating 50 percent of these as repeats and "false hits," one is still nearly overwhelmed with the worldwide concern with this topic. But what is it? How does it relate to educators and prospective educators? One way of answering these questions is to note that many of the sites pertain to the education gap between Whites and Blacks—this is true

whether the country in question is the United States, England, Scotland, South Africa, Brazil, or Canada. In each and every instance, the concern is with understanding or reducing *inequality* due to "race" and/or racism.

But "race and education" is a much more comprehensive and complex notion than relations between "Black" and "White," or racism and inequality. The phrase "Race and Education" refers to the education and schooling that were created because of and influenced by ideas about certain minorities. One way of describing this topic or field of study is in terms of its major dimensions:

- perspective
- policy
- pedagogy

Race and education is, first and foremost, a *perspective*—a way of looking at the desired, actual relation of schooling to a given identity. That identity we call "race." As we shall see, the idea of "race" has changed over the centuries; today, the word is often used in parentheses to indicate that it has no one certain, unchanging meaning. I will speak further about this particular facet of the word when we take up race and education as a **discourse**. It is partly because there are competing perspectives of race that we have a discourse. But why are there different ways of looking at race and education?

As a perspective, race and education is rooted in racism (Coloma, 2006; Hilliard, 2001). This is the underpinning of race and education; it is the reason that society has to talk about "race" and its relation to education (Ladson-Billings, 1994). But to say this immediately raises challenges, counterstatements, or interpretations: For many, "race" is something real and concrete; it pertains to physical characteristics such as eye color, hair texture, and skin pigmentation. These observed differences have been associated with differences in intelligence and achievement, and with presumed differences in what one needs to know and what one can learn. For these observers, racism has nothing to do with race and education. They would tend to support, therefore, educational policies and practices that deemphasize things such as reducing racism in schooling.

The *policy* dimension of race and education refers largely to the school-related decisions that societies make based on "race." Educational policies typically evolve from social policies (Curti, 1966; House, 1999; Karier, 1967).

Discourse

This term refers to a broad-based discussion of a topic, but not just any spontaneous discussion. Rather, the discussion in question has been influenced by various groups and interests, and the positions have been largely established and passed along to others. Education as a discourse, generally, reflects a wide range of ideas, including the role of schooling in realizing *the American Dream*; the responsibility of parents and society to provide for the education of the young; and the vested interest big business has in educational excellence.

For instance, when societies segregate their minorities with regards to housing, employment, and entertainment, they often prefer segregated schooling as well (Orfield & McArdle, 2006). These policies rely on laws. The law has been a critical aspect of policy in race and education.

Laws have controlled race and ethnic relations in the United States over the centuries. How these laws have impacted what goes on in education is also an important part of race and education policy. Beginning with laws allowing and enforcing slavery and those permitting the taking of Native American and Mexican lands, American law has been at work in setting the terms of education for minorities.

Education and law have been both beneficial and detrimental to minorities:

> Education was widely regarded as essential for a democratic society, yet it was systematically denied to African Americans on the basis of race. In the northern states, laws excluded free blacks from schools even though they were obliged to pay taxes to support them. In the South, laws punished anyone who taught African Americans to read. Education was one of the key tools of race oppression before the Civil War, and a key tool for their "elevation" after the War. (http://www.clements.umich.edu/womened/Religion.html, taken on October 19, 2007)

A wide range of important court cases have impacted the historical relation of race to education in the United States. These include issues such as:

- Desegregation (*Brown v. Board of Education,* 1954)
- Language needs (*Cisneros v. Corpus Christi Independent School District,* 1972)
- Busing (*Milliken v. Bradley,* 1974; *Riddick v. School Board of Norfolk,* 1986)
- Bilingual education (*Lau v. Nichols,* 1974)
- School finance inequities (*San Antonio Independent School District v. Rodriguez,* 1973)
- Assessment and placement (*Larry P. v. Riles,* 1972)
- Zero-Tolerance and school discipline (*Seal v. Morgan,* 2000)

As *pedagogy,* race and education pertains to instruction beliefs, values, decisions, and practices. These may be consistent with or resistant to the dominant perspectives and policies. During the period after the Civil War, for instance, the North controlled minority schooling in

the South. Then, the colonial education model was introduced to teach former slaves and Native Americans basic work skills in domestic and manual areas; but courses of study that would prepare them for leadership roles in mainstream American society were not a part of the curriculum (Anderson, 1988; Watkins, 2001).

Pedagogy also pertains to the resistance of the messages contained in teaching practices that seem to devalue or track students into one direction or another. For instance, after the apparent failure of integrated education for many African American children in the 1970s, **Afrocentric education** was introduced to help African American youth overcome a variety of perceived flaws in traditional schooling (Dunn, 1993; Morris, 2003b). Chapter Five will explore further dimensions of race and pedagogy.

What is shared by these various dimensions of race and education is a concern with the relation of "race" to schooling. Because they cover such a wide range of issues and diverse beliefs and values, these dimensions and meanings of race and education have evolved into a large conversation. This larger conversation pertains, in part, to the five areas identified by Kowalczewski as well as others that arise from time to time about minorities in education. This larger conversation constitutes a discourse; it is important to grasp it as such because the prospective teacher has been placed at its center and often finds herself or himself unable to make sense of how to act in the best interest of self and student.

Afrocentric Education

An educational movement began in the 1970s as a reaction to the failure of traditional education to meet all the needs of African American students. The emphasis is on African cultural traditions that are relevant to African American youth's present environment and their past, including achievements associated with Africa prior to European contact and conquest.

The Discourse of "Race" and Education

As a discourse, race and education pertains to the ongoing debate about the place of race and racism in human affairs, especially in nations with a significant minority population (Arora, 2005; Gabe, 1991). Some have referred to this broad-based discourse as "race education" or, more recently, as "race"-education (Gabe, 1991). In the United States, this discourse began with concerns about the place of enslaved Africans and captured Native Americans and has been extended to many other minorities, including Latinos and Asian Americans.

As mentioned above, racism is the driving force behind the importance of race and education as discourse. This means that race and education is not a value-neutral topic, one that we may choose to either engage in or disregard as

we please. Knowledge has been defined by the times and conditions shaping the periods in which scholars, researchers, teachers, policymakers, and politicians were living and performing their crafts (we will take up this theme in Chapter Two).

Thus, race and education has many, often competing, perspectives. For example, some describe the "education gap" as a failure in the minority community; others locate the flaw within society's racial attitudes and practices. Yet others will point to the class and gender factors in society. Finally, some question whether or not there is a real gap at all. These competing views have their strengths, weaknesses, and different degrees of persuasiveness. You, ultimately, must decide these for yourself. This attitude of *criticalness* is important for future teachers and informed citizens. One way of gaining a critical attitude about race and education as a discourse is to see it in historical perspective. From this view, we might ask: How does the "beginning" of interest in race in education help us to understand the problem it has become? In Chapter Two we consider this beginning with the nineteenth-century interest in civilization and progress. As a prelude to this discussion, let us return to an earlier period, the eighteenth century.

"Origins" of Race in American Education

I have found it useful to think of race and education origins or beginnings in terms of two broad orientations toward what it means to be human and how learning has been related to it within the United States. One orientation emphasizes a belief in inherent and essential *racial* qualities that underlie culture, civilization, and accomplishment (Bederman, 1995). The other attends to the shifting, changing, and evolving nature of understanding, skills, and accomplishment among groups, especially those fighting against external oppression such as unfairness in housing, employment, and social services (Alridge, 1999; Dunn, 1993).

These different perspectives have evolved two competing educational thrusts or traditions with regards to race in education: *indoctrination* and *liberation* (Willie, 1978). The first thrust sees education and schooling as tools to control what is known or thought; the second employs education as a tool to insure freedom of thought and the pursuit of

full inclusion in the social and political life of the community and nation.

These two thrusts no doubt overlap at times, but they can also be seen as distinct trajectories. Moreover, they characterize all American education in a broad or general way; that is, women, the poor, as well as racial and ethnic minorities have had to struggle or compete to make schooling a liberating rather than oppressing experience (Allison, 1995). Nonetheless, through the thoughts of two very important men, Thomas Jefferson and Frederick Douglass, we gain a sense of how these two motives have become central to the topic of "race and education." In their reflections on education, moreover, we can see the beginnings of the public discourse of race and education as perspective, policy, and practice.

Thomas Jefferson on Slave Education

In the early days of the new nation, after he had served as governor of Virginia, Thomas Jefferson wrote his famous reflection *Notes on the State of Virginia*. This was a long, detailed account of various issues facing the new nation. Even though it was to continue for nearly a century after nationhood, slavery's moral and political limitations had been raised by some. And forward-looking men such as Jefferson had put their minds to imagining the future (Takaki, 2000). It was within this context that Jefferson considered the question of the slave as future American citizen:

> It will probably be asked, Why not retain and incorporate the blacks into the state, and thus save the expense of supplying, by importation of white settlers, the vacancies they will leave? Deep-rooted prejudices entertained by the whites; ten thousand recollections, by the blacks, of the injuries they have sustained; new provocations; the real distinctions which nature has made; and many other circumstances, will divide us into parties, and produce convulsions, which will probably never end but in the extermination of the one or the other race. (Kurland & Lerner, 1987, 534)

Jefferson offers a strongly felt sobering reflection on what enslavement of Africans and racism meant for the future of race relations in the new nation. But why was Jefferson so pessimistic about the possibilities of change? To be sure, race relations continue to be tense and difficult in the United States. Still, much important advancement,

including integration, has come about since the eighteenth century. The source of Jefferson's pessimism is provided in a further observation he made:

> Comparing them [enslaved Africans] by their faculties of memory, reason, and imagination, it appears to me that in memory they are equal to the whites; in reason much inferior, as I think one could scarcely be found capable of tracing and comprehending the investigations of Euclid; and that in imagination they are dull, tasteless, and anomalous. It would be unfair to follow them to Africa for this investigation. (Kurland & Lerner, 1987, 536)

In this passage, Jefferson captures the motive or "origin" for later policies and practices with respect to schooling and education on the basis of "race." This "origin" or "foundation" for relating to the African as human and learner had two dimensions. First, there was the belief or assumption that the important achievements of mankind were due to Whites and, perhaps, Asians. Second, there was a refusal to recognize that Africans and Native Americans had a world, a life before their enslavement that merited attention.

The orientation toward race and education reflected in Jefferson's words sees an essential, unchanging, and hostile relation between peoples defined as races. This view assumed that the cultures and traditions established by peoples from Europe and Asia to be superior to those from Africa. Moreover, even where slavery was not seen as a necessary consequence of this superiority-inferiority among cultures, it was felt that the apparent *differences* precluded equitable, fair, just, and harmonious relations. Much of the development of group relations in the United States seems to support this assessment as many Whites have systematically devalued and assigned various groups according to perceived differences (Slotkin, 1973).

But this is not the full story of White attitudes and actions toward non-Whites. Benign or humanistic actions by Whites have, in fact, formed a crucial dimension of the other orientation with respect to race and education. Minorities struggling against inferior schooling and other social inequalities have always had their White supporters (Banks, 2002). But, contrary to a widespread misperception, minorities, especially African Americans, have assumed a leadership role in their own education. This self-help has constituted an alternative orientation toward

race and education (Williams, 2005). Frederick Douglass was one of the early leaders in this alternative orientation toward race and education.

Frederick Douglass on Race and Liberation

In his autobiography, *Narrative of the Life of Frederick Douglass,* Douglass (1845, 14) describes his "awakening" to the relation between race and education that characterized the enslaved African's life:

> Very soon after I went to live with Mr. and Mrs. Auld, she very kindly commenced to teach me the A, B, C. After I had learned this, she assisted me in learning to spell words of three or four letters. Just at this point of my progress, Mr. Auld found out what was going on, and at once forbade Mrs. Auld to instruct me further, telling her, among other things, that it was unlawful, as well as unsafe, to teach a slave to read. To use his own words, further, he said, "If you give a nigger an inch, he will take an ell. A nigger should know nothing but to obey his master—to do as he is told to do. Learning would spoil the best nigger in the world. Now," said he, "if you teach that nigger (speaking of myself) how to read, there would be no keeping him. It would forever unfit him to be a slave. He would at once become unmanageable, and of no value to his master. As to himself, it could do him no good, but a great deal of harm. It would make him discontented and unhappy."

One of the great contradictions in American race relations is the declaration of "Black inferiority" and the insistence that no White person teaches or otherwise aids African American learning. One of the enduring lessons for minorities is this contradiction. Douglass's *Narrative* stands as a classic statement of the refusal to be contained by the "peculiar institution"—slavery. His documentation of the horrors of slavery, however, is only one aspect of the fascinating stories he shares. Equally compelling and certainly more instructive are his insights on freedom and the central place of learning in the attainment of the attitudes and habits necessary for the liberation of oneself and others.

In his own words, Douglass (1845, 31) mirrors the attitude shared by many generations of minorities trying to make their way in the ambivalent America Jefferson described in his reflections:

> These words sank deep into my heart, stirred up sentiments within that lay slumbering, and called into existence an entirely new train of thought. It was a new and special

revelation, explaining dark and mysterious things, with which my youthful understanding had struggled, but struggled in vain. I now understood what had been to me a most perplexing difficulty—to wit, the white man's power to enslave the black man. It was a grand achievement, and I prized it highly. From that moment, I understood the pathway from slavery to freedom. It was just what I wanted, and I got it at a time when I the least expected it.

Here, Douglass makes several important observations. First, he recognized that there were Whites who were helpful and hurtful to him and his interests. Second, he learned that White society had certain fundamental group interests that might compromise their better intentions such as treating slaves kindly or teaching them to read. Finally, and most important for generations of minorities seeking to be full citizens, he recognized education as the road to liberation.

Douglass influenced generations of African Americans through his own liberation through education, and his contribution to the ongoing saga of *racial uplift*—the belief and insistence by both Blacks and Whites that African Americans must take the lead in changing their racial plight. In addition, Douglass, like Jefferson, addresses certain issues that have characterized discussions of, and actions on, the relation between race and education in the United States. At the heart of their discussions or perspectives on race and education is the concern regarding the construction of "essence" and "possibility."

Thomas Jefferson illustrated the dominant group's construction of the "essence"—the important, unchanging, and defining qualities—of the enslaved Africans. This essence was one of inferiority to the White man. On the other hand, Frederick Douglass reflected on "possibility"—the potential to learn the A, B, and C's; the need, drive, and determination to reject enslavement. Through his rejection of the construction of "Blackness" as an essence, Douglass exposes and explodes the accepted master-slave, superior-inferior constructions. This threat is seen when the wife tries to teach Douglass: her husband says don't do it. He explains the pragmatic reason: the chosen, forced role for the slave as free laborer will be undermined. He also cites the operating structural barriers—the laws against teaching slaves to read, their systematic exclusion from other "humanizing" or "equalizing" experiences. These laws

Student Teachers and the Study
of Race and Education

Some years back, one of my White male students began his narrative essay on race and education with the following: "Every Monday and Wednesday I come here to learn about what an asshole I have been throughout history" (Gresson, 2004, 2). Many diversity educators report a corollary experience: pain and resistance by students to be confronted with ideas, beliefs, or even "truths" they don't or can't see as "truth" or as "relevant" to their lived experience (Alridge, 2003). Perhaps one reason why many students experience pain and turn away from looking fully in the face of the complexities of race is society's modeling of this attitude.

Today, it has become increasingly more favorable and preferable to say there is no real race issue—this is as true in the minority society as in the dominant society (Carr & Klassen, 1997; Gresson, 2004; Thomas, 2000). In the face of this societal denial, it is reasonable to feel overwhelmed by negativity of information about the present and its relation to the past when discussing inequality in the United States. But it is important to find ways of confronting the issues. This can be done without undue guilt, shame, or despair. In the following chapters, you will be introduced to a wide range of material on the relation among race, education, and life choices and chances in the United States. The material may or may not move you toward a clear, clean conclusion regarding the reasons that race has played such an important role in American society, or why some of the things attributed to "race effects" are persuasive or otherwise to you. That is, you may not see why most African Americans can't seem to "achieve like Asians in school," or what makes "minorities so difficult to get through to about the importance of schooling, behaving in class, and not being violent."

I believe that a crucial task for education in general and teacher education in particular is making clearer the relation between "personal troubles" and "public issues" (Lewin, 1948; Mills, 1959). Kurt Lewin, a psychologist and Jewish émigré to the United States from Europe, used these terms to describe the plight of Jewish families in the early twentieth century as they tried to assimilate to a Gentile and often anti-Semitic society. Lewin (1948) found that Jewish parents often tried to train their children for acceptance by people who held prejudiced beliefs and practiced

discrimination toward them. He said that they were trying to treat a "social issue," something due to the values, beliefs, institutions, and practices of society, as "personal troubles" that could be solved by being nicer, "more like Gentiles," or by making other changes in Jews themselves. But, he argued, these "social issues" required group-level solutions.

The sociologist C. Wright Mills expanded on the scope of these social psychological notions introduced by Lewin. He wrote in *The Sociological Imagination,* "When, in a city of 100,000, only one man is unemployed, that is his personal trouble, and for its relief we properly look to the character of the man, his skills, and his immediate opportunities. But when in a nation of 50 million employees, 15 million men are unemployed, that is an issue, and we may not hope to find its solution within the range of opportunities open to any one individual" (1959, 9).

By thinking about the topic of race and education as interplay of personal troubles and public issues, we can see that the various positions taken by individuals and groups reflect different experiences with schooling, education, the workplace, and social life in general. What *The Sociological Imagination* asks of you is to look for the ways that "personal troubles"—individually experienced pain and difficulties—conceal larger, broader societal forces. This approach will also invite and even press you to consider what ways your own ideas, concepts, and presuppositions have been inherited or adopted without much reflection on their validity beyond your own immediate experience. You will be asked to consider your own lived experience as valuable and valid, but no more so than that for others very different from you. These expectations are not without costs or pain; but they carry, I believe, benefits worth the sacrifice. Willem L. Wardekker's (1995, 1) reflection is pertinent here:

> In the course of his or her development, each individual learns to handle the facts of change and contradiction in a certain way: either negating them or valuing them negatively, or understanding them as opportunities for development and using them in a positive way. Thus, people learn to manage their own development. Education can play a crucial part here by stimulating certain ways of handling contradictions.

Literacy

The ability to read and write is the base meaning. But increasingly the term has been understood as the information shared by a given group regarding how to do something or survive within one's context. Thus, we speak of "streetwise" to indicate that knowledge and skills vary and are valuable depending on what is needed.

The ability to understand the ins and outs of one's society and culture is called **literacy**. Reading and writing are often what we think of when referring to literacy. But it is more: all people have specific understandings of the way things work according to their own lived experiences. Thus, there are competing literacies (Reder & Wikelund, 1993; Snavely & Cooper, 1997). Education is a two-edged sword in this regard: it can both hinder and help learning and enlightenment. If education or schooling is broad, inclusive, and permitted to enlarge and include expanding and evolving realities, it can be a force of personal and collective growth. If it tends toward a narrow, distorted, or "one size fits all" attitudes, it can conceal the contradictions that must be tackled in life (Becker, 1971).

In race and education, there are themes and issues that are addressed and those that are not. Prospective teachers must grapple with the social, historical, cultural, and political significance of knowledge—information, curricula, texts, media—they encounter on the issue of minorities and their schooling. The following chapters introduce you to some of these themes and issues.

GLOSSARY

Afrocentric Education: An educational movement began in the 1970s as a reaction to the failure of traditional education to meet all the needs of African American students. The emphasis is on African cultural traditions that are relevant to African American youth's present environment and their past, including achievements associated with Africa prior to European contact and conquest. There are various versions or perspectives on this general emphasis on Africa, including some that define the movement as misguided and ineffectual.

The American Dream: A term coined in the 1930s by James Truslow Adams in *The Epic of America,* to indicate the belief or hope in the United States as a land where life could be better for everyone, where opportunities abounded and one could achieve according to one's efforts.

Brown v. Board of Education, 1954: In 1954, the U.S. Supreme Court struck down *Plessey v. Ferguson (1896)* by declaring that separate was not equal, thus ending official or legalized segregation in public affairs such as housing, transportation, and schooling. The case itself pertained to segregated schooling in Topeka, Kansas, and the effort of the African American

Brown family to receive a quality education for their children.

Civil Rights Act of 1964: Signed into law on July 2, 1964 by President Lyndon Baines Johnson, this was the most important Civil Rights legislation passed since the nineteenth century. The Act prohibited discrimination in public places. Employment discrimination became illegal and integration of schools and other public places became possible.

Colonial Education Model: Colonialism is essentially the subjugation of a people or group in order to exploit their resources, including labor. People living under colonialism exist for the pleasure and profit of the ruling elite. Thus, the American colonies existed for the British Empire. Colonial education pertained to the model of education America deemed appropriate for the former slaves and all other minorities. It emphasized manual labor as a supportive role and sought to reinforce the idea of inferiority and second-class citizenship. The development of practical skills, in this instance, are not seen as tools aimed at increasing one's mental acumen or moving one beyond the caste or class circumstances one is in. For African Americans, in particular, this meant an emphasis on practical skills that went with an impoverished rural life style.

Criticality: We all understand. But to see beyond what we have inherited or been taught to believe calls for the ability to apply ideas that are often against what we initially learned. Ideas—including notions such as "gender," "race," and "class"—can help us to see things from a broader perspective. Also implied in this term is seeing ourselves as part of what we seek to understand, explain, or interpret.

Cultural Competence: This term refers to both a perspective and a range of remedial efforts aimed at preparing primarily nonminority teachers and human service personnel to adequately understand the diverse cultural backgrounds of their students or clients. The rationale is that more effective teaching or client advocacy can obtain where there is a respectful recognition of how different backgrounds, values, and norms impact choices, perspectives, and behaviors.

Dialectical: "Dialectics" has many definitions that broadly refer to the idea of contradiction. In much educational and social science literature, it pertains to the fact that most ideas or actions contain a challenging or subversive [see definition of subversive below] quality. I like to use the illustration of how Judaism, the belief in one God, derived from Hellenic, polytheistic religious systems; Catholicism evolved from Judaism;

and Protestantism was born when a Catholic monk, Martin Luther, challenged corruption in the Catholic Church. In each case, a contradiction or flaw in thinking or practice led to resistance, revision, or renewal.

Discourse: This term refers to a broad-based discussion of a topic, but not just any spontaneous discussion. Rather, the discussion in question has been influenced by various groups and interests, and the positions have been largely established and passed along to others. Education as a discourse, generally, reflects a wide range of ideas, including the role of schooling in realizing **the American Dream**; the responsibility of parents and society to provide for the education of the young; and the vested interest big business has in educational excellence.

As discourse pertains to education and race, it includes the various discussions of where "race" and "education" fit into daily life, how we understand different issues such as what is fair treatment of different groups, what they are capable of achieving, and what they merit in terms of society's understanding and support. By naming "race and education" as a discourse, we are also tying it to the idea of "ideology." This decision is intended to draw attention to the way that talking, debating, and writing about this topic help to reproduce it or keep it alive in the minds and hearts of the citizens. It is important to understand that a discourse starts at specific times and in particular places. Thus, Thomas Jefferson's and Frederick Douglass's lives and reflections are identified as specific points or places where discourse of race and education are given life or vitality. The position taken by Jefferson persists: the discourse of Black Inferiority. This discourse continues, although its form has changed.

Education Gap: The differences in achievement test scores or outcomes among different groups are called an achievement or education gap.

Empowerment: This term has various definitions, but *power* is central to them, as is the idea that power relations can change and expand. The expansion of resources and assets to include minorities or those traditionally denied access to these is the overriding idea in our use of the term. To empower thus means to help people recognize their own abilities, potentials, and interests and the opportunities available for pursuing them.

Ideology: This is defined as set of ideas or beliefs that are accepted at face value. It is what guides a group or society's under-

standing and interpretation of a wide range of issues, events, circumstances, or relations. Ideologies are thus values that imply what people believe is right, correct, and even necessary. Ideas of "chosen people" and "manifest destiny" are aspects of this ideology. The former concept derives from the biblical allusion to Jews as the chosen people of God; the latter concept was a mid-nineteenth century belief that the United States was destined, because it was chosen, to expand to the Pacific Ocean.

Literacy: The ability to read and write is the base meaning. But increasingly the term has been understood as the information shared by a given group regarding how to do something or survive within one's context. Thus, we speak of "streetwise" to indicate that knowledge and skills vary and are valuable depending on what is needed.

Scientific Racism: This term refers historically to the effort to use scientific concepts and theories to prove biologically based differences in intelligence. Efforts to legitimize White supremacy and racism through science continue unto the present, even though it has been largely discredited by many.

Societal Contradictions: A contradiction is an idea, action, or position that goes in two opposite directions. A societal contradiction is one that is seen as emanating from society itself. For instance, the idea that a man ought to provide for his family may be contradicted if the given society prevents a large percent of the males from gainful employment. Education is also the site for societal contradictions when teachers are prevented from having the power and resources needed to achieve the teaching outcomes demanded by society.

Subversive: This term refers to activities aimed as undermining or overthrowing the established institution or authority. Any form of opposition may be considered subversive if it challenges the status quo or what has been set up as the ideal. Clearly, many important and progressive actions have been considered subversive at the time of their inception, including the abolition of slavery and the winning of the vote by women.

CHAPTER TWO

"Race" and Education

Origins, Beliefs, and Themes

The real problem is hegemony, not "race"!

—*Asa Hilliard (2001,1)*

Hegemony

Simply put, "hegemony" pertains to predominating influence or control exercised by some over others. Gramsci conceived the term to refer to the mechanisms or strategies of the dominant class to persuade subordinates to go along with their plans, for example, the way wealthy people get poor people to agree with them and vote for a leader who seems to belong to the dominant group.

Now that we have some idea of the meanings of "race and education," we can take on the next part of *the problem.* That problem, as suggested by Asa Hilliard, is **hegemony.** We already have some hint of what this term means to the prospective teacher from Chapter One, where Peter S. Kowalczewski pointed out that the teacher is handicapped when addressing "race and education" by a society that has not resolved what it wants to do about social injustice. Why is it so hard for everyone in the United States to get an excellent education? Why has education always been something both attractive and problematic for those at the margins of society? Why must there be a special law aimed at leaving no child behind?

For the student of race and education there is a need to understand the backdrop to questions such as the above. As Diane Ravitch (2000, 14) writes in *Left Back: A Century of Failed School Reforms:* "We cannot understand where we are and where we are heading without knowing where

we have been. We live now with decisions and policies that were made long ago."

In this chapter, we consider some of the early and seemingly eternal themes and tensions pertaining to race and education. These themes and beliefs have a context that must also be understood. Thus, we will begin by asking how scholarship on race and education emerged to give support and challenge to these recurring beliefs (Banks, 2002).

Guiding Concerns and "Race" Scholarship

America was and is a nation of immigrants and diverse, heterogeneous peoples (Takaki, 2000). The leaders felt it imperative to find acceptable but unequal positions in society for its various minorities. William H. Watkins (2001, 80) describes the race and education position taken by the influential Columbia University sociologist Franklin K. Giddings in these terms: "As ideologist and social engineer, Giddings offered a blueprint for the social order. America needed planned racial segregation alongside citizen participation and economic development. The successful joining of hierarchy to democracy would be America's destiny." Taking this position has been especially crucial to the kinds of information, facts, and solutions to problems that those in charge have pursued. This has been done, most often, while maintaining that the betterment of society is the goal, and the advancement of "civilization."

Modernity, Positivism, and Race Relations

In her book *Manliness and Civilization,* Gail Bederman (1995, 25) offers a powerful statement on the meaning of "civilization" to the emerging American nation: "By about 1890, the discourse of civilization had taken on a very specific set of meanings which revolved around three factors: race, gender, and millennial assumptions about human evolutionary progress." For post-1890 Americans, civilization meant the forward movement of humanity toward improvement in all areas of life.

Elsewhere, Bederman (1995, 27) wrote: "Scientific theories corroborated this belief that racial difference, civilization, and manliness all advanced together. Biologists believed that as human races slowly ascended the evolutionary ladder, men and women evolved increasingly

differentiated lives and natures. The most advanced races were ones that had evolved the most perfect manliness and womanliness."

Civilization was an ideology, a belief that saw some men as superior to others and called to develop the world community even as they exploited others. This belief was, in part, related to the idea of **modernity**. Modernity has been seen as a hope and faith in the ability to progress, to use reason and science to make a better world. The achievements of science, especially improvements in the material conditions of certain nations, were seen as a rationale for continued rational exploitation of the earth's natural and human resources. Edwin Lemert (1999, 22) observed in this regard: "For one thing, the modern world brought destruction. Throughout the century, lands were taken to build the railroads that fueled the factory system. In America native civilizations were destroyed in the name of progress."

One important idea accompanying modernity was the belief in the ability to achieve a unified and uniform truth. Because of this orientation toward knowledge and truth, differences—skin color, religions, diverse ideas and traditions—were devalued. The goal was to make everyone as much like the "ideal" American as possible. This was, of course, more feasible with some than others. Assimilation versus **pluralism**—one of the enduring themes in race and ethnic relations—is directly linked to this orientation. The ongoing conversation about a **core curriculum** goes back to the question of what is worth knowing and who gets to determine this.

What appears in the course of study/curriculum or, more recently, in the emphasis on diversity in the curriculum across the educational spectrum (K-12, postsecondary) is directly related to the ongoing resistance shown by various groups of Americans to being forced to accept a particular version of truth and knowledge. Americans, whose values, including versions of past accomplishments and achievements, are represented in the dominant social conversation, may not see a need for alternative realities or positions. Recall how Thomas Jefferson's and other slave owners' understanding of slavery differed from that of Frederick Douglass. They did not see the world from the slave's perspective.

The resistance of generations of minorities and their advocates to Eurocentric versions of reality—that is,

Modernity

A belief or value system that proceeds from the idea that the world moves forward toward progressive perfection or improvement through the application of reason, logic, and the observation and measurement of things that can be manipulated.

Pluralism

This term refers to the many different ideas that tend to focus around the presence and relative equality of a multitude of perspectives, positions, values, and cultures. Within education, recognition that we have not achieved a true "melting pot" status has led to the rise of multicultural education and diversity-focused curricula and the inclusion of educators from different groups.

Core Curriculum

This term refers to the information, knowledge, and skills necessary for successful high school completion. Over the years, this body of information and abilities has changed as society and various states have adjusted their goals to achieve a particular end, say, more mathematicians and scientists to compete with Russia during the race to reach the moon.

Eurocentrism

The term means literally Europe-centered. Because of Europe's historical domination of much of the known world at one time or another, the term has achieved a specifically negative value for those countries or people who were once colonies of Europe. Within educational contexts, the term pertains to the production of knowledge favoring things European over those favoring indigenous or local peoples.

Eurocentrism—has partly contributed to the rise in the 1970s of multiculturalism. Multiculturalism as the pursuit of equal attention to the cultural traditions of everyone has produced several challenges, especially among those committed to the traditional version of truth. The spirit of this challenge to alternative versions of truth and the social good is seen in a reflection by former Supreme Court judge nominee Robert Bork. Bork (1996, 311) argues in his *Slouching towards Gomorrah: Modern Liberalism and American Decline:*

> Multiculturalism is a lie, or rather a series of lies: the lie that European-American culture is uniquely oppressive; the lie that culture has been formed to preserve the dominance of heterosexual White males; and the lie that other cultures are equal to the culture of the West. What needs to be said is that no other culture in the history of the World has offered the individual as much freedom, as much opportunity to advance; no other culture has permitted homosexuals, non-Whites, and women to play ever-increasing roles in the economy…. What needs to be said is that American culture is Eurocentric, and it must remain Eurocentric or collapse into meaninglessness.

Bork and many who see the world from his perspective have argued that reason and science are largely Western creations that have found their highest form or perfection in Anglo-Americans. While this form of group chauvinism is not the sole province of any one group, among Europeans this attitude has contributed to the rise of social science as a means of furthering the march toward the improvement of the species.

Thomas G. Dyer (1980, 143) provides an especially telling example of the fusion of social science thinking and the development of the nation in his study *Theodore Roosevelt and the Idea of Race:*

Race Suicide

Simply put, race suicide is a collective term for all those practices such as birth control and mixed mating that diminish the numbers of a given racial grouping.

> Few social science theories gripped the Western imagination more completely at the turn of the century than the idea of **race suicide**. In enthusiastic discussions on both sides of the Atlantic among laymen as well as scholars the concept combined much viable thought from anthropology, sociology, history, and other disciplines and stressed the notion that entire "races" of men faced extinction through failure to fulfill the reproductive function. Foremost among the true believers in this doctrine stood the American race theorist, amateur sociologist, and politician Theodore Roosevelt. . . .

Theodore Roosevelt was the nation's twenty-sixth president. He was an energetic, dynamic man, the leader of the famed Rough Riders who invaded Cuba in 1898 during the Spanish American War. He was also concerned with *eugenics*—selective breeding of humans. As part of the early twentieth-century eugenics movement, several *contextualizing* events—Asian immigration, declining birth rate among Whites, racial and ethnic intermarriage—stimulated fears of race suicide.

Academics, notably Edward Ross, had a major role in fueling this race anxiety. The term "race suicide" was coined by Ross in 1900. Since the 1860s, antagonism had been growing toward both the Chinese and the Japanese, at home and abroad. Japanese immigration stimulated an upsurge in **nativism.** Ross believed that Chinese and Japanese immigration lowered American character as defined by the "high American standard of living." Because they couldn't or wouldn't assimilate, these groups represented a threat. Americans responded by intensifying the "we/they" sentiment characterizing nativism.

The nativist impulse went deeper. Many feared that things were falling apart: African Americans were moving northward from the South to newly evolving urban centers such as Chicago to take their place alongside the new immigrants coming from various parts of southern Europe (Baldwin, 2005; Banks, 1995). There was yet another side to this anxiety—the need to manage a *contradiction:* prosperity for those *racialized* as "White" and poverty for those deemed as "colored." This tension continues today because of **capitalism,** as more and more White Americans share the economic fears traditionally associated with certain racial minorities.

Capitalism has long been a source of enduring tension—one that fuels the current rhetoric on "the disappearing middle-class." Certain jobs were for men, others for women (Gonäs & Karlsson, 2006; Wallerstein, 1987). Some were for different White ethnics: Anglos could be bankers and lawyers; Irishmen could be soldiers and policemen; and Italians could be bakers, restaurateurs, or laborers (Roediger, 1999). Still other jobs were for the minorities: maids, fieldworkers, mailmen, and preachers.

Capitalism promoted public education to both stabilize social relations and produce workers for the factories. Public education both stabilized and destabilized the status

---

Nativism

The term refers to attitudes and policies that favor native born Americans over immigrants. First emphasized in the late nineteenth century when earlier groups of American immigrants considered themselves "natives" and newer immigrant groups as foreigners.

Capitalism

This is an economic system defined by two concepts: individual rights and private property. Goods are privately produced and owned. The critical point here is that human beings have been considered private property under slavery and even since then, workers' lives are significantly influenced by the processes governing private enterprise.

quo (Counts, 1927; Ellwood, 1927). Schools could both help people to learn their place in society and help them to be socially mobile (Pinar & Bowers, 1992). Thus, the forward movement associated with progress was rife with tension, including the saving of "civilization" from being overwhelmed by various minorities and the competition they constituted for those already identified as "American."

Other academics, including William James and G. Stanley Hall, shared the overall concern for saving "civilization" as exemplified in upper-class, White Protestant males. During this period, moreover, fears of the "**feminization of culture**" (Douglas, 1978/1988) expressed itself as part of this conservative moment. In this instance, fears that women and effeminate men had gained control of the Protestant Church in America led to the so-called Muscular Christianity Movement (Putney, 2001). Both the Boy Scouts of America and the Young Men's Christian Association were begun, in part, to reclaim or reaffirm White male dominance. The broader social goal—again in the service of "civilization"—was to reverse the rise of *sentiment* (emotion) over *reason* (logic), a rise some felt had taken place (Bederman, 1995).

These cultural and social changes in the early twentieth century had implications for race in education. In particular, social studies and science curricula were more conscientiously *politicized* (Apple, 1990; Giroux, 1981). The restriction of females from teaching male students, for instance, was among the ideas that gained prominence among some educators at this time. Reflecting this attitude, G. Stanley Hall (1901, 660) wrote: "The progressive feminization of the high school is perhaps also seen in the standardization of Tennyson's 'Princess,' [a nineteenth-century English poem] much of which the standard boy of the middle teens regards as saccharinity [*sic*] ineffable."

Academic involvement in the shaping of the nation was a natural outgrowth of the faith in reason and science as sources of human betterment. Theoretical frameworks were a way of making sense out of the world, of studying, understanding, and predicting the relations among various elements, events, and phenomena. Hall and other social and behavioral scientists were anxious to bring clarity to our views on the human condition and to foster better relations. These sentiments and incursions went beyond the experimental laboratory, however, to the larger social

Feminization of Culture
The term refers to the belief that women are sentimental and men are rational; and when women try to influence religion and public affairs, they infuse sentiment over reason into issues that require rational responses.

Social Theory
Scholarly derived explanations, assumptions, and beliefs that attempt to interpret and forecast about people in groups.

arena. It was here that **social theory** arrived. Historian Davarian Baldwin (2005, 313), reflecting on the origins of American sociology at the University of Chicago in the 1890s, observed, "The racial contacts and conflicts between White residents and African American migrants, but also non-White and White immigrants, profoundly shaped the U.S. social sciences."

Today, the social sciences concern themselves with much broader matters than "race." Still, "race" continues to be a way for Americans to understand so much about themselves as groups, citizens, "good" and "bad." Issues such as school violence and zero-tolerance policies, for instance, are very much about "race." At the beginning of the twentieth century, "race" also held a special place in the nation's imagination. Again, Baldwin (2005, 318) comments: "The most common organizing principle for understanding social differences was 'race.' At this time, any group with a specific ancestry and geographical origin in common, such as Irish, Polish, or Jewish, was referred to as a 'race.'"

The emphasis on "race" in scholarship aimed at explaining social inequality and race relations largely followed the dominant race ideology. In the early days of the social sciences, notably sociology, there was little attempt to explain the problems between groups in terms of economics or politics, or simply in terms of the desire of some to dominate others. Rather, *nature* was called upon to explain race relations. And like the idea that civilization was naturally given to the "White race" because it was genetically superior, the idea that social science could chart a road toward cultural cohesion was one of the guiding concerns. Social science was chosen to achieve this cohesion by fiting the various groups together in a hierarchical arrangement (Watkins, 2001).

Social Theory, Critical Theory, and the Disciplines

When Thomas Jefferson made his statement (see Chapter One) about the limitations of enslaved Africans' intelligence and achievements, he said that one ought not to follow them back to Africa to see what they had produced or how they lived. He and the other slave owners did not want to talk or think about the cultures and traditions Africans had in place at the time of their enslavement. By neglecting unpleasant or contradictory information, Jefferson exposed an important feature of race and educa-

tion as a scholarly initiative: *methods of creating, collecting, and interpreting knowledge have often been carried out in a manner aimed at reinforcing the status quo or the preferred position* (McKee, 1993; Mills, 1959).

The earliest theorizing on race and education seemed to take place within the spirit of Thomas Jefferson. Although some people rejected the inferiority of Native Americans and enslaved Africans, the dominant perspective accepted the superiority of some groups over others (Bederman, 1995; Slotkin, 1973). Because of a faith in the **scientific method**, the inability of biology to explain so many things about race relations did not prevent the continued effort to explain things "racial" in a scientific manner. Enter sociology.

John Rex (1994, 647) recently wrote: "The problem of race was passed from biology to sociology, and sociologists were called upon precisely to understand the real nature of the groups and intergroup processes which were misleadingly called 'racial.'" Because biology could not offer significant evidence for the alleged or constructed "racial" basis for differences among human groupings, the task fell to sociology and other social-behavioral sciences. Why did groups create different cultures? Why were some more aggressive or assertive, and others more malleable and amenable to control? Why did many identified as "White" or "superior" despise those who were darker and more "primitive"?

These questions dealt with what has continued to be a mainstay of race relations—the nature-nurture debate over human diversity formation. Michael Banton (2003, 492–493) noted regarding this biology-culture tension:

> In the United States ethnic and racial studies.... started as a criticism of the belief that the relations between African Americans and Whites were best explained as the outcome of biological differences. Research demonstrated that racial prejudice was learned rather than inherited; that popular conceptions were molded by stereotypes; that individuals desired to keep members of different groups at varying degrees of distance from them.

These are important ideas. First, they remind us that knowledge is a complex affair. It is not self-evident much of the time: it must be both produced and interpreted. This leads us to another point: scholarship on race and education is both highly contested and often neutralized in terms

---

scientific method

Observation and measurement are the twin pillars of this approach to knowledge production and validation. The method involves several systematic or sequential steps, including the identification of a researchable problem, the formulation of a statement of expected findings (a hypothesis), the controlled observation and/or manipulation of possible factors (called variables), and the interpretation of the outcomes in terms of established theories or previous research.

of its pragmatic value because of these competing interests. In the final analysis, *power* comes into play.

Power influences both knowledge creation and interpretation. Returning again to Jefferson and Douglass, we might note that what Douglass knew about himself, the slave owner, and slavery were unimportant. He had been defined not only as unlearned but as uneducable as well—yet it was forbidden to teach him. Whatever contradictions marked the slave master and his agenda could not, however, be challenged: the presence of slave breakers—men with weapons—kept the slave silent, and *other truths* unvoiced.

The social theory and scholarly inquiry that have emerged with respect to race in education have significantly followed the path laid down by powerful men (Baldwin, 2005; Banks, 2002; Young & Braziel, 2006). Only gradually has the resistance seen in the lives and struggles of men and women such as Frederick Douglass succeeded in voicing alternative perspectives on "the truth." But many women and men have pursued ways of talking, thinking, and emphasizing these other perspectives on reality. One important group of such scholars has been called critical theorists and the perspective they espouse is known as **critical theory** (Endres, 1997; Kincheloe, 2004).

There are many different versions of and ideas regarding critical theory (Apple, 1990; Endres, 1997; Giroux, 1981; Guess, 1981). For the most part, they all argue that there is an underlying conflict of power between groups within society based on economics, race, gender, religion, class, and education (Kincheloe & McLaren, 2000). Because this is felt to be the truth, critical theorists and researchers insist that these factors *contextualize* socially significant discussions on issues such as the relationship of race to education (Ladson-Billings, 1994). They argue that social oppression in various forms, including discriminatory school practices, can be fully dismantled or destroyed only if we understand how ideas and discourse (language and conversation) are framed in ways that influence how people think, believe, and behave. Benjamin Endres (1997, 1) wrote in this regard:

> Critical theorists, inside the educational field and out, link their accounts of oppression and hegemony to **positivism** as a method of social science. All of these accounts portray positivism as "unreflective" and "uncritical" in such a way that it disregards oppression as an object about which

Critical Theory

This term pertains to a broad range of perspectives, including feminist theory, the Frankfurt School, and Afrocentrism, that share a concern with knowledge creation and dissemination by those who dominate. Thus, they share an interest in critiquing domination and aiding emancipation or freedom. Critical theory tries to identify and share analysis (interpretation) of social and cultural issues.

Positivism

This term refers to a belief and practice in the concrete, empirical, or touchable and measurable things. Knowledge is thus based on what can be observed rather than what one intuits or believes to be true through means other than what is determined by the scientific method.

we can have genuine knowledge, thus reinforcing the attitudes and institutions that underlie oppression.

Some take this critical theory approach to education and curriculum as sound; others reject it outright (Pinar & Bowers, 1992). Finally, there are those who agree that it is very important to understand that knowledge and instruction are created and performed by humans who are a part of the process (what is taking place). Being part of the context implies that we all have a vested interest in shaping what is seen as right, correct, or desirable.

Research is one of the ways that we produce knowledge. But what is it that critics of researchers in education want to make clear? According to Lynn Schofield Clark (undated), there are different research agendas or purposes; and

> Research that aspires to be critical seeks, as its purpose of inquiry, to confront injustices in society. Following a tradition associated with **Antonio Gramsci**, critical researchers aim to understand the relationship between societal structures (especially those economic and political) and ideological patterns of thought that constrain the human imagination and thus limit opportunities for confronting and changing unjust social systems.

Gramsci, Antonio

Gramsci was an early twentieth-century journalist and a political activist who was imprisoned by the Fascists for his writings against totalitarianism and others forms of domination of the weak by the more powerful. Gramsci was especially concerned with understanding why people who should rebel against their oppressors often cooperate or collude with them.

In this passage, Clark impresses on us that the economy, politics, and the various other ways that societies arrange people into roles, rules, and relationships influence human behavior. How people view their options and choices is not merely dependent upon their individual motivation, family psychology, or cultural traditions. Rather, some—though not all—behavior is influenced by the environment created by humans to benefit some at the expense of others.

From this view, inequality, notably in our society among various groups defined as "races" and "ethnicities," has led to social struggle. Social change occurs because of this struggle. And "good" social theory should help to understand these dynamics. "Bad" social theory has been seen as that which refuses to frame reality in critical terms that will help account for things that happen. For instance, it has been argued that sociology failed to adequately acknowledge the nature of racism and the struggles against it; hence, the Civil Rights Movement was not anticipated by this discipline (McKee, 1993).

In a related vein, Young and Braziel (2006) have examined how "race theory" has influenced how knowledge in various disciplines has been shaped, sometimes erroneously. In particular, Young and Braziel (2006, 2) draw attention to the academy's role in fostering a loss of memory, or cultural forgetfulness, about important events or realities from the past:

> The Americas still suffer from historical amnesia, a deep unwillingness to face and confront the inflicted wounds of the past: the legacies of genocide, slavery, and colonialism committed against indigenous or Native Americans and enslaved Africans. And these wounds have been academic, intellectual, and **ontological** as well as material or physical.

Some say that this past is irrelevant; things have changed. We are now both "color-blind" and "raceless" in this nation. Others say, "just get over it!" Of course, some psychological perspectives say that the past has neither changed that much nor can it without the healing that has yet to come (Gresson, 2004; Stoler, 1995). Thus, for instance, the late Frantz Fanon, Martinquan psychiatrist and revolutionary, wrote in *The Wretched of the Earth:* "Colonialization is not satisfied merely with holding a people in its grip and emptying the native's brain of all form and content. By a kind of perverted logic, it turns to the past of the oppressed people, and distorts, disfigures and destroys it" (1963, 170).

Where one stands on this issue can have great significance for how one views efforts to challenge traditional **"official knowledge."** That is, are things okay the way they are or do they need to change? Recalling the relation of politics to curriculum in schooling, Pinar and Bowers (1992, 18) recalled how some critical scholars saw things before the curriculum was revised: "Generally, the ideas and culture associated with the dominant class were argued to be the ideas and content of schooling."

So much of what is going on today in curriculum and pedagogy pertains to the belief that the school curriculum has been dominated by values, beliefs, and practices that contribute to the continuing social inequality within American society. Again, people will differ on whether or not this is a true interpretation of things and how much it can be changed. We will take up this issue further in Chapters Three and Four. Here the important point is that

---

Ontology

This is the branch of philosophy that deals with "reality." Reality, from a philosophical perspective, is not readily evident; it has many facets that must be thought about and analyzed, including what is real and what is illusory. Education too must grapple with issues

---

Official Knowledge

Education theorist Michael Apple used this term to refer to knowledge—information, history, and facts—that appears in mainstream media such as books, television, and other media. Knowledge considered suitable for all or everyone, moreover, gets scrutinized or vetted by those in official positions; thus, it attains the status of "official" knowledge.

early shapers of the course of study in public and private education paid little regard to the importance of racial attitudes in determining what was being taught. Through a series of important intellectual and activist steps, education scholars such as Michael Apple and Henry Giroux influenced a generation to consider the impact of ideology on schooling.

Following recognition and discussion of how curriculum was influenced by ideology, these scholars focused on **resistance** and **reproduction** as possible outcomes. Their thinking and writing have many important nuances or aspects. But their essential argument is that much of what schools do, intentionally and unintentionally, is to recreate the attitudes, relationships, and social arrangements that exist. There is little real change in the status quo through the social knowledge gained in schools (Anyon, 1981).

But students, especially those from the working and lower classes, do resist some ideas and attitudes circulating in schools. Theses ideas and values often pertain to things that seem to devalue their family backgrounds, culture, and lived experience. Together, reproduction and resistance as forces or factors that influence school relationships offer one way of understanding the life of minorities who have been racialized or marginalized. We see these forces, for instance, in the life of Frederick Douglass: he accepted some and rejected other things the dominant society tried to represent as the truth, the necessary, and the inevitable.

Some scholars understood that civilization was not necessarily good for the poor in the nineteenth century. Oppressed people could get lost in the processes aimed at bettering things for mankind. Edwin Lemert (1999, 23–24) recalls the social origins of sociology in this way: "Emile Durkheim [one of the founding fathers of the discipline]… let it be known that scientific sociology was urgently needed not just because progress was at hand but also because the lawlessness of modern society had devastating effects on the weaker, more marginal individuals."

Two broad fields of scholarship have evolved from this effort to understand, manage, and improve race relations: these are "Race and Curriculum Studies" and "Race Education and the Social Sciences." Before a review of these two fields that evolved from the efforts to under-

Resistance

Not every social practice achieves the reproduction of the past; there are many ways in which what is intended gets sidetracked or derailed. Partly intended to recognize that individuals have some interests and power (agency), this perspective on social relations emphasizes that resistance to controlling influences also exists.

Reproduction

This term was introduced to describe those social practices, including schooling, that recreate the past or keep the status quo. Tracking females into home economics courses or Native Americans and African Americans into industrial education are two examples of reproduction.

stand and manage race in education, it will be useful to consider some of the beliefs and themes generated by the guiding concerns discussed above. As we shall see, these beliefs and themes have led to conflicting perspectives in many instances.

Some Beliefs and Themes in "Race" and Education

Hilliard (2001, 1) has written: "we must understand that the structure of society and the embedded structure of education/socialization systems in hegemonic societies are designed to maintain hegemony." Of course, not all educators or leaders of society share this view of reality or the need for teachers to be alert to the problem of hegemony. Some educators, including myself, believe that because the prospective teacher often lacks a personal experience with social injustice in the educational context, she or he can also, unwittingly, be complicit with it (Gresson, 2004; Kincheloe, 2004). So, future teachers and other human service professionals need to understand the role of beliefs in shaping what has brought about both the historical emphasis on "race" in education and the contemporary forces reproducing educational inequality (Diller & Moule, 2005).

Ideologies are important in this regard. They contain many unexamined values and beliefs. Moreover, ideologies serve as lens or glasses through which we see and interpret so much of the world around us. This is why teachers in training, especially, need to be alert to ideologies through an awareness of their guiding beliefs. Beliefs are powerful forces in everyday life. Beliefs may inspire the noblest qualities in the species, including imagination, courage, and compassion; they may also contribute to massive human destructiveness and inhumanity. Beliefs about "race" are a case in point.

"Race" made its way onto the Western world stage in the seventeenth century. From this time to the present, it has been defined, refined, and redefined initially—as one group and then another sought to understand itself and others. Over the centuries, *difference* has survived as a defining characteristic of who an American is, and what she or he can hope to experience as citizen, student, and human being.

Two core concepts—biology and culture—were embedded in the ideas giving significance to the idea of

racial difference. Biology pointed to the physical, seemingly permanent character of humans. Culture—values, beliefs, institutions, artifacts—was the way of communicating one group's grasp on the world in contrast with another's, resulting all too often in chauvinistic comparisons of one's own culture with another.

Intellectual and scholarly attempts to understand, describe, and proscribe "racial differences" or diversities have resonated to these two concepts. Nowhere, perhaps is this more evident than in education and schooling. From the beginning, education—as knowledge, instruction, and learning—held a special position in shaping how individual Americans experienced their country and their calling before family, community, and God. This was equally true of those already inhabiting this vast nation, the Native Americans, the Europeans who supplanted them, and the various forced and voluntary groups that completed the mosaic the United States became. From this view, the couplet "race and education" has been a formative aspect of the creation and recreation of American identity, dreams, hopes, and expectations.

According to Ernest House (1999, 1): "Beliefs about race have played a central role in American history, literature, and education. Racial beliefs are embedded in the national identity in complex and disguised ways." House identifies several aspects and outcomes of these beliefs:

1. Minorities, notably, African Americans, are seen qualitatively different in character and ability from Whites;
2. Education policies result from these beliefs that separate, differentiate, and mandate different curricula and treatment for minorities;
3. School organization, finance, and administration are influenced by these beliefs;
4. These policies are claimed to be fair and democratic.

Within this broad statement on "race and policy," House touches on several of the more enduring features of "race and education" as a site for competing ideas of truth. These beliefs include:

- Race is real and crucial to how people organize their lives and relations with each other.
- Race determines human intelligence, ability, and where people belong in a hierarchical society that places

humans in a "pecking order" as a way of assigning them society's resources and valued goods.

- Education, or schooling, is both democratic and fair— even when unequal—because of racial differences that can be modified but not eliminated completely.
- Equality of treatment is an ambivalent, back-and-forth issue with respect to race in schooling.

These ideas are held as true by many and as totally incorrect or misleading by others. What they all suggest, nonetheless, is that race in education is significantly about identity and character—how we define ourselves and others in relation to us. This point is particularly crucial to gaining a perspective on the massive material constituting the field of race and education. Specific themes or issues and the facts chosen to champion one or the other position can deflect attention away from the enduring truth that race and education is first and foremost about identity (Hilliard, 2001). This fact points to other beliefs about race in education.

Education as Multipurposed and Contradictory

Thomas Jefferson's ideas regarding African slaves reflect a basic, seemingly enduring contradiction: Africans were supposedly less than Whites yet fully human, with the qualities of other humans, including the capacity to know that they had been wronged and to hold long memories. Moreover, the very qualities—hard work, know-how, loyalty—that made Africans useable as slaves were denied by Whites such as Douglass's master and enforced through laws aimed at preventing the growth and development that would prove African Americans as equal in humanity and potential to Whites. This contradiction in beliefs and behaviors is dialectical: contain contradictions that are challenged by resistance and alternative realities. Frederick Douglass successfully learned to read and write. This achievement challenged Jefferson's and other Whites' claims. Together, Douglass and Jefferson also expose the complex nature of education.

There are many purposes for education, including workforce preparation and containment of the poor and minorities in the underclass (Kincheloe, 1999). As time goes by, things change and the needs of the society change as well. Education for everyone, improvement of mathematics and science education, identification and education of the

gifted and talented, and education for the children of illegal immigrants are all examples of educational interests that reflect specific periods and particular dominant concerns. Education, then, is like race: a complex idea, shifting in its meanings and significance (Hilliard, 2001).

Education has its contradictions (Ginsburg, 1988). Education for the slave, for example, was necessary in order to achieve certain work-related tasks; "… As Booker T. Washington recalled in a 1903 essay, "Industrial Education for the Negro…" [from "Industrial Education for the Negro," October, 1903, Retrieved August 27, 2008, from www.TeachingAmericanHistory.org.] much of the skilled labor on the plantation was located within the slave class. Still, as Frederick Douglass's former master correctly reasoned, teaching the slave too much or too well defeated the exploitation of him. This basic contradiction—genuine education versus strategic exploitation—has remained a dominant theme in race and education (Willie, 1978). So many other issues—equitable resources and quality teachers for all—often come back to this basic issue.

The education of prospective teachers, most of whom are White, working, middle-class females, is a part of this contradiction. Mark Ginsburg (1988) reported a familiar finding in his important study of student teachers: students' values, beliefs, and experiences prior to entering teaching, including their preservice experiences, often fail to prepare them for the society-changing roles they must assume (Banks, 2002; Freire, 1970).

"Race" Is Both Real and a Social Construction

"Race" is a *construct;* it is created by humans who give it meaning and power. Social scientists argue that "race" exists because humans say it does and act in ways that make race real. This is what is meant by the now popular statement that race is a "social construction" (Omi & Winant, 1986). Beginning with Native Americans, who were made into "uncivilized, ungodly, savages" (Slotkin, 1973; Spring, 2004), the dominant tendency has been to define Anglo-Americans apart from and above all others. Location of this attitude within a religious, Christian framework not only rationalized the sense of "chosenness" but also explained the basis for treating others in the most "ungodly" ways as a means of insuring their salvation.

Some historians maintain that from its beginnings, the nation has seen a succession of groups being first demonized and then going on to participate in the demonization of others (Marone, 2003; Roediger, 1999). James Marone, in *Hellfire Nation: The Politics of Sin in American History,* chronicles how social movements such as temperance—the prohibition of alcohol—were successful by demonizing African Americans, the Irish, and other immigrants as drunkards and criminals.

Recent portrayals of Muslims as radical, crazed terrorists seem to be following this pattern of constructing race as a means of mobilizing a diverse population to identify with each other and to pull together against the constructed other as enemy. Of course, in recent decades, some apologists have argued that White Americans have been more demonized than Jews throughout the thousands of years they have suffered religious and political oppression (Roberts, 2002).

The education of Native Americans, African Americans, and other *racialized* groups has been and continues to be very much about *character* (Spring, 1994). Character has been largely considered from a racialized viewpoint. Racialization has been recognized as essential to being an American; African American philosopher Cornel West has said: "It is impossible to be an American and not racialize how you feel" (cited in ATS, 1997).

From this view, what goes on in schools has been recognized as something much more than reading, writing, and arithmetic. Even these topics, or skill areas, come under the gaze of character: girls and minorities are not good in math and science; poor kids find their way to "the shop" (vocational education) and Blacks and Latinas/os end up in special education, especially classes for the socially and emotionally disturbed or for those with attention deficit disorder.

Because of the importance of identity to learning, much of education for minorities has addressed issues such as self-esteem and the role of schooling and peer relations in the socialization of pupils into gender, sexual, class, and racial identities. Recent scholarship and debate have emphasized the shifting, changing quality of what is meant by "race" and the corresponding fact that racial identity in the school context often belies much of the official thinking about this quality (Gresson, 2004; Kincheloe, 1999; McCarthy, 1990a).

As a result, some social critics and scholars have taken up the challenge to document the ways students struggle especially with negotiating their racial identities from situation to situation despite the school's efforts to essentialize—find an unchanging core—identity (Pollock, 2004).

"Ethnicity" Is Both a More "Real" and Useful Concept than "Race"

Race has lost much of its value as a scientific concept outside of the social and political contexts (ASA, 2002). It simply reflects a desire to group humans in terms of certain cherished physical characteristics: hair texture and color, eye color, skin color, and so forth. Still, it continues to be an important concept for many types of social discourse, including medical research, economic surveys, and so forth. But **ethnicity** is a much less controversial and, to some, more useful way of grouping people in ways that sometimes includes, but largely goes beyond, physical features.

Ethnicity

This term is used to describe groups or collectivities that share a common background, as described by such elements as religion, common ancestry, and cultural traditions (foods, music, sports, and so forth). Culture over biology is the distinguishing factor determining one's ethnicity.

As a classification scheme ethnicity refers to the classification of groups in terms of shared habits and values such as nationality, language, religion, eating preferences and habits. Ethnic groups, moreover, traditionally share both *history* and *myth* as the basis for their "origins." For example, Romans traditionally identify their origin with the feral twins, Romulus and Remus, alleged founders of Rome. It is this *perceived shared past* and culture that stands out in the definition of ethnicity.

The use of "race" to refer mainly to "Black" and "White" as essence—definite, unchanging—without a context is important to note at this point. Recall that the initial and seemingly critical moment was the gradual construction of two distinct clusters of presumed essential qualities: *Black* and *White*. In a way, Jefferson symbolized this when he described the essential character of enslaved Africans one way, and the more fluid yet equally essential nature of Whites and Asians in another manner. Although it has taken centuries for these constructions to take hold (Bederman, 1995), they persist and have been challenged as people insist that what is "White" or "Black" or some other color can be understood only in *context*.

The concept *ethno-race* has been seen to address this need to tie "Black" down to specific cultures and groups (Ginorio & Martínez, 1998; Goldberg, 1993). Because

"Black" has no culture or historical context, it has been rejected by many as they attempt to introduce specific cultures and "Blacks" into the discourse (Sansone, 2003; Spencer, 2006). Thus, for instance, a "Black Brazilian" is not the same as a "Black Puerto Rican" or "Black Nigerian." The U.S. Census Bureau has actually exposed the limits of categorizing according to race and ethnicity by allowing people to name and classify themselves. While this procedure is not without its own problems, it is nonetheless worth noting when confronting the thorny matter of "race" and "ethnicity."

Two important ideas have resulted from the various inquiries into "race" and "ethnicity" as meaningful concepts. First, these classifications have limited value with respect to innate biologic qualities or predispositions. Second, social relations are captured by these terms with respect to how people both identify and relate to each other. In this latter sense, the classification points to the larger, thornier matter of *racism* (Hilliard, 2001; Jones, 2001; Kaufman & Cooper, 2001). The practice of racism in education goes back to the beginning of intergroup relations in the United States.

Segregation, Education, and the "American Project"

Democratic governance and social justice are for many the hallmarks of what America stands for. These twin notions are so ingrained in most of us that we cannot see any other way; we are indeed "true believers" for the most part. The current, ongoing rhetoric that America is in Iraq to "bring democracy" to the Middle East is an excellent illustration of the pervasive persistence of this mentality. The easy slide from fighting to remove "weapons of mass destruction" to "bringing democracy to the Middle East" was possible because Americans largely value democracy as sacred and correct. And any project aimed at spreading democracy deserves at least a hearing from this perspective.

But democracy is an American ideal that has a long history of violation by Americans toward each other. Segregation of people into different groups defined by race, class, gender, and so forth has often led to nondemocratic practices by Americans. Segregation in education is one area in which we see this nondemocratic practice. Joel Spring has written in this regard: "The history of African-

American education is highlighted by both the denial of education in order to continue economic exploitation and the use of segregated education to assure an inexpensive source of labor" (2004, 53). Of course, working-class Whites have also been exploited or denied equitable educational opportunities as part of a **cooling-out process** that tracks groups into the labor force (Clark, 1960)

There has and will be challenges to this view. The successes of African Americans such as Oprah, Condoleezza Rice, and Michael Jordan will be ushered forth to argue the goodwill of the American project and the possibilities accruing from hard work and talent. I agree; still, as I often remind my students, my two doctoral degrees and relative successes do not blind me to the nature of my success: My good fortune, hard work notwithstanding, could not get me very far without patrons, mentors, and people with their own agenda who have helped me. I do not recognize my achievements as either solitary or commonplace.

A strong belief among people who have dominated others is the rightness to rule others. Within Anglo-American traditions, the "Divine Right of Kings" is one expression of this type of thinking. Here the king or aristocrat was believed to rule through God's selection. Race, gender, and other criteria have been used to put forth ideas or ideologies regarding dominance and subservience. There is overwhelming evidence that Americans as a group believe in self-reliance as the essential ingredient for success. This belief has persisted despite evidence that governments and specific initiatives have underlaid the gains realized by most in terms of housing, social welfare, and the like (Coontz, 1993; Warren & Tyagi, 2003). Yet the continuing ebb and flow of economic well-being among the nation's population can make for interesting bouts of competition. This competition is very much a part of schooling. In an incisive reflection on race and education, Linda Darling-Hammond (1998, 28) wrote in *The Brookings Review:*

> W. E. B. Du Bois was right about the problem of the 21st century. The color line divides us still. In recent years, the most visible evidence of this in the public policy arena has been the persistent attack on affirmative action in higher education and employment. From the perspective of many Americans who believe that the vestiges of discrimination have disappeared, affirmative action now provides an unfair advantage to minorities. From the perspective of others who daily experience the conse-

---

Cooling-out Process

This term was taken from the crime world lexicon to describe the strategy used by extortionists to prevent victims from revealing that they have been illegally exploited. As Burton Clark used the term, it was intended to address the ways schools use counselors and others to prevent some students, especially those at risk, from pursuing education after high school.

quences of ongoing discrimination, affirmative action is needed to protect opportunities likely to evaporate if an affirmative obligation to act fairly does not exist. And for Americans of all backgrounds, the allocation of opportunity in a society that is becoming ever more dependent on knowledge and education is a source of great anxiety and concern.

This "allocation of opportunity" has always been a concern for thriving societies; the need and desire to grow and expand has fought with that to retain or conserve and remain "untainted" and uncorrupted by outside forces. Countries such as England and the United States have chosen to move beyond their borders, touching and taking from other lands and, in turn, being modified and enlarged by peoples from diverse places. All of this activity, especially what is now called **globalism**, alters what can be hoped for by the average American in terms of her or his share of knowledge, education, and the material well-being associated with them. In Chapter Five, we take a closer look at globalism as a force that is reshaping traditional notions and experiences of "race," "racism," and education.

Globalism

This term refers to networks of interconnections that span geographies or national boundaries. This includes connections achieved by the Internet and having multinational corporations, for example, having McDonald's retail outlets in countries other than the United States.

Numbers, Immigration, and Nativism

Benjamin Franklin, one of the founding fathers, wrote in 1751:

> The Number of purely white People in the World is proportionably very small. All Africa is black or tawny. Asia chiefly tawny. America (exclusive of the new Comers) wholly so. And in Europe, the Spaniards, Italians, French, Russians and Swedes, are generally of what we call a swarthy Complexion; as are the Germans also, the Saxons only excepted, who with the English, make the principal Body of White People on the Face of the Earth. I could wish their Numbers were increased. (cited in Crawford, 2000, 1)

Franklin was concerned with a recurring theme in American history: who has the numerical advantage and what powers can and should accompany numerical dominance? Because it is very difficult to maintain or control power if one is in the numerical minority, various societies concerned with power have devised various strategies for the control of numbers. As "race" and "ethnicity" are ways of controlling relations among people and managing the issue of power, "racial homogeneity" and "racial heterogeneity" have been important strategic notions. The

ability to maintain "racial homogeneity" or similarity has, in particular, led many societies to restrict practices such as immigration that might lead to the commingling of cultures and racial and ethnic groups. The United States differs from countries such as Germany and Sweden that have been especially careful who they permit to enter their national boundaries or attain power within the country.

Quotas—a specified number or proportion of goods assigned to a group—have had a long and powerful role in the management of power in relation to numbers. Many are familiar with the introduction of quotas in the 1960s by laws and court decisions to insure that a certain percentage of minorities gained access to the mainstream. Intended to redress centuries of both institutional and individual discrimination, the quota lost much of its moral and persuasive impact as opponents of "forced equality" claimed reverse discrimination against White males (Gresson, 1995). Claiming that affirmative actions such as quotas were **preferential privilege** and unfair to nonminorities; advocates of racial practices similar to those preceding the Civil Rights Act of 1964 have largely succeeded in forcing institutions such as colleges and universities to abandon scholarships and "sit asides" for minorities.

Educational quotas are popularly believed to be *affirmative* statements of social progress, inspired by altruistic motives: the dominant group wants everyone to be equally successful although many believe in inherent differences in intelligence, ability, and achievement potential (Herrnstein & Murray, 1995). Quotas used to get women and minorities in jobs and educational institutions loom large as an unfair gesture by well-meaning but unfair and unconstitutional activists (Gresson, 1995; Lynch, 1989). But quotas actually entered education during the early twentieth century when Jews were tracked and contained at the nation's Ivy League institutions. Presidents from Harvard, Princeton, Johns Hopkins, and other schools decried the felt overrepresentation of American Jews at these elite Gentile institutions and said quotas would help lower an increasing presence of anti-Semitism on campus (Karabel, 2005).

Again, during the 1990s, several American universities, including Brown, Williams, and UCLA, were cited by the then active Department of Education for applying quotas. In this apparent abandonment of the ideology of **meritocracy**, we see support for a basic argument of

Preferential Privilege

This term refers to initiatives such as affirmative action or quotas in education that are seen as privileging some over others without examining an issue on its own merits. The term came into popular use by those feeling that Whites were discriminated upon by efforts aimed to help redress historical discrimination.

Meritocracy

By definition, a meritocracy is a system of governance that distributes goods or rewards based on achievement or what has been accomplished. While much success in the United States and elsewhere is due to merit, much more is not. Given this fact, routine allusions to achievements by Whites, for instance, as due to merit alone is inaccurate, or an ideology.

those who believe that the dominant groups do not necessarily practice all that they preach about fairness in schooling (Wang, 1988).

Still, quotas remain a favored strategy for those concerned with controlling minority access to things such as higher education. Introduced into American education in the early twentieth century to control Jewish entrance to the prestigious colleges and universities dominated by Anglo-Americans, this practice is seen by some today as resurging with both Jewish and Asian American students (Lee, 2002). In contemporary America, once again there is concern with the changing demographics: it has been estimated that by 2045, nearly half of the nation's projected 420 million people will be "minorities," with more than a quarter of these Latinos (Pew Hispanic Center, 2004).

The changing demographics would certainly concern the founding fathers such as Benjamin Franklin; they have continued to influence those Americans who feel that the nation belongs to them as a birthright that they have earned over and over again, against various new immigrant groups. Nativism, although a specifically nineteenth-century movement, pertains to a "we-they" attitude that continues even today. However, it was not a new development.

Beginning in the 1790s, for instance, the dominant group passed *The Naturalization Act,* which defined an American citizen in very strict terms. Columbia University historian Eric Foner (2002) has argued:

> The Naturalization Act suggests that by narrowing the gradations of freedom among the white population, the Revolution widened the divide between free Americans and those who remained in slavery. Race, which had long constituted one of many kinds of legal and social inequality among colonial Americans, now emerged as a convenient justification for the existence of slavery in a land ideologically committed to freedom as a natural right. By the nineteenth century, the idea of innate black inferiority, advanced by Jefferson in Notes on the State of Virginia as a "suspicion," would mature into a full-fledged ideology, central to many definitions of American nationality itself.

In 1896, just decades after passing the thirteenth, fourteenth, and fifteenth amendments, the Supreme Court declared in *Plessey v. Ferguson* that "separate is equal." This clear assault on the thirteenth and fourteenth amendments was changed only in 1954 in the historic *Brown v. Board*

of Education case. Now, many see the historic declaration of "separate as unequal" as a new wave of assault on the affirmative actions implemented after the Supreme Court decision of 1954.

As the nation's leadership and dominant groups have adjusted laws and policies toward minorities to reflect the changing times, minorities have continued to press forward in their search for recognition as fully human and for greater inclusion. The position taken by Frederick Douglass was and continues to be instructive in this regard. This position might be defined as one of resistance.

Resistance, individual and group, institutional and scholarly, has been around for a long time. Because of people's specific experiences, they come to different interpretations of the real and the possible. Frederick Douglass, born into slavery, saw the operation of greed, selfishness, and inhumanity among people claiming to be superior, godly, and humanistic. He also saw his own humanity—the desire and need for freedom and ways of gaining it, including learning to read. Douglass resisted someone else's notions of slave education and potential. He also worked to achieve the freedom of others through his writings, speeches, and lobbying among powerful and supportive Whites.

The Civil Rights Movement influenced the race and education discourse in a major way. It has been recognized, moreover, as the movement among movements with respect to pushing the nation to live up to the implications of the Constitution and the ideal of democratic governance (Banks, 1997; 2003; Carson, 1981; Lewis & D'Orso, 1998). Beyond this, the various initiatives undertaken to bring about greater social justice in all sectors of American life can be significantly understood in terms of the Civil Rights Movement. For instance, the student's, women's, gay and lesbian, and anti-ageism movements were all identified in the 1960s and 1970s with the **Black Power Movement** (Gresson, 1995).

The point is that recurring themes reflecting enduring beliefs and values are essential parts of the race and education discourse. Those discussed above are but a few of the many we might note. Indeed, throughout this primer, we shall come upon new or revised themes based on the guiding concerns of modernity, reason, and the dominance of Western civilization. In the next chapter, we turn to the

Black Power Movement

Dated from roughly 1965, this phase or dimension of the Civil Rights Movement emphasized "Black" self-definition and self-assertion. Associated often with Malcolm X, the Black Panthers, and other groups, the movement is significantly defined in terms of the willingness to use violence to protect themselves and press the struggle for social and racial justice.

role social science and other scholarly fields play in forwarding the interests of these guiding concerns.

GLOSSARY

Black Power Movement : Dated from roughly 1965, this phase or dimension of the Civil Rights Movement emphasized "Black" self-definition and self-assertion. Associated often with Malcolm X, the Black Panthers, and other groups, the movement is significantly defined in terms of the willingness to use violence to protect themselves and press the struggle for social and racial justice.

Capitalism : This is an economic system defined by two concepts: individual rights and private property. Goods are privately produced and owned. The critical point here is that human beings have been considered private property under slavery and even since then, workers' lives are significantly influenced by the processes governing private enterprise.

Cooling-out Process : This term was taken from the crime world lexicon to describe the strategy used by extortionists to prevent victims from revealing that they have been illegally exploited. As Burton Clark used the term, it was intended to address the ways schools use counselors and others to prevent some students, especially those at risk, from pursuing education after high school. Clark considered this tracking away from higher education metaphorically equivalent to a criminal action.

Core Curriculum : This term refers to the information, knowledge, and skills necessary for successful high school completion. Over the years, this body of information and abilities has changed as society and various states have adjusted their goals to achieve a particular end, say, more mathematicians and scientists to compete with Russia during the race to reach the moon. "In the mid-1980s, the issue of a shared national core curriculum became heated following the formation of the Core Knowledge Foundation by E. D. Hirsch, eventually leading the state governors to adopt, in 1988, the National Education Goals. Stressing math and science, Goals 2000 established shared standards in the different subject areas, provoking numerous controversies about what they should (and should not) include." http://www.answers.com/topic/curriculum?cat=health taken March 8, 2008.

Critical Theory : This term pertains to a broad range of perspectives, including feminist theory, the Frankfurt School, and Afrocentrism, that share a concern with knowledge creation and dissemination by those who dominate. Thus, they share

an interest in critiquing domination and aiding emancipation or freedom. Critical theory tries to identify and share analysis (interpretation) of social and cultural issues.

Ethnicity : This term is used to describe groups or collectivities that share a common background, as described by such elements as religion, common ancestry, and cultural traditions (foods, music, sports, and so forth). Culture over biology is the distinguishing factor determining one's ethnicity.

Eurocentrism : The term means literally Europe-centered. Because of Europe's historical domination of much of the known world at one time or another, the term has achieved a specifically negative value for those countries or people who were once colonies of Europe. Within educational contexts, the term pertains to the production of knowledge favoring things European over those favoring indigenous or local peoples. Hence, for example, it was considered Eurocentric to force Native American students to learn English, accept Christianity, and adopt White names and dress.

Feminization of Culture : The term refers to the belief that women are sentimental and men are rational; and when women try to influence religion and public affairs, they infuse sentiment over reason into issues that require rational responses. The 1880s was one period when some perceived a "feminization" of American culture because middle-class women and certain Protestant clergymen were getting involved with public affairs. In education, the fear was that having female teachers for male students could lead to undermining normal development of American males to be strong leaders. The Boy Scout and YMCA were initiatives aimed at correcting this perceived feminization of culture.

Globalism : This term refers to networks of interconnections that span geographies or national boundaries. This includes connections achieved by the Internet and having multinational corporations, for example, having McDonald's retail outlets in countries other than the United States.

Gramsci, Antonio : Gramsci was an early twentieth-century journalist and a political activist who was imprisoned by the Fascists for his writings against totalitarianism and others forms of domination of the weak by the more powerful. Gramsci was especially concerned with understanding why people who should rebel against their oppressors often cooperate or collude with them. He developed a theory of "cultural hegemony" to explain this observation.

Hegemony : Simply put, "hegemony" pertains to predominating influence or control exercised by some over others. Gramsci conceived the term to refer to the mechanisms or strategies

of the dominant class to persuade subordinates to go along with their plans, for example, the way wealthy people get poor people to agree with them and vote for a leader who seems to belong to the dominant group.

Meritocracy : By definition, a meritocracy is a system of governance that distributes goods or rewards based on achievement or what has been accomplished. While much success in the United States and elsewhere is due to merit, much more is not. Given this fact, routine allusions to achievements by Whites, for instance, as due to merit alone is inaccurate, or an ideology. As an ideology, meritocracy helps to conceal how factors other than merit influence the path to success in many spheres of life; who one is or who one knows seems to account for promotion and other social rewards.

Modernity : A belief or value system that proceeds from the idea that the world moves forward toward progressive perfection or improvement through the application of reason, logic, and the observation and measurement of things that can be manipulated.

Nativism. The term refers to attitudes and policies that favor native born Americans over immigrants. First emphasized in the late nineteenth century when earlier groups of Americans immigrants considered themselves "natives" and newer immigrant groups as foreigners.

Official Knowledge : Education theorist Michael Apple used this term to refer to knowledge—information, history, and facts—that appears in mainstream media such as books, television, and other media. Knowledge considered suitable for all or everyone, moreover, gets scrutinized or vetted by those in official positions; thus, it attains the status of "official" knowledge.

Ontology : This is branch of philosophy that deals with "reality." Reality, from a philosophical perspective, is not readily evident; it has many facets that must be thought about and analyzed, including what is real and what is illusory. Education too must grapple with issues of what is real. This is partly seen in the struggle to determine what is real—thus one is faced with questions such as: Does God exist? How can we know? Should we teach the idea of "Intelligent Design" in science class as an alternative explanation to human existence and evolution?

Pluralism: This term refers to the many different ideas that tend to focus around the presence and relative equality of a multitude of perspectives, positions, values, and cultures. Within education, recognition that we have not achieved a true "melting pot" status has led to the rise of multicultural edu-

cation and diversity-focused curricula and the inclusion of educators from different groups.

Positivism : This term refers to a belief and practice in the concrete, empirical, or touchable and measurable things. Knowledge is thus based on what can be observed rather than what one intuits or believes to be true through means other than what is determined by the scientific method.

Preferential Privilege : This term refers to initiatives such as affirmative action or quotas in education that are seen as privileging some over others without examining an issue on its own merits. The term came into popular use by those feeling that Whites were discriminated upon by efforts aimed to help redress historical discrimination.

Race Suicide : Simply put, race suicide is a collective term for all those practices such as birth control and mixed mating that diminish the numbers of a given racial grouping.

Reproduction : This term was introduced to describe those social practices, including schooling, that recreate the past or keep the status quo. Tracking females into home economics courses or Native Americans and African Americans into industrial education are two examples of reproduction.

Resistance : Not every social practice achieves the reproduction of the past; there are many ways in which what is intended gets sidetracked or derailed. Partly intended to recognize that individuals have some interests and power (agency), this perspective on social relations emphasizes that resistance to controlling influences also exists. Frederick Douglass's resistance to being denied a chance to learn to read, write, and achieve his freedom is an illustration of the possibilities implied in this term.

Scientific Method: Observation and measurement are the twin pillars of this approach to knowledge production and validation. The method involves several systematic or sequential steps, including the identification of a researchable problem, the formulation of a statement of expected findings (a hypothesis), the controlled observation and/or manipulation of possible factors (called variables), and the interpretation of the outcomes in terms of established theories or previous research.

Social Theory : Scholarly derived explanations, assumptions, and beliefs that attempt to interpret and forecast about people in groups.

CHAPTER THREE

Minorities and the "Education Gap"

"I'm sure those are not the right words," said poor Alice, and her eyes filled with tears again as she went on, "I must be Mabel after all, and I shall have to go and live in that poky little house, and have next to no toys to play with, and oh! Ever so many lessons to learn! No, I've made up my mind about it; if I'm Mabel, I'll stay down here! It'll be no use their putting their heads down and saying 'Come up again, dear!' I shall only look up and say 'Who am I then? Tell me that first, and then, if I like being that person, I'll come up: if not, I'll stay down here till I'm somebody else'—but, oh dear!" cried Alice, with a sudden burst of tears, "I do wish they would put their heads down! I am so very tired of being all alone here!"

—*Lewis Carroll, Alice in Wonderland*

The racial achievement gap is as old as slavery.

—*Charles Lawrence (2003, 1)*

As demographic data makes clear, the gap is everyone's concern. By the end of the decade, Black and Hispanic children will make up 34% of the school-age population. Our nation's

economic strength and social cohesion depend on *all* children being well-educated.

—*Nancy Kober (2001, 13)*

The first epigraph is from the well-known book *Alice in Wonderland* by Charles Dodgson (Lewis Carroll), a nineteenth-century mathematician and clergyman. Alice has just eaten a mushroom that has made her grow into a giant and lose some of her abilities such as reciting poems she previously learned. Because she has lost her ability to recite poetry, she is frightened and begins imagining what life would be like for her outside the hole she has fallen into.

I find this episode in Dodgson's fantasy about a little girl in a rabbit hole an excellent illustration of the challenge facing race and education policy and practice today. In particular, Alice's plight in the hole highlights three important themes related to race and education:

- Pecking order/class and knowledge are related (Alice associates Mabel's intelligence and school performance with her poverty: poky house, few toys)
- Identity is unstable; it can and does change depending on circumstances (Alice recognizes that her own identity as smart has been affected by the mushroom and how people will treat her outside the hole; hence, she says "I must be Mabel")
- Resistance to real or perceived threat from others is expressed in many ways, including those that seem self-defeating (Alice says she will remain in the hole if she can't be somebody valued by those outside the hole)

Each of these themes is relevant to the one issue that dominates contemporary race and education: minority underachievement. Described as an "educational gap," minority underachievement has been seen as partially the result of minority students' position in society's pecking order (Schmid, 2001). These students' school-related identities—how they are treated and act within schools—moreover, have often been seen as the reason they fail to achieve as well as their nonminority peers (Steele & Aronson, 1995). And, as seen in the previous chapter, resistance has always been a continuing factor in race and education, particularly the resistance to being taught

things that seem to threaten one's sense of self (Gresson, 2004; Pollock, 2004).

The gap in achievement has stimulated a number of responses that impact on the topic of race and education. These perspectives and initiatives are not always dealt with in the typical teacher education program or within mainstream textbooks on education. Thus, for many, they are treated as marginal and inconsequential. But they are not truly inconsequential because they address issues that will erupt in volcanic fashion if not addressed in a more proactive—thoughtful, forthright, and comprehensive—manner (Guinier & Torres, 2002).

The Education Encyclopedia states it this way: "In order to examine how students' race, ethnicity, and culture might influence learning, however, one must first examine the assumptions that underlie these concepts" (2002, 1). In this chapter, we begin with a brief overview on the education gap. We then consider how this phenomenon relates to specific minorities. Next, a brief overview of some of the explanations for the gap is presented as a prelude to later chapters that focus on the relevance of the gap to teacher education.

What Is the "Education Gap"?

Charles Lawrence (2003) believed the education gap began with slavery. It is perhaps evident that a gap would exist between slave owners, free citizens, and those forced into slavery. Times change, but certain questions still remain. For instance, a recent ABC television program on race and education out of California posed the following questions:

- Do Latinos and Blacks have the same access to quality education as other students?
- Are the expectations for students of color different than those for White students?
- Do people of different races value education differently? (www.News10.net, "Race and Education," taken July 28, 2006)

These questions illustrate the range of issues associated with the "education gap." There are many different ideas about the meaning of education gap. Simply, it is the observed difference between test scores and graduation rates for African American, Latino, and Native American

students when compared to non-Hispanic Whites and Asians. White and Asian American achievement is typically seen as the benchmark by which others are assessed, although certain Asian American groups do considerably better than Whites (Herrnstein & Murray, 1995; Kincheloe et al., 1996).

The size of the gap between different groups of students varies according to who is doing the testing, but the primary finding does not significantly vary: certain minorities do less well on tests than others. Harvard economist Ronald Ferguson (2006, 1) has defined the gap like this:

> There are a lot of different achievement gaps. The achievement gap that I focus the most on is the gap between students of different racial groups whose parents have roughly the same amount of education. It concerns me that black kids whose parents have college degrees on average have much lower test scores than white kids whose parents have degrees, for example. You can take just about any level of parental education and we have these big gaps.

The American Educational Research Association (2004, 1) reported a similar pattern:

> By 12th grade, the average African American and Hispanic student can only do math and read as well as a white eighth grader. In addition, high school completion rates remain markedly lower for students of color. Substantial research has tried to explain the test score gap. We know that it begins early; for example, there is a significant gap in vocabulary knowledge even as children enter school. This confirms earlier findings that family and community differences have a significant impact on student achievement.

Nancy Kober, author of "It Takes More Than Testing: Closing the Achievement Gap" (the Center on Education Policy's report), offered yet another take on the gap:

> On the 1999 reading trends test of the National Assessment of Educational Progress (NAEP), the average score of Black students at age 17 was roughly the same as that of White students at age 13. In science, the average scores of Black and Hispanic students at age 13 were lower than the average score of White students at age 9.
>
> Because most of the discussion about the gap centers on school-age children, many people think the gap is entirely the product of what happens in school. In fact, assessments of young children have uncovered a sizable achievement gap *before* children start school. (2001, 14)

Kober goes on to note that the achievement gap is a very sensitive issue, one characterized by misinformation and inaccurate understanding of the causes and cures for the gap. Because the achievement gap is a sensitive topic and because misconceptions can have damaging effects, it is critical that policies to close the gap be based on solid evidence rather than conjecture. A major flaw in this regard is the widely held belief that the gap has not changed positively over time. Nancy Kober, however, observes:

> The fact is, U.S. students as a whole are performing better on key tests than they did 30 years ago, especially in mathematics.... Every racial/ethnic subgroup has made gains in achievement during the past 25 to 30 years.... We shrunk the gap once and we can do it again.... In a nutshell, the size of the gains gap depends not only on trends in minority student achievement, but also on rates of improvement or decline for other subgroups. (2001, 10)

Kober makes a particularly important point above when she observes that different minorities as well as White subgroups reveal different gaps. Too often minority diversity is neglected when discussing the gap. More precisely, the gap has seldom been framed in terms of the unique educational histories of various minorities, but these do bear on the meaning of the gap for any specific group (Coloma, 2006). This neglect can add to the misunderstanding and misrepresentation of why there is a gap. Thus, it will be helpful to briefly consider some of the unique historical aspects of minority education and the gap.

Minority Diversity and the Education Gap

Between 1619 when African slaves came to America and the conclusion of the Civil War in 1865, schooling for minorities, and for poor Whites, was not a priority. In fact, some have argued that only with attempts to expand education for the former slaves were important strides made toward the education of the less privileged Whites, especially in the South (Banks, 2002; McKee, 1993; Watkins, 2001; Williams, 2005).

But if poor Whites have often received inferior education (O'Connor, 2001; Williams, 2005), what is the meaning of "minority education"? To answer this question, we need to consider the meaning of "minority" in the American context. According to Charles Marden and Gladys Meyer (1968, 23), minorities

1. are subordinate segments of complex societies;
2. have special physical or cultural traits which are held in low esteem by the dominant segments of the society; and
3. are self-conscious units bound together by the special traits which their members share and by the special disadvantages these traits bring.

From this view, minority education may be viewed as education for second-class status. It was created to achieve the dominant groups' need for minorities to accept their place and not offer too much resistance. From this view, minority education can be defined as schooling experiences that society has deemed appropriate for those who were not at the top of the social hierarchy. African American historian Carter G. Woodson (1935/2000), speaking of the African American, referred to this form of education as the "miseducation of the Negro."

Americanization is the term traditionally used to describe the primary objective that schools assumed in this process. Some will disagree with this formulation of the purpose of schooling for minorities. Instead, they would argue that it was intended to help "new Americans" become a part of the whole, to achieve an "American identity." Thus, boarding schools for Native Americans (Adams, 1995) or English-only education for Japanese immigrants to Hawaii in the early twentieth century (Asato, 2003) were seen as the right thing to do.

But minorities are not mere pawns; they can and have initiated educational changes on their own behalf (Coloma, 2006). In so doing, they manifest not only the capacity for resistance but also the need for empowerment or a share in the resources and power of society (Anderson, 1988). Because of the back-and-forth struggles between the dominant society and various minorities, their education has gone through many different phases or stages since missionaries first attempted to school Native Americans to European values regarding Christianity and since political leaders seduced some of them into capitalism and notions of private property (Spring, 2004). These phases have been shaped also by the different ideas that dominant group members held. For instance, abolitionists (those against slavery) and suffragists (supporters of women's rights) were often among those who fought for educational equity for minorities.

Americanization

Assimilation or schooling newcomers and immigrants to the dominant cultural tradition within the United States is the overriding definition of this term. It has a more nuanced meaning as the forcing of "American culture" (McDonalds, conspicuous consumption of goods, Eurocentric arrogance, etc.) onto other groups and nations.

Clearly, definition of who holds minority status has changed over time and circumstance, and so has the group's vulnerability to the education gap. For instance, both Italians (Guglielmo & Salerno, 2003) and Jews (Freedman, 2000) were once considered minorities and had experiences that were considered part of "minority education." But neither Italians nor Jews are typically identified today as minorities or as part of the achievement gap.

For the most part, only certain minorities are identified when speaking of the education gap. But even these groups are not homogeneous; they have differences among them. For instance, Mexicans are different from Cubans, and Vietnamese from Japanese, although we typically call the first two groups "Latinos" and the second two "Asian Americans."

Because minorities have both similarities and differences in their racialized histories, it is important to place the achievement gap within a historical context. African Americans, for instance, have evolved attitudes toward education that reflect the history and experience of racism and slavery, but they have not developed one response to it (Watkins, 1993). For teachers to see the education gap in perspective, it is useful to understand how the particular challenges of different minorities have impacted their schooling and achievement. What, then, is the gap as it pertains to minorities? In answering this question, let's consider a few important events associated with the more well-known minority subgroups.

Native Americans

Dartmouth College is one of the historic Ivy League institutions. Located in New Hampshire, it was founded in 1769 by Reverend Eleazar Wheelock, a Congregational minister from Connecticut. Today it is a highly endowed, elite institution. But on a Web site describing its current Native American Program, we read:

> Samson Occom, a Mohegan Indian and one of Wheelock's first students, was instrumental in raising substantial funds for the College. The Royal Governor of New Hampshire, John Wentworth, provided the land upon which Dartmouth would be built and on December 13, 1769, conveyed the charter from King George III establishing the College. That charter created a college "for the education and instruction of Youth of the Indian Tribes in this Land...and also of English Youth and any others."

(http://www.dartmouth.edu/~nap/about/ taken September 29, 2007)

The Web site goes on to note that Dartmouth evolved as an institution for privileged White males; it graduated only nineteen Native American students for 200 years. John G. Kemeny, thirteenth president of Dartmouth College, in his 1970 inaugural address, pledged to redress this injustice. This was an important gesture. But poverty, underemployment, alcoholism, and depression and other mental illnesses are among the many social ills that continue to affect most Native Americans who have struggled to make a success under severe oppression (LaGrand, 2002).

This current condition has generated many explanations; chief among these is **deculturation** (Spring, 2004). Between 1880 and 1935, Native Americans were part of a great educational experiment: "killing the Indian" and the creation of a "new man." Through boarding schools, thousands of Native American youths were forced to leave their families and homes to study "the ways of the White man" (Adams, 1995; Archuleta, Child, & Lomawaima, 2000; Weinberg, 1977). Enculturation flourished because of a commitment to racist beliefs. But the experiment failed: living far from home, some died of homesickness; others dropped out and returned home or "returned to the blanket," as it was put by Captain Richard Henry Pratt.

Founder of Carlisle Indian School in Pennsylvania, Pratt reflected a common insensitivity to the near overwhelming burden deculturation can be for the conquered outsider. In the case of Native Americans, these "new Indians" were not accepted by White society nor were they able to return to the reservation and take up their former lives as "Indians." Concurrent with the numerous laws enacted to steal Indian lands and with their forced internment on "reservations" was an apparent belief that Native Americans should get over it. Recalling the Indian reform efforts of the late 1880s, J. C. Bard (1997, 1) wrote:

> An important side effect of the passage of the Dawes Act was that membership in the national Indian organizations declined. Martin (1969:185) explains that as with other American reform movements, once the law they sought was enacted, reformers complacently felt that their work was complete. Apparently the average American believed it was now time for the Indian to help himself.

Deculturation

This term has been used by various authors, notably Berry (1980) and Spring (1994), to describe a condition where a group's initial or beginning culture has been stripped away and a new one inadequately substituted for it. Spring (1994) saw this as characterizing Native Americans, African Americans, and other groups.

This is an important point to recall when dealing with minorities in schools: the violence done historically to minorities is expected to be "forgotten" or glossed if they are to fit it (Abdelhamid & Choudhury, 1998; Toth, 1997). This expectation seems to hold even if the effects of the oppression continue unto the present. This is the perennial requirement: to fit in or be deemed oppositional. The importance of this point cannot be stressed too much because, as we shall see in the next chapter, teacher-student interactions affect minority student achievement.

Joel Spring viewed deculturation as a process affecting not only Native Americans, but also African Americans and others whose cultures were devalued. But he saw deculturation also as part of an intentional plan of destructiveness. Bard (1997, 1) notes regarding Native American deculturation:

> What anthropologists refer to as the process of acculturation can be also viewed as the process of deculturation. By the 20th century, the Indian world had been all but replaced by that of the white men, whose civilization, also changing rapidly, raced on at a quickening pace sweeping Indian traditionalists aside.... In evocative terms, Ruby and Brown (1988:271) pictured the Indians, in huts or on street corners, sitting in sullen silence dreaming of the past as the white men rushing by them planned for the future. The once-proud horsemen of the interior, dreaming of their free-riding past, saw their horses rounded up and shipped off to canneries and the Indians saw road and town builders destroy the graves of their ancestors.

Ruby and Brown (1988) were thinking of Native Americans from the Pacific Northwest—Bella Bella, Chiook, Tillamook, Eyak, Coast Salish, and the Tlingit. But, as Jody Marinucci (2001, 1) points out: "the term 'Native American,' a label *given* to all tribes, is extremely generic in nature and scope. Customs, beliefs, languages and ideas can (and do) vary enormously among the tribes; what is acceptable in one tribe may be totally unacceptable in another."

But the losses associated with deculturation applied to most Native Americans. Moreover, given the near extermination of hundreds of tribes and the loss of their lands and culture, the Native American achievement gap has been described as more severe than that of other minorities. Schooling on both reservations and in urban schools yields similar patterns. Beaulieu (2000) identified various factors that are related to the Native American achievement gap:

- High staff mobility [turnover] in schools;
- Students disproportionately affected by violence and substance abuse; and
- Lack of appropriate knowledge base for providing professional development and curricular development to meet students' cultural and language needs.

Dorothy Lesvesque (1994) identified two related factors associated with the achievement gap among Native Americans:

- differing views on the purpose of education; and
- a lack of Native American values reflected in the educational system.

By and large, the gap seems to be found across Native American tribes. There is evidence that some tribes differ from others in their efforts to overcome the factors associated with low academic achievement (Miller, 2005; Olsen, 1997). But limited English proficiency continues to be the major issue; in particular, the mismatch or disjunction between what and how Native youth learn at home and at school (Cairney, 2000).

This issue of literacy styles and practices seems to be the entry issue. However, other issues include:

- cultural dissonance between Native cultures and the "White" or dominant culture
- assimilation and integration of Native cultures
- Anglo-American cultural perceptions of Native cultures
- Classroom climate

Sherman (2002) reported a narrowing of the achievement gap between White and American Indian students when a school reform model was implemented that focused on cooperative learning and celebration of American Indian culture. Other scholars have made similar observations regarding the benefits of cultural acceptance and sensitivity.

Latinos and the Gap

The March 6, 2001 issue of *The Michigan Daily* carried the following from the Census Report for that year:

> Overall, 57 percent of Latinos 25 and older are high school graduates, compared with 88 percent of non-Latino whites. About 11 percent of Latinos have a college degree, compared with 28 percent of non-Latino whites.

Within the Latino population, there are differences associated with their country of origin. Those of Cuban origin have the highest levels of income and education, while those of Mexican origin have the lowest relative income and education, the survey said. (http://media.www.michigandaily.com/, taken September 1, 2007)

A Pew Report found that underpreparation in early childhood negatively impacts both high school and post-secondary education among Latinos:

Achievement test scores suggest that the average Latino child is about two grades behind the average white child by age 9. Growing recognition of the importance of early learning has stimulated a surge in preschool and nursery school enrollment in recent decades, but such programs are nowhere near universal. About 55 percent of white 3-to 4- years-olds are enrolled compared with 35 percent of Latinos the same ages. Part of the gap can be explained by the fact that a greater proportion of white mothers with young children work. However, affordability is also a barrier. In most jurisdictions nursery school is not part of the regular public school programs, and parents must pay for it. (http://pewhispanic.org/factsheets/factsheet.php?FactsheetID=3, taken October 12, 2007)

These statistics reflect the "education gap" that pertains to Latinos. But these figures do not tell us nearly enough. For instance, based on her reading of the literature in both educational research and fiction, Sonia Nieto (1998) identifies four interrelated and contrasting issues or themes that have emerged from the long history of stories told about Puerto Ricans in U.S. schools:

- colonialism/resistance
- cultural deficit/cultural acceptance
- assimilation/identity
- marginalization/ belonging

Of course, Puerto Ricans have traveled a different road than other Latino groups. Given that Puerto Rico is a commonwealth and its people are statutory citizens, they are not typically considered in issues such as illegal immigration. But their experiences parallel those of some other immigrants whose low socioeconomic backgrounds tend to combine with negative reaction from mainstream American society to place them in weak social and political circumstances (Schmid, 2001).

The problem with lumping together so many different ethnic or immigrant groups into a broad category such

as Latino is the range of vast differences that sometime accompany their experiences in the United States. Mexican Americans, Puerto Ricans, and Cuban Americans are the main groups that come to mind when discussing Latinos. There are others, and their different experiences—including class, race, and gender experiences—are pertinent to understanding how they relate to the larger American culture. Thus, Cuban Americans are generally perceived as better integrated into mainstream American society than Mexican Americans.

The education gap reflects these important differences. Looking at immigrants more broadly, Schmid (2001) identifies several factors that interact to influence immigrant academic achievement:

- Cultural characteristics
- Social class
- Language
- Gender

According to Schmid, these factors do not interact in the same way for different immigrant groups. While some immigrant groups do well in the academic and economic arenas, other immigrant groups do quite poorly. Comparing Asian immigrants with Mexican immigrants from 1970 to 1990, Schmid found that differences in achievement among immigrant groups seemed related not only to their cultural histories, but also to their class background, and how the dominant society received them—were they valued or devalued, treated positively or negatively in terms of "ethnic markers" such as skin color or religion. Additionally, their relative success depended on the political and economic capital they had developed in the U.S. context. Thus, if they had already achieved a relatively high status, as the Japanese or Cuban Americans have, then they tended to do well. However, if their existing status was fairly low, as has been the case for Mexican Americans, Puerto Ricans, or Filipinos, then they tended to be less successful.

The positive support from the ethnic enclave—the already established ethnic community in the United States—and the affirmative reaction from the dominant society tended to work well for Asian American immigrants. Conversely, a negative reaction from American society and their weaker economic background tended to associate Mexican immigrants with less socially valued

groups of Americans. As a result, they face greater difficulty in developing social and human capital.

The possible effects of being negatively received by the dominant society are important to understanding the historical context. As with the Native Americans who failed to be educated at Dartmouth as planned, Mexican Americans have experienced discrimination in education that predates the contemporary anxiety about having to educate "illegals" from Mexico. Robert R. Alvarez, Jr. (1986, 1) wrote:

> The history of school desegregation legislation in the United States is not often associated with the Mexican Community in Southern California and is usually thought to have begun with the 1954 landmark Supreme Court case of *Brown vs. the Topeka school board*. It has recently come to light that the earliest court cases concerning school desegregation occurred in the Southwest and California in the 1930s. In these cases Mexican immigrants and their communities were the targeted groups of segregation by school officials. A case of particular importance, which has begun to take its place in the social history of civil rights, occurred in San Diego County during the 1930s, in the then rural community of Lemon Grove. This case: *Roberto Alvarez vs. the Board of Trustees of the Lemon Grove School District,* was the first successful school desegregation court decision in the history of the United States.

The Latino education gap points to one question that future educators face when trying to make sense this phenomenon. What does it mean to label a given group as academic underachievers? To better understand this question, consider Cuban Americans. There have been three major waves of Cuban immigration to the United States (García, 1996). Some of the early Cubans who came to the United States were among those who fled when Fidel Castro came to power. They were often both upper-class and light-skinned. They also often identified with both the pre-Castro regime and the U.S. government. Later generations of Cuban immigrants were often both poorer and dark-skinned.

Differentiation of income, education, and occupation among Cubans is instructive to understanding race as a construct and its expression in education. This is so, in part, because Cubans are also differentiated according to skin color (Espino & Franz, 2002; Montalvo, 2004; Stepick, 2002). For example, Espino and Franz (2002, 612) conclude their study on the role of skin color among Latinos in the job market this way: "Our findings indicate that darker-

skinned Mexicans and Cubans face significantly lower occupational prestige scores than their lighter-skinned counterparts even when controlling for factors that influence performance in the labor market."

The point is that cultural background among various Latino groups remains important in the United States, but skin color can further intensify differences within these Latino groups, resulting in a greater absorption of "White"-skinned Latinos into the White American dominant group. One potential consequence of this differential treatment and experience among Latinos is that some groups show greater identification with African Americans. This is true despite the very great differences in historical background. This movement of some Latinos toward "White" and some toward "Black" reminds us that specific contexts and ongoing racialization construct identity. The school is important as a site where this identity construction takes place and it is in the school context that we see some of the educational gaps that characterize Latinos.

Asian Americans and the Gap

"Many people don't realize that students from Southeast Asia and the Pacific Islands don't tend to fit the stereotype of the educationally advanced Asian American. This publication should help policymakers and teachers get over some of those stereotypes and provide support to students," comments Robert Underwood, former U.S. Congressman from Guam and one-time Chair of the Congressional Asian Pacific American Caucus (CAPAC). Mr. Underwood remains a leader in the fight for policy changes and funding to help Pacific Islander and Southeast Asian American students reach academic achievement levels comparable to Caucasian Americans. He is now working with colleagues on a publication focused on the status of Pacific Islander and Southeast Asian Americans in higher education.

Asian Americans cover a wide range of national groups, including Chinese, Japanese, Koreans, Taiwanese, and Vietnamese. There are some hundred or more recognized Asian American groups; they have different cultural traditions and have had different experiences in the United States. Their achievement patterns also vary across subgroups. But the most notable Asian American groups from a historical perspective are the Chinese and the Japanese and, more recently, Koreans and East Indians.

Chinese and Japanese Americans have known considerable discrimination because of their racial and national ancestries. Several national policies have been enacted, and later repealed, that affected Asian American immigration and assimilation. For instance, Cheryl Brown Henderson (2000, 1) recalled the history of Japanese immigration in this way:

> Japanese Americans have suffered from discriminatory practices, legislation and restrictions. They immigrated to the United States as a source of labor without plans for them to stay and participate actively in the life of society. The Asiatic Exclusion League mounted a campaign in 1905 to exclude Japanese and Koreans from the United States. Under pressure from the league, the San Francisco Board of Education ruled that all Japanese and Korean students would join the Chinese at the segregated Oriental School established in 1884. There were 93 Japanese students in the 23 San Francisco public schools at that time. Twenty-five of those students had been born in the United States.

The internment camp experience of World War II reflects the constructed nature of race and how crisis can negotiate the boundaries of race. Germans and Italians remained "White" for the most part and were not questioned; Japanese were interned. Education continued in the camps (James, 1987). Asian Americans were also a labor-focused challenge: they were needed to assist in the expansion of the West, but this required acceptance of them as immigrants and as a potential challenge and threat to cultural and economic dominance/hegemony by Whites.

Because of their academic successes and their families' economic achievements within the larger society, Asian Americans have been often called the **model minority**. This term recognizes the comparative successes of Asians with respect to other minorities and many White ethnic groups. For this reason, educational researchers have considered issues such as student achievement motivation.

Kiyoshi Asakawa and Mihaly Csikszentmihalyi (2000), for instance, believe that Asian American students' commitment to their families and cultures partly account for their accepting or buying into the values that favor high achievement. By internalizing—or taking on as their own—values held by their communities and forebears, some believe that good study habits as well as persistence and fear of failure influence success.

Model Minority

This term has been applied to Asian Americans who have seemingly overcome the challenges of immigrating to the United States by quickly moving into the middle class through high academic achievement and prestigious career advancement.

High expectations of success have been found to distinguish Asian group academic performance. That is, some Asian American students and their families seem to believe, while others do not, that they will do well. Using data from the National Educational Longitudinal Study of 1988–1990, Goyette and Xie (1999) found:

- High achievement among students seemed to go with high parental educational attainment and socioeconomic levels;
- All Asian groups have higher educational expectations than did whites. For instance, 58.3% of white students expected to graduate from college, while all Asian groups reported higher percentages, ranging from 67.9% of Southeast Asians, to 84.8% for Japanese and Koreans, up to 95.7% of South Asian students who expected to graduate from college.

Goyette and Xie (1999) found intra-group differences important. In particular, some Asian Americans such as Southeast Asians and Chinese have lower average incomes than White students and yet outperform them academically. Ironically, while many see African American and Latino lower academic performance as suggestive of genetics, expectation is the preferred explanation for Asians doing better than Whites. They also found that Chinese Americans—although having lower educational and economic statuses than the South Asian, Korean, and Japanese families—scored the highest in mathematics.

This brief overview of some of the specific historical factors influencing how we think and talk about the gap is especially telling when considering African Americans. Indeed, this subgroup is the primary focus when discussing the education gap across various developed nations (Arora, 2005). But, as historian V. P. Franklin has noted, "historically, there has been some similarity in the way these…['races'] have been educated or 'miseducated' in American public schools, but there were also significant differences in their educational experiences" (1978, 289).

Because they have been the primary focus of scholarship and intervention, the major explanations for the gap have been formulated around African Americans. We turn now to some of the explanations and solutions offered for the gap.

Some Responses to the "Education Gap"

Each of the major minority groups has experienced movement through similar storied histories (Weinberg, 1977). For the African Americans, the three themes or tensions were: slavery for labor, social, and cultural integration with Whites. As freed men and women, African Americans would both compete within the economic sphere and explode cultural notions of White superiority as they achieved and assumed, at times, equality with Whites. Education under slavery was minimal and characterized by a few basic needs and interests: indoctrination into a weak, submissive Christian faith and practical skills needed to fulfill tasks on the plantation. After slavery, African American public schooling assumed a basic profile: colonial education (Anderson, 1988). The Brown decision of 1954 marked a decisive shift in education for African Americans (Patterson, 2001).

The continuing economic and social inequality experienced by African Americans and some other minorities have resulted in diverse explanations, including those that consider genes, culture, and motivation. But institutional inequality remains a potent concern even when described in seemingly less economic terms. For instance, Linda Darling-Hammond (1998, 28) places debate regarding the institutional inequality and the education gap in these terms:

> Educational outcomes for minority children are much more a function of their unequal access to key educational resources, including skilled teachers and quality curriculum, than they are a function of race. In fact, the U.S. educational system is one of the most unequal in the industrialized world, and students routinely receive dramatically different learning opportunities based on their social status. In contrast to European and Asian nations that fund schools centrally and equally, the wealthiest 10 percent of U.S. school districts spend nearly 10 times more than the poorest 10 percent, and spending ratios of 3 to 1 are common within states. Despite stark differences in funding, teacher quality, curriculum, and class sizes, the prevailing view is that if students do not achieve, it is their own fault. If we are ever to get beyond the problem of the color line, we must confront and address these inequalities.

Darling-Hammond has been a leading figure in the movement to ensure that teachers are well-trained and only

the very best teachers are placed in schools serving minority children. This passage is from her important essay for The Brookings Institution, the world-renowned private organization devoted to analyzing public policy issues at the national level. And her insights regarding the importance of excellent teachers and school-based resources have received wide support. Still, other explanations for the education gap abound:

- Parental noninvolvement and irresponsibility
- Undermotivated students
- Teachers' low expectations, inexperience, cultural bias, and lack of caring attitude toward minorities
- Administrators' lack of creativity and preparedness to challenge the status quo
- Society's ambivalence about achieving educational equity or social equality, especially through institutional support of teachers and administrators

These various perspectives on the nature and causes of the education gap reflect how complex a matter it is. There is no one clear or accepted perspective regarding what are the ultimate indicators of the gap (Ferguson, 2006; Hilliard, 2001), who is to blame, or what set of strategies will eliminate or nearly close the gap as currently defined. What can help the prospective teacher is to understand that progress for minorities has been an ongoing struggle, one characterized by resistance to being pigeonholed as inferior, disinterested, and incapable of assuming a place of equality within the national mainstream (Anderson, 1988).

Nancy Kober (2001, 3) concludes:

> What, then, are the most probable explanations for the gap? A complex combination of school, community, and home factors appears to underlie or contribute to the gap. For example, African American and Hispanic students are less likely than White or Asian students to take challenging courses or be exposed to rigorous instruction. They have less access to experienced and well-qualified teachers. Teachers tend to expect less of Black and Hispanic children than of White and Asian children. Black and Hispanic children also attend schools with fewer resources and higher rates of disruption and student mobility. They have less access to learning activities at home and in the neighborhood.

In her 2006 presidential address before the American Educational Research Association, Gloria Ladson-Billings (2006) reframed the achievement gap as the education debt.

From her perspective, the focus on achievement disparities is misplaced. Rather, the "education debt," which has accumulated over time, is the real issue. According to her, "this debt comprises historical, economic, sociopolitical, and moral components." In particular, focus on "inequalities in health, early childhood experiences, out-of-school experiences, and economic security are also contributory and cumulative."

Harold Berlak (2001) has argued that using standardized tests to measure achievement perpetuates a system of institutionalized racism and lends the cloak of science to discriminatory practices. His reasoning is that there is a difference between academic achievement and academic performance. The first pertains to what is measured on tests; the second refers to how a given student may actually perform in class.

For the prospective student these various findings are not easily resolved: obviously, the past three decades show tremendous advancements for millions of minorities. In part, the apparent arrival of a firmly established Black middle class leads many countries to express puzzlement and even despair at minority underachievement among Afro-Canadians, Afro-British, and Afro-Americans, to name a few. Black males, in particular, stand out here, although other minority males as well as some minority females also fair poorly when evaluated on a variety of standardized tests. But the prospective educator must try to make a difference in the classroom against complex, sometimes overwhelming challenges.

Explanations for the gap and proposed solutions have been and continue to be sources of both serious commitment and creative innovation; they have also often resulted in controversy. As a result of efforts to explain the gap as the fault of the particular individual, minority group, or dominant society, several important themes have surfaced:

- Racism no longer exists (D'Souza, 1995)
- Affirmative action has narrowed the gap (Bowen & Bok, 2000)
- Segregated schooling for Blacks may be better (Asante, 1991; Nobles, 1990)
- Public School policies and practices are deadly for most African American students (House, 1999)

Beyond these issues, a newer theme has been raised regarding the differences found among different *Black*

Americans. For instance, immigrants from the Caribbean may be seen as either Latino or Afro-Carribean because of their African or European ancestry. This can, of course, refer largely to skin color, although immigrants from the Dominican Republic and Haiti have made the distinctions more difficult to make because they may identify culturally with their Spanish or French ancestry more than with Africans or African Americans. The point is that migration from Latin American and the Caribbean introduce an added dimension to the immigration and racial relations picture.

The different experiences various "Black American" groups have with the dominant and other minority groups can influence their attitudes toward and relations with school. The role of different experiences in how school knowledge is understood and related to has been observed by various scholars. William Watkins (1993), for example, has identified six historical orientations toward curriculum among African Americans. These range from those that emphasized gaining industrial knowledge and skills to those focused on knowledge of African heritage and the ways of achieving power and status in a racist society.

Watkins argues that these six orientations "have evolved, and that they survive and impact the cultural underpinnings of the contemporary African-American educational experience" (Watkins, 1993, 321). Watkins's point is that how a specific group has oriented itself toward learning, particularly the content or curriculum, depended upon what its needs were or are. In a similar vein, it has been observed that resistance to school norms varies among African American students in important ways. For instance, Patricia S. Kusimo (1999, 1) observed in her review of African Americans and rural education:

> Instead of submitting to the norms of a school establishment many students experience as oppressive, some students reject European American speech patterns and devalue high academic achievement, inadvertently limiting themselves.... However, other African American students respond in the opposite way. These high-achieving African American students cite their awareness of racism and prejudice as a reason to excel, thus preparing themselves to fight these evils.

This passage points to the idea that there is a significant, perhaps unbridgeable, gap between different subgroups of African Americans. In Chapter Four, for instance,

John Ogbu and his associates argue that oppositional values underlay African American underachievement. The point is that "cultures" are not fixed contents. Any given "culture" is made up of things—ideas, values, objects, and practices—that are in constant flux. Moreover, no member of a culture necessarily embraces everything about it. This is true for those born into the culture as well as those who acculturate—take up the beliefs, values, and perspectives of another, often dominant culture. Racial and ethnic minorities can be understood, in part, in terms of how they retain older cultural ways or take on newer ones (Landrine & Klonoff, 1996; Pinderhughes, 1989).

Conclusion

The education gap is real. But it is also a complex notion. Its causes and cures are seen differently by various observers and activists. Scholars also differ in their understanding of the gap and their recommendations for change. In this chapter, we have gleaned clues to some of the factors involved in the discussion of the gap and the lens through which it has been appraised. In the next chapter, we return to the guiding concerns raised in Chapter Two. Our goal will be to see how social theory and research were shaped to address the education of minorities, including the gap that has existed since the beginning of American education and the institutionalization of slavery.

GLOSSARY

Americanization: Assimilation or schooling newcomers and immigrants to the dominant cultural tradition within the United States is the overriding definition of this term. It has a more nuanced meaning as the forcing of "American culture" (McDonalds, conspicuous consumption of goods, Eurocentric arrogance, etc.) onto other groups and nations. Part of this negative sense of the term pertains to the relations of the dominant group toward various minorities and to the sense that the dominant group has unjustly asked for greater accommodation to Anglo-American tastes and values than is necessary. Whether fair or not, the term has also suffered from the historical tensions associated with racism toward Native Americans, African Americans, Latinos, and Asian Americans.

Deculturation: This term has been used by various authors, notably Berry (1980) and Spring (1994), to describe a condition where a group's initial or beginning culture has been stripped away and a new one inadequately substituted for it. Spring (1994) saw this as characterizing Native Americans, African Americans, and other groups. Some scholars seem to challenge the idea that an initial culture can be fully or effectively destroyed (Del Pilar & Udasco, 2004).

Model Minority: This term has been applied to Asian Americans who have seemingly overcome the challenges of immigrating to the United States by quickly moving into the middle class through high academic achievement and prestigious career advancement. Sensing an undesirable comparison of their successes to the relative failures of some African Americans and Latinos, Asian American scholars have challenged that their minority plight is distorted by this term.

CHAPTER FOUR

The Study and Practice of "Race" in Education

> Knowledge does not grow naturally or inexorably. It is produced through the inquiries of scholars—empiricists, theorists, practitioners—and is therefore a function of the kinds of questions asked, problems posed, and issues framed by those who do research.
>
> —*L. Shulman (1990, 1)*

Reflecting on the place of knowledge in the preparation of future generations of teachers, Carl A. Grant and Kim Wieczorek (2000, 4) observed, "the knowledge that teacher candidates receive needs to be socially moored to enable teachers to be effective in our multicultural society." Another term for "socially moored" is **contextualized.** Lee Shulman, in the opening epigraph, contextualizes knowledge: it is a human creation. Moreover, at least three things define its context:

Contextualization

This is the process of giving meaning or structure to ideas, events, and circumstances. Implicit in the concept is the fact that few things are self-explanatory; it is in the very nature of the human beings to see and interpret things—both physical and abstract—against some background.

- Issues
- Questions
- Problems

Each of these contextualizing factors influence what becomes knowledge and knowable by those seeking under-

standing or enlightenment. Some things do not become problems or issues for those controlling information; hence, certain questions do not get asked or answered (Hartmann, Croll, & Guenther, 2003). For instance, during slavery the educational achievement of enslaved Africans or Native Americans was not a major issue or problem for most people in society. Hence, questions regarding the educational gap between them and Whites were not worth studying or trying to answer.

The context of knowledge about race and education, moreover, has been shaped by both certain guiding concerns and the scholarship they have inspired. In the previous chapter, we examined some of these guiding concerns, and certain beliefs and themes that emerge from them. In this chapter, we focus on the two fields of scholarship most pertinent to understanding the relation of race to education. I hope, as a result of reflecting on the material in this chapter, you will have a more complete or useful understanding of why so much controversy accompanies the issue of minorities and the education gap.

Scholarship and the Guiding Concerns

In Chapter Two, we saw that social theory was partly the fruit of modernization: it was an attempt to apply to progress an increasing confidence in using science. In race and education, theoretical frameworks date back to the early attempt to explain the presumed and valued relations between the races. Various disciplines or fields of study and inquiry have had a very important role in the evolving understandings of race and education and the ultimate structure and process of schooling. The initial focus was on the curriculum.

Curriculum Studies and "Race Education"

Curriculum Studies is a multi- and interdisciplinary field of inquiry concerned with the impact of the curriculum on learning. It draws from several fields, including sociology, history, social studies, reading, literacy, language instruction, science, and psychology (Pinar et al., 1995; Schubert, 1986). This field has largely evolved from an increasingly sophisticated understanding of the relation of schooling to the quality and character of life in a democratic society. With respect to minorities, Curriculum Studies was

largely ignored (Pinar, 2003). It began with a concentration on a course of study appropriate for second-class citizens; it later moved to a critical assessment and intervention initiative aimed at inequalities in education perpetrated through the curriculum itself (Ornstein & Hunkins, 1998; Parkay & Hass, 2000).

School Knowledge and the Oppressed

Traditionally viewed by many as a static thing, the curriculum is today seen as dynamic and changing. Moreover, the school knowledge that makes up various curricula has a history. According to political sociologist William Watkins (2001, 40), "School knowledge is a product of complex power politics, popular ideas, ideological struggle, negation, consensus, and compromise. Along the way powerful individuals and groups affect the process."

Watkins is speaking directly to the influence of the powerful businessmen from the North who concerned themselves with the reunification of the nation after the Civil War of 1861–1865. The North won and the South was devastated both socially and economically. One part of the task pertained to fitting newly freed Africans into society. In the South especially, the emphasis was on accommodating African Americans to the traditions and social arrangements of that region. This has been called "accommodation."

G. Stanley Hall, introduced earlier in Chapter Two, had strong views regarding the feminization of the curriculum. He also cautioned against too much enthusiasm for teaching Latin to teenage boys. It was in this context that he clarified the dominant perspective held toward "race education" in 1900:

> This superstitious reverence of Latin has a second illustration in the autobiography of Booker Washington, who says that during the reconstruction period from 1867 to 1868 [sic], the colored people had two crazes—to know the classical languages and to hold office. It was felt, he adds, that "a knowledge, however little, of Latin, would make one a very superior human being, bordering almost on the supernatural," and he conceived a large part of all his own [sic] mission among his race to be the overcoming of these two passions. (1901, 665)

The popular understanding of Washington's emphasis on teaching African Americans was not limited to a few

psychologists such as Hall. Educational historian Merle Curti (1966, 309) observed in his book on social ideas that shaped American education:

> Probably the most representative and influential educational leader of the period, William T. Harris declared that Washington's solution for the Negro problem was of "so universal a character that it applies to the down-trodden of all races, without reference to color."

The curricular significance of these ideas about what was important education for African Americans, nay, the "down-trodden of all races," is that the role of race in curriculum studies did not begin in earnest until the mid-twentieth century (Pinar, 2003). Because the idea of separate and inferior education for minorities was not generally viewed as a problem or issue, the questions asked were not about what was happening to and for "Negro Education." Thus, curriculum has been a central focus in "race education" (Counts, 1927; Watkins, 1993), although "race" has only recently become a prominent feature of curriculum studies.

The creation of a cadre of African American leaders such as Frederick Douglass who might participate in their own racial uplift was a motive among what James Anderson calls "missionary philanthropists" (1988, 149). After the war, subjugation and containment through the creation of an African American educated group that would not challenge or create tensions within the South was the goal of the northern business leaders behind the creation of Negro schools (Bullock, 1967).

Character and labor training for African Americans was the "special education" of the period. This is part of the backdrop for the rise of Hampton Institute in Virginia and Tuskegee Institute in Alabama, the latter under Booker T. Washington (Anderson, 1988; Watkins, 2001). Of course, there were other models of education that appealed to African Americans and some Whites, such as "liberal education"—the middle-class focused curriculum combing study of the arts and sciences. But the important model is the one that evolved into the well-known industrial education curriculum (Caruthers, 2006).

The **Washington-Du Bois Debate**, popularly characterized as a clash between industrial and liberal education views, was derived from the influence of White industrialists and philanthropists in the construction

---

Washington-Du Bois Debate

The historic debate was not a one-to-one meeting but a series of speeches made by Booker T. Washington and W. E. B. Du Bois over a period of years regarding the proper educational focus for African Americans. Washington focused on the industrial education model that some called "colonial education." Du Bois emphasized the need for African Americans to receive a broad educational experience comparable to that received by the White elites who would be leaders, not just followers.

of African American and other minority education. The Hampton model, for instance, was later applied to Native Americans at the Carlisle School in Pennsylvania, where Pratt applied the perspectives, policies, and practices conceived by Armstrong at Hampton.

From this view, the course of study for most groups in the United States has been shaped by educational purposes very much responsive to dominant group interests. To be sure, there have been competing dominant group interests; social mobility among the less well off has been aided by curricular changes that increased their chances for employment that would enrich their lives. Nonetheless, educational policies traditionally reinforced this attitude that the various minorities were largely similar in terms of their needs. Consider the 1896 ***Plessey v. Ferguson*** decision; it institutionalized "Separate but Equal" as the official position on minority involvement in mainstream social institutions, including education. Most minorities suffered as a result of this policy. Moreover, IQ testing and tracking students into different courses of study deepened this policy's impact by insuring that even within segregated schools, class differences might persist (Weinberg, 1977).

Various minorities resisted both—the definition by the dominant society and forced second-class education (Weinberg, 1977). The seeds of resistance to the colonial model of education were especially prevalent among African American intellectual leaders. For instance, Harvard educated sociologist W. E. B. Du Bois championed liberal education for African Americans. He also believed that scholarship was a crucial key to changing race relations, notably White myths, misrepresentations, and misunderstanding of African peoples. But, as educational historian and Du Boisian scholar Derrick Alridge (1999, 361) wrote:

> The historical context that Du Bois faced when he set out on his mission in 1895 had not changed much by 1930. It was during this period that he began to move away from the utopian view of social science research as a primary method of educating Negroes and Whites about the irrationality of racism, and slowly move away as well from using scientific research to dismiss and debunk views of Negro inferiority. What Negroes needed, he surmised by 1930, was a hardheaded, pragmatic, and culturally grounded educational perspective that would yield them social, economic, and political power in America.

Plessey v. Ferguson

In 1896, the Supreme Court upheld racial segregation in public facilities by deciding against Plessey, a mulatto, who had attempted to be seated in a Whites-only section of the train. The court declared that segregation was just and legal as long as the "separate but equal" doctrine (requirement) was met.

Educational thinkers such as Du Bois were not alone; there were also influential practitioners such as the African American educator and administrator Horace Mann Bond. Bond was the first African American president of his alma mater, Lincoln University, in rural eastern Pennsylvania. Curriculum scholar William Pinar (2003, 11) has observed that Bond's "understanding of the profoundly conservative character of American education, particularly in the racial sphere, represents a significant moment in the advancement of curriculum knowledge. Bond's work foreshadowed the establishment of race as a central curriculum discourse."

In particular, Bond "stressed the social sciences, since these areas of study provided the means for analyzing the problems African Americans faced and pointed the way to their possible amelioration" (Pinar, 2003, 11). What Bond and others saw as important about the traditional emerging scholarship were the insights on relations between the races as well as scholarship on society and human behavior in general. At the curricular level, Historically Black Colleges and Universities (HBCUs) attempted both to prepare minority leaders for racial uplift and to help modify the White man's bigotry and discrimination.

Du Bois and Bond reflected the scope of the faith and loss of faith in scholarship's ability to influence how the majority chose to view and treat minorities, notably African Americans. This was seen in the fact that the influence of the assimilationist model held sway until the *Brown v. Board of Education* decision of 1954. V. P. Franklin (1978, 287–288) wrote in the second decade after *Brown:*

> The movement of Afro-Americans to cast aside their second-class status inspired other racial and cultural minorities to work for the removal of discriminatory statuses and laws that prescribed their position in the American social order.... **De jure** and **de facto** segregation not only facilitated the provision of inferior educational services to culturally and racially different groups, it also crippled minority attempts to participate in the allocation and utilization of the material resources of the larger society.

With the arrival of multicultural education in the United States and England (Arora, 2005), efforts turned toward national and educational policies that seemed to respect minority reality. In particular, there was the recognition that countries such as the United States, Canada,

De jure

This term, literally meaning "from law," is the counterpart to the concept below. It simply means to be according to the rule of law; reality should be what has been adjudicated by the courts as the meaning of specific pieces of legislation.

De facto

This term, literally meaning "from fact," has a particular place in the race and education legal context: it signifies that what exists in fact or reality may differ greatly from what it is supposed to be. Thus, where one was supposed to have equal protection under the law, vast differences have always existed for various groups.

and Australia are diversities that require some treatment in the school curriculum (Banks, 2004).

Since then, a "fight for the curriculum" has more prominently characterized both public and postsecondary education. That is, various groups struggle to control or influence what is considered worth knowing. This struggle reflects a conflict regarding the legitimate charge of the curriculum at both K-12 and postsecondary levels (Ornstein & Hunkins, 1998; Ravitch, 2000). Some believe that the traditional knowledge base—reading, mathematics, science—is beyond criticism with respect to diversity. Some believe that schools cannot and should not get involved in controversial, **social deconstructionist** curriculum work.

Others believe that these subject areas, as well as history, social studies, and the humanities must be constructed and presented in ways that reflect social justice. This means a curricular orientation that is nonracist, nonsexist, nonclassist, and nongendered. This battle of perspectives is part of what is meant by "**cultural wars**."

Culture wars were apparent very early in the formation of curricula in various schools. Different regions of the original colonies, for example, emphasized different courses of study and reflected different religious influences as well. Cultural wars with respect to curriculum pertain ultimately to the question of values in education.

Race in education has been especially shaped by cultural values. In the next chapter, we will return to this controversy as we consider some of the emerging perspectives in curriculum and schooling. What they will all show is that curriculum as a field of study dating from 1918 has emphasized scientific principles and progressive thinking. One aspect of these emphases has been a self-critique—the recognition that curriculum creators and scholars are vested in the knowledge they plan, produce, and teach. A parallel recognition has been that the politics of curriculum has always been operating in schooling, including that of minorities. And as a result, the production and dissemination of knowledge continues to be a contested matter in pre- through postsecondary education.

Social Deconstruction

It is the process of exposing the way a given social fact or reality has been constructed to appear natural, normal, and perhaps inevitable. This process relies on the use of specific concepts or ideas designed to help uncover other possibilities. Power and truth are the focus of social deconstruction: the goal is to free what is true from the control and packaging of those who have had the power to determine its form and presentation to us.

Cultural Wars

The term has most recently gained popularity with respect to clashes between groups with different values: those who believe in abortion and those who are against it; supporters of gay marriage and those who say marriage is only between a single male and a single female; and those who favor open borders and those who challenge this policy.

Social Science and Race Education

Social Science and Education pertains to scholarship carried out in several disciplines: anthropology, economics, education, pedagogy, psychology, political science, and sociology.

To a large extent, sociology was the axis discipline for this cross-disciplinary focus in the early decades of the twentieth century. Writing in the inaugural volume of the *Journal of Educational Sociology,* Charles A. Ellwood (1927, 29) charged:

> Educational sociology…will place social intelligence first among the aims of education, and it will demonstrate that social intelligence is impossible in our modern world without social information; that to understand culture and to make education promote a well-balanced culture we must make basic in it the knowledge of human history and of human institutions afforded by such studies as history, sociology, economics, and politics.

The confidence placed in the social sciences by Ellwood and others reflected a modernist perspective. The idea of a "well-balanced culture" reflected a belief that all cultures were distinct and that the "American" or European culture needed to assimilate other cultures into it if things were going to work out favorably.

Although many of the early scholars shied away from explicit criticism of traditional views of "race relations," some of their philosophical or moral views increased the tensions due to the contradictions in society's positions regarding democracy and justice, on the one hand, and the dominant treatment of racial, ethnic, and other disenfranchised groups, on the other.

Thus, Ellwood (1927, 30) concluded in his defense for seeing educational sociology as a **social philosophy** of education: "Science aims at universal generalizations, and it necessarily contains a philosophical element if it attains to the stage of **universal truth**." And George S. Counts (1927, 16), writing on the relation between curriculum and sociology, considered the limits of the scientific methods of sociology and psychology for human progress in this manner:

> The reason is to be found in the fact that education has to do with welfare, and when one approaches the question of welfare, one seems to pass outside the confines of objective science. The critic immediately asks whether, in the formulation of the doctrines of welfare, equal regard is to be paid to the interests of all classes, sects, and races…. Scientific method can give no satisfying and conclusive answers to these questions. In vain have we sought an objective definition of progress. The difficulty lies in the fact that progress implies movement forward, and the direction in which one moves in advancing depends upon

Social Philosophy

Social philosophy is a philosophy (love and study of wisdom) that focuses on man and society. In particular, it attempts to identify and speak on the nature of man, especially what makes him "human." Its purpose is to help humans make a better world by identifying behaviors that benefit us as a species and those that hurt.

Universal Truth

This term is associated with philosophy, particularly those branches—epistemology and ontology—that deal with final things such as God, Heaven, and Hell. It pertains less to a specific truth or fact than to the pursuit of such a possibility. Thus, it refers to that truth or fact that goes beyond all finite truths.

one's orientation. Every man sees the world through his own eyes.

Counts wrote these words at the dawn of the professionalization of education, the curriculum, and the social science study of education. I have quoted them at length because they are prophetic: they offer great insight into contemporary educational issues and battles. Already we have seen in Chapter Two that *lived experience* is something too little considered when trying to make sense of racial and social inequality in a society claiming to be a meritocracy. In Chapter Two, we went further into the validity of this claim as we examined the debates around the "education gap."

Sociology, as noted previously, has had a special place in knowledge production about race and ethnic relations in general and about race in education in particular. Early forays into thinking and writing about school life focused on providing sociological insights for future teachers; it then gradually took on the problems in schools (Shimbori, 1979). This area of interest was called "educational sociology" (Ellwood, 1927).

But these views did not make a great impression on the early scholarship in American sociology. Race relations were viewed in terms of the social problem minorities constituted for a developing nation (Baldwin, 2005). Taking the position of the national leaders and the dominant racial perspective, the emphasis was on understanding race and education as a part of the assimilation of minorities into a legally sanctioned pecking order.

Assimilation, Race, and Social Science

During the 1920s and the 1930s, Robert Park, a professor at the University of Chicago, and his students addressed assimilation. Historian Davarian Baldwin (2005, 313–314) has written about the importance of the sociological work of Park in this way:

> The "Chicago School's" theories of race consciousness, cultural assimilation, and urban organization are integral to what is called a sociological outlook and celebrated as challenges to the dominant biological theories of social difference at the turn of the last century. The institutionalization of these ideas emerged with the rise of Harvard- and German-trained, White scholar Robert Park, the "father" of urban sociology and race relations in the U.S. He challenged fixed genetic visions of social relations with

a theory of cultural evolution informed by the idea that race is a dynamic and changing product of socio-historical conditions.

These scholars proposed to describe how human migration and immigration was characterized of several phases that went from separation and hostility to inclusion and oneness (Park, 1928). Park was an advocate for better race relations and his argument did describe a typical pattern for many new immigrants who found their way through various stages or phases to full inclusion. But the wished-for integration of the African American and Native American was a more challenging possibility. His theory did not adequately explain dominant relations with Native Americans, African Americans, and other similar groups (McKee, 1993; McCarthy, 1988). Why? Davarian Baldwin (2005, 314) suggests:

> Park's discussions of Black people in this critical period reveal a "cultural turn" that was infused with equally rigid categories of identity and distinction. The dynamic events of Black migration, urban racial violence and "New Negro" resistance posed direct threats to his paradigm of cultural cohesion and order. To maintain scientific certainty, Park incorporated race conflict and racial traits into his overarching social system, as natural elements to be overcome by the inevitable force of cultural assimilation.

Park's African American students, the men who entered the African American communities and collected the data, challenged his perspective. Their work was largely **marginalized**. They did not get their knowledge published in the prestigious journals or book series; they did not gain the prestigious jobs. And few trained in sociology are likely to know the names of men such as E. Franklin Frazier, St. Clare Drake, or Horace Cayton. Many minorities, including Jews, have had similar experiences in academia. This has been and continues to be a challenge for those who write for both the majority and the minority (Banks, 1997; Gresson, 2006).

Partly for these reasons—Park's emphasis on cultural cohesion and the marginalization of minority social science perspectives—conceptual clarity on the matter of assimilation was not popularly received until J. Milton Yinger and George Simpson (1978) proposed it. A more nuanced view of assimilation in American society was offered by Yinger and Simpson They recognized several levels of assimila-

Marginalization

This is the process of being forced to the outside or the ends of the page, so to speak. Socially, the term refers to lacking a primary share in the creation, interpretation, and use of the material and cultural wealth of the society.

tion—cultural, psychological, biological, and structural. Both structural (housing, entertainment sites) and cultural (values, habits, and language style) segregation characterized African American-White relations. Over time, structural segregation continued as cultural segregation diminished: African Americans and Whites shared many values—likes and dislikes in terms of clothing, religion, politics, and so forth—but remained physically separated on a *hierarchical* basis.

Culture, Difference, and Education

Beyond the assimilationist efforts of men such as Edward Ross and Anthony Giddens, there was little substantive work on race and education prior to the 1960s that dealt with race (Shimbori, 1979). Interestingly, some of the earliest important work on race and education was conducted by anthropologists concerned with culture. Hervé Varenne, Columbia University professor of the anthropology of education, has noted: "When one takes as broad a view of the anthropology of education as I take, much of the work on **socialization** and **enculturation** of the 30s and 40s could be placed within the literature. They are certainly at the root of what must count as the opening of the field itself: the work on Jules Henry, the Spindlers and Solon Kimball" (2000, 1).

According to Michiya Shimbori (1979, 393), the established subdiscipline of sociology of education occurred after World War II. It had three approaches to understanding teachers, schooling, and educational problems. These included

- Cultural anthropological—studying cultural differences through ethnography
- Social psychological—studying individual behavior due to group influences
- Historical-institututional—studying institutional influences such as the family and religion

The cultural anthropological approach, according to Shimbori, overlapped with the anthropology of education perspective mentioned above by Hervé Varenne. Both educational sociology and educational anthropology eventually overlapped in the interests and their methods of inquiry—notably in the study of groups and cultures through observational methods, interviews, and case studies.

Socialization

This is the process of educating people to the values, beliefs, and ways of a given society; it is the process of getting people to want to do what they must do for the society to work.

Of course, this is an imperfect process; people do not always buy into what is presented to them, especially when there are competing messages or socializing agents.

Enculturation

This is the process of learning one's own culture. Babies and small children must learn their culture; they are not born speaking a particular language, practicing a given religion, or preferring a particular type of wine.

Anthropology had begun the observation of schooling practices early, although largely through ethnography. This emphasis on viewing behavior within its important contexts served as a corrective to some of the limitations attributed to early sociological inquiry.

Understanding Race, Education, and Social Structures

The crisis of education associated with the radical sixties saw the sociology of education focus on the crisis and the planning of remedies for it. This crisis pertained to a wide range of educationally important events, including movements aimed at changing the relations of minorities, women, youth, the elderly, gay and lesbian, as well as others to the dominant society (Gresson, 2004). Because these various movements challenged the preferred way of seeing the nation and relations among its people, we refer to this period as a "crisis."

Moreover, because schools figured as sites where much of the resistance to the **status quo** was happening, studies of education became a major concern. This was the context for the emergence of several important studies on race and education. Sociology made an important shift at this point (McKee, 1993). Its early concern had been with quantifying data on various minorities and their relations to the dominant society. Now, sociologists of education needed to consider some of the more pressing and less positive aspects of the inconsistencies between stated educational goals and typical educational practices. This meant, in part, a move from survey research to observational inquiry.

The crisis also served to turn race and education scholarship toward issues of power and specific school practices. Sociology also began looking at the specifics of social inequality in the context of the school itself. Case studies, participant observation, structured and semistructured interviews began to replace more quantitative methods

Between 1954 and the 1960s, scholarship was much influenced by the studies of the late James Coleman at Johns Hopkins University. Ideas regarding social structure and inequality predominated in much of the literature. The important work of the preceding decades had been in the field of the social psychology of racism. Groundbreaking scholarship by Mamie and Kenneth Clark, and their colleague Thomas Pettigrew, reestablished the obvious: racist propaganda and practice had a negative impact on minority,

Status quo

This term refers to the way things are. It is traditionally seen as representing a conservative position, one characterized by fear or complacency.

notably African American, self-esteem and social behavior. Citing research from the now famous doll-preference studies, the Clarks and their colleagues argued before the Supreme Court as to the ill-effects of racial discrimination and oppression. Evidence that African American girls often preferred White dolls and considered African American dolls as negative was a powerful statement.

The Supreme Court decision to reverse *Plessey v. Ferguson* was partly based on the social psychological evidence presented by the Clarks and their colleagues. Chief Justice Warren Burger said that segregation "generates a feeling of inferiority in their [African Americans'] hearts and minds in a way unlike ever to be undone" (cited in Gresson, 1995). Within years after this decision, President Lyndon Baines Johnson signed the Civil Rights Act of 1964. This act impacted all areas of public life that had been previously segregated by law. It also led to a shift in the educational context: discrimination in schooling was no longer law; efforts to achieve racial parity in access to education were now important.

The U.S. Department of Education commissioned a study to reflect this altered context. James S. Coleman was a Johns Hopkins sociologist and the lead researcher on this education report—*Equality of Educational Opportunity*. This report, popularly called "The Coleman Report," argued that disadvantaged African American children benefited from integrated education (Coleman et al., 1966). Mass busing was one consequence of this widely regarded finding. Although Coleman later reversed his belief in the efficacy of forced integration because of mass "White flight" to the suburbs, the study remains a landmark illustration of sociological inquiry in education.

The *social context* of education was the new focus of much of the sociology of education after the Coleman Report. A recent reflection on the Coleman era notes in this regard:

> Equality of opportunity, for instance, was traditionally taken to mean equality of schools' resources, such as the number and quality of textbooks. Unlike his predecessors, who focused on the equality of what was going into the school system, Coleman evaluated the equality of what was coming out. He also examined student performance, for the first time using test scores as an indicator of equality. (Kiviat, 2000, 1)

The direction of inquiry inspired by James Coleman and others sensitive to the social context of race in education continues to emphasize the use of large data resources—usually surveys based on a combination of interviews and observation—to make sense of what affects school effectiveness. Social dynamics within the classroom and school as within the community and society as a whole are the focus of scholarship in this tradition. And the results of these findings have often yielded as much contradiction and controversy as useful knowledge.

For instance, James Coleman's (1981) study of Catholic versus public school education suggested that minority youth who had recently begun attending Catholic schools in greater numbers benefited more from this education than in public schools. He based this argument on data collected from over a thousand public, private, and Catholic schools. Some were elated to learn that African American and Latino students might be able to close the achievement gap with Whites through the traditional Catholic education. But the study raised a number of questions and stirred up much controversy.

Some research challenged the long-term effectiveness of the apparent improvement in language and mathematics achievement (Peterson and Llaudet, 2006), yet some have concluded otherwise, as Ilg and Massucci (2003, 71) recently commented: "Although a convincing resolution to the debate has yet to emerge, the flood of new research on nonpublic and public schooling has consistently confirmed one reality about the effects of Catholic education on student achievement. Poor and minority students have the most to gain from Catholic schooling."

Scholarship such as that produced by Coleman and others help affirm or deflate certain popular assumptions around race and education. Ideas such as **social capital** is one outcome of such inquiry; in the present case, Coleman and others have found that the Catholic school context routinely provides a traditional type of discipline, self-esteem, and parental involvement that poor minorities seem to benefit from (Neal, 1997).

One important study from this period used both anthropological and sociological methods and is illustrative of the kinds of critical statements coming from observational studies. In 1970, Ray Rist and his associates reported on a participation-observation of working-

Social Capital

Like cultural capital, social capital pertains to exchange values. In this case, however, emphasis is not on the knowledge dimension but on the social relationships, the individuals or groups one knows that can enhance one's productivity or skills.

Cultural Capital

"Capital" is, therefore, anything that can be used to produce more of something that is valued. Linking the term culture to capital is intended to describe in monetary or exchange-valued terms a wide range of cultural artifacts: skin color, religion, hair texture, height, facial features, athletic prowess, and academic abilities.

class, inner-city students. According to Rist (1970), in a large class of African American kindergarten pupils, their African American teacher sorted them according to class features: skin color, hair texture, body scent, and the like. These qualities, which have been called **cultural capital,** served as the basis for the children in being designated as more or less bright. Moreover, the more bright pupils were placed in the front seats and received more positive attention from the teacher than did other classmates.

Rist's findings continue to fire the imagination of many concerned with race and education. The operation of **class** in the school and in the classroom has been and continues to be an important aspect of the discourse of race and education. For example, a recent study reports that not only low-achieving but also high-achieving children from poor families show academic underachievement, including school dropout and over time (*Education Week,* 2007). But class is only one variable or factor that impacts on school achievement.

Culture and Power in School Achievement

Class

Among this term's meanings is a basic one: one among several interconnected or related positions in society defined in terms of cherished values such as money, education, and prestige. In education, class becomes important because schooling has been seen as the site for both keeping people in and helping them to change their class positions.

Oppositional Behavior

The term refers to behavior against that which is desired or required by the context. John Ogbu used the term to describe what he felt to be the characteristic or normative behavior of some minorities who had suffered oppression.

The late John Ogbu and other anthropologists focused on deepening our understanding of the education-culture-minority interface. Ogbu, in particular, emphasized the different educational results of being a voluntary immigrant versus a nonvoluntary minority. His basic argument was that African Americans and some other minorities who have experienced slavery and severe discrimination eventually adopted attitudes and behaviors that are self-protective but ultimately self-defeating. He called this **oppositional behavior**.

Ogbu, who spent the greatest part of his academic career at the University of California, Berkeley, used comparative methods to study minority education across various countries. As per his view (Ogbu, 1992, 5)"...the crucial issue in cultural diversity and learning is the relationship between the minority cultures and the American mainstream culture. Minorities whose cultural frames of reference are oppositional to the cultural frame of reference of American mainstream culture have greater difficulty crossing cultural boundaries at school to learn."

Ogbu, like James Coleman, stimulated both supporters and detractors for his theory. Among scholars whose work overlapped and somewhat reaffirmed his is Signithia

Fordham. Fordham, who has conducted several important ethnographies of schools and students, found that some African American students resist achieving to their potential because of the peer group context. She found that among those African American students who were high achievers, many were rejected by their peers and accused of "acting White."

Fordham (1982, 1991) adopted the concept of "racelessness" to talk about how successfully African Americans had been socialized to consider academic achievement as beyond their province. According to her interpretation, these students attempted to distinguish themselves from Whites by rejecting all things "White," notably academic achievement. From the youth she studied, Fordham gathered that they felt their "African Americanness" threatened if they performed as Whites do.

Certainly, there has been evidence that some youth succumb to peer pressure and act in ways that are not to their long-term benefit. But other scholars have found a more complex set of factors (Noregua, 2002). For example, Donna Ford and her colleagues (Ford, Harris, and Schuerger, 1993) view African American academic performance as adaptive; that is, it is designed to cope with the complex environment these students find themselves in. Moreover, according to Ford (1992), student perceptions of their performance and peer influence do not necessarily lead to reports of peer or environmental pressures.

Like Coleman, Ogbu and Fordham took on a very rich and complex issue: minority student achievement and its relation to the persistence of racial and social inequality in the United States. The plethora of different findings and interpretations of recorded differences across racial and ethnic groups is, in fact, the main contemporary issue in the field of race and education. In the next chapter, we take up some of the instructional challenges created by these diverse perspectives on minority underachievement. .

GLOSSARY

Class: Among this term's meanings is a basic one: one among several interconnected or related positions in society defined in terms of cherished values such as money, education, and prestige. In education, class becomes important because

schooling has been seen as the site for both keeping people in and helping them to change their class positions.

Contextualization: This is the process of giving meaning or structure to ideas, events, and circumstances. Implicit in the concept is the fact that few things are self-explanatory; it is in the very nature of the human beings to see and interpret things—both physical and abstract—against some background. In education, context pertains most immediately to the many social factors or conditions that may influence whether and how a child learns, achieves, and matures into an optimally fulfilled adult.

Cultural Capital: The French sociologist Pierre Bourdeiu (1993) is credited with first using this term to show that knowledge as well as money, diamonds, and jewelry are things valuable and exchangeable for other valued things. "Capital" is, therefore, anything that can be used to produce more of something that is valued. Linking the term culture to capital is intended to describe in monetary or exchange-valued terms a wide range of cultural artifacts: skin color, religion, hair texture, height, facial features, athletic prowess, and academic abilities. These are all qualities that draw their value or cherishedness from social groups; and this fact connects cultural capital to the companion term "social capital." In education, "cultural capital" has been seen as contributing to the process or reproducing both society and culture, that is, the social relationships and the values, ideas, and material creations used by the population.

Cultural Wars: The term has most recently gained popularity with respect to clashes between groups with different values: those who believe in abortion and those who are against it; supporters of gay marriage and those who say marriage is only between a single male and a single female; and those who favor open borders and those who challenge this policy. In truth, there has always been some degree of conflict among diverse groups and collectivities where there are different ways of seeing and constructing knowledge and institutions by which to carry on social life. Still, it is worth noting the resurgence of the idea in recent times and its frequent use in discourse relating to race and education. As one blogger has noted: "These 'culture wars,' however, are only the current incarnation of what in gentler times (the 1950s!) was called 'The Great Conversation,' an argument about education and citizenship, and about individual freedom and social order, stretching back over the centuries at least to Socrates's strictures on what the poets should and should not say about the gods" (Dorfman, 1997).

De facto: This term, literally meaning "from fact," has a particular place in the race and education legal context: it signifies that what exists in fact or reality may differ greatly from what it is supposed to be. Thus, where one was supposed to have equal protection under the law, vast differences have always existed for various groups. Similarly, despite the requirement to desegregate all public areas, *de facto segregated housing* continues.

De jure: This term, literally meaning "from law," is the counterpart to the above concept. It simply means to be according to the rule of law; reality should be what has been adjudicated by the courts as the meaning of specific pieces of legislation. Hence, the Brown v. Board of Education decision in 1954 meant we would have *de jure integration.*

Enculturation: This is the process of learning one's own culture. Babies and small children must learn their culture; they are not born speaking a particular language, practicing a given religion, or preferring a particular type of wine.

Marginalization: This is the process of being forced to the outside or the ends of the page, so to speak. Socially, the term refers to lacking a primary share in the creation, interpretation, and use of the material and cultural wealth of the society. Lacking a voice, a presence, and a piece of the rock is another way of visualizing life on the margins. Of course, various scholars have perceived strength and extraordinary insights as flourishing at the margins (hooks, 1990; Park, 1928)

Oppositional Behavior: The term refers to behavior against that which is desired or required by the context. John Ogbu used the term to describe what he felt to be the characteristic or normative behavior of some minorities who had suffered oppression. A wide range of behaviors have been described as oppositional, including a refusal to do well academically because it is presumably not acceptable in certain groups. Some scholars have challenged this type of behavior as by any means characteristic of African American youth, but the term remains a favorite among some clinicians who prefer to describe youth rejection of authority figures and controlling situations as oppositional.

Plessey v. Ferguson: In 1896, the Supreme Court upheld racial segregation in public facilities by deciding against Plessey, a mulatto, who had attempted to be seated in a Whites-only section of the train. The court declared that segregation was just and legal as long as the "separate but equal" doctrine (requirement) was met. This decision enabled

the continuation of segregation in public places and the markedly inferior education Blacks and other minorities received in underfunded schools.

Social Capital: Like cultural capital, social capital pertains to exchange values. In this case, however, emphasis is not on the knowledge dimension but on the social relationships, the individuals or groups one knows that can enhance one's productivity or skills. Sociologist James Coleman used the term to advance his theory that specific features of social organization—family structure, kinship relations, norms or standards for behavior, and shared values—are the bases for success in schools. From Coleman's perspective, if one belonged to or was able to avail oneself of a social network such as the Catholic parochial school system, for example, one might benefit from the long tradition of values that Catholic education has forged to achieve optimal performance from its students. Thus, because the Catholic school traditionally values and even demands a certain type of parental engagement for its students, parents who interact more with the school as volunteers in the classroom or as members of the parent-teacher association will see greater educational outcomes for their students. Research has not fully validated this theory; the findings are mixed.

Social Deconstruction: It is the process of exposing the way a given social fact or reality has been constructed to appear natural, normal, and perhaps inevitable. This process relies on the use of specific concepts or ideas designed to help uncover other possibilities. For instance, recalling the case of Frederick Douglass's initial lack of self-confidence to learn just like the Whites, we might try to make sense of why he felt inferior. When he had a series of experiences over time that exposed that not all Whites were smarter than him and that some, like his master, actively worked to keep him ignorant, he began to "deconstruct" the story/myth that Blacks were inherently inferior to Whites. He saw that specific things had to be done to make him "inferior." From this view, we see that power and truth are the focus of social deconstruction: the goal is to free what is true from the control and packaging of those who have had the power to determine its form and presentation to us.

Socialization: This is the process of educating people to the values, beliefs, and ways of a given society; it is the process of getting people to want to do what they must do for the society to work. Of course, this is an imperfect process; people do not always buy into what is presented to them,

especially when there are competing messages or socializing agents.

Social Philosophy: Social philosophy is a philosophy (love and study of wisdom) that focuses on man and society. In particular, it attempts to identify and speak on the nature of man, especially what makes him "human." Its purpose is to help humans make a better world by identifying behaviors that benefit us as a species and those that hurt.

Status quo: This term refers to the way things are. It is traditionally seen as representing a conservative position, one characterized by fear or complacency.

Universal Truth: This term is associated with philosophy, particularly those branches—epistemology and ontology—that deal with final things such as God, Heaven, and Hell. It pertains less to a specific truth or fact than to the pursuit of such a possibility. Thus, it refers to that truth or fact that goes beyond all finite truths. Its relevance to modernity as historically envisioned is the belief that through the scientific method and other techniques we can approach, if not attain, a more perfect world.

Washington-Du Bois Debate: The historic debate was not a one-to-one meeting but a series of speeches made by Booker T. Washington and W. E. B. Du Bois over a period of years regarding the proper educational focus for African Americans. Washington focused on the industrial education model that some called "colonial education." He saw Negro progress as dependent upon gaining skills and jobs that did not directly threaten or compete with Whites. Du Bois emphasized the need for African Americans to receive a broad educational experience comparable to that received by the White elites who would be leaders, not just followers. Although the two men differed in their emphases, they shared a vision of Negro social progress; Du Bois later agreed more with the Washington model than he did initially, although he remained a champion and model of high academic attainment for African Americans.

CHAPTER FIVE

Race and Pedagogy

We blame P-12 teachers and university professors for the "failure" of the schools. We blame them on a lot of levels. We blame their professional teacher education; we blame what they teach; we blame how they teach. The simplistic and punitive reform efforts that have resulted in the creation of standards and the development of high stakes testing reflect the fact that, for over twenty years, teachers in public schools and institutions of higher education have been blamed for all that is wrong with education.

—*Perry Marker (2003, 1)*

When Frederick Douglass's master insisted that he not be taught to read and write, he was addressing the role of pedagogy in learning. Defined broadly as the theory and practice of teaching, pedagogy has been alternatively defined by Henry Giroux (1994, 281) as "a vehicle for transmitting knowledge." According to Giroux, pedagogy not only transmits knowledge: it shapes, enhances, and limits what we are aware of and how we use and broaden our minds.

Given this view of pedagogy, Douglass was exposed to several pedagogies: the master's; the master's wife's; and his own evolving lived experience of slavery and White people. From these diverse pedagogies, he learned to challenge slavery and yet remain positive toward the White abolitionists who helped him gain his own freedom and advocate for slavery's termination. Further, Douglass's life was clear evidence that the education gap created by slavery could be overcome. For hundreds of years, moreover, African Americans have achieved academically and assumed a significant role in the growth of the nation (Benson-Hale, 1986).

But, as we saw in Chapter Three, a major achievement gap continues to exist between African Americans and White Americans. As a result, "race and pedagogy" has become an increasingly significant subtheme in the race and education discourse. This subtheme of "race and pedagogy" is made more complex and pressing for prospective teachers because of another issue: blaming teachers for a wide range of national problems.

In the epigraph, Perry Marker identifies the main race-related issue raised with respect to teachers: the role of curriculum and instruction in continuing the gap in achievement. Given that people have very different notions of what "race" and "pedagogy" do or ought to mean, there are tensions that continue to plague efforts to reduce the education gap. Some put the failure of certain minorities to do better in school down to human factors, including cultural, familial, and individual flaws (Thernstrom & Thernstrom, 2003). On the other hand, some see racism as the continuing underpinning for both social and educational inequality (Bell, 1992). In this chapter, we will review some of the tensions and interventional trends associated with the topic of "race and pedagogy." We begin with a closer look at what it means to be an effective teacher for those students identified as academically underachieving.

Some Aspects of Effective Teaching for Educational Equity

Pedagogy is concerned ultimately with teaching. What makes for quality teaching? Different people will identify different things: teacher preparation or excellence, teacher care, supportive administrators, sufficient material

resources, parental and community involvement, and so on. Some of these elements have already been covered in previous chapters. Here, I want to focus on several that bear more specifically on the matter of equitable education—that is, an education that allows all students to achieve to their abilities and potential.

Scholars have identified many critical elements of quality teaching that move toward or promote equity. These are:

- Teachers' content knowledge and pedagogy (Saphier, 1997; Wiggins & McTighe, 1998).
- Teachers' cultural responsiveness (Gay, 2000; Howard, 2003; Ladson-Billings, 1994; Milner, 2003)
- School organization and structures that promote and support ongoing collaborative learning among the stakeholders—students, parents, teachers, and community
- Teacher-pupil relationships

These four foci or elements have been identified as essential for quality teaching. They have been viewed as especially significant for students identified as struggling or at risk of failure in public schools. Minorities, especially African American and Latino students, have been among the most often cited groups requiring quality teachers (Darling-Hammond, 1998; 2006). For this reason, reform efforts have paid particular attention to these four elements. But what precisely do these elements refer to?

School Knowledge and Pedagogy

The first of these elements pertains to the observation that beyond school knowledge as curriculum content and material, there is a "school knowledge" (Anyon, 1981) that gets expressed differently in schools according to class and other differentiating characteristics. That is, quite often, very different content is presented to different students according to their class. For instance, consider Jean Anyon's study of five schools, distinguished by class (working, middle, elite). She found that even when the textbooks were similar in some courses, the way the material was presented was very different, with important consequences for how students saw themselves both as learners and as future citizens and workers.

Research has shown that student achievement and performance is very much influenced by teacher assump-

tions and beliefs (Rist, 1970; Brophy, 1983; Brophy & Good, 1986). This is important to understand because a variety of reforms have been based on understanding and influencing teacher beliefs. We will return to this issue below. Summarizing research on the importance of quality teachers, the following passage from the Teachers 21 Web site illustrates a basic attitude and pedagogical orientation characterizing effective teaching:

> Teaching rigorous content knowledge means teaching not only facts, but also deconstructing and explicitly teaching the habits, skills, and practices...associated with a discipline or academic practice. For example, a science teacher might break apart and teach discrete aspects of writing a laboratory report, including understanding terms and concepts (e.g.: hypothesis, conclusion), the purpose and function of each section of the lab report, communicating results in different forms (text, graph, pictures), etc. If the laboratory report required students to work in groups, the teacher might also explicitly discuss and teach expectations, roles, and routines regarding working in groups, and have in place a system for students to discuss with the teacher not only benefits, but also problems or obstacles that arise through working in groups.

Rigorous teaching, as described above, can and does take place across classes and racial groups (Haberman, 1995; Ladson-Billings, 1994). In addition to the strategic deconstructive skills described as important for effective teaching, effective practitioners have been identified by others. For instance, Martin Haberman has identified excellent teachers of minority children identified as "star teachers." These teachers are both warm and fair; they also model or personify discipline. They do not blame the students' underachievement on possible personal weaknesses, family background, or the community at large. Rather, they provide safe, secure environments for their students and identify ways of avoiding the institutional pitfalls that can hurt their pupils.

The reform implication of this element—teacher mastery of knowledge and pedagogy—is simple: the teacher must not only know what and how to teach subject matter content (math, science, social studies), she or he must also recognize that students learn from teachers things not in the books. This has been called "the hidden curriculum" (Jackson, 1968) because these ideas, values, and beliefs are not always stated. Nonetheless, students learn attitudes and strategies about life and learning through the things said and done in schools by teachers, administrators, parents, and other students (Meighan, 1981).

Efforts have been made to make sure that all teachers are well prepared, especially those chosen to teach minorities. Citing the research evidence for this policy goal, Linda Darling-Hammond (1998, 1) notes:

> Studies of underprepared teachers consistently find that they are less effective with students and that they have difficulty with curriculum development, classroom management, student motivation, and teaching strategies. With little knowledge about how children grow, learn, and develop, or about what to do to support their learning, these teachers are less likely to understand students' learning styles and differences, to anticipate students' knowledge and potential difficulties, or to plan and redirect instruction to meet students' needs. Nor are they likely to see it as their job to do so, often blaming the students if their teaching is not successful.

Darling-Hammond's ending thought echoes Martin Haberman's view cited earlier. Recall how Haberman's star teachers do not blame the students for their own lack of preparation. But the problem goes further: teacher expertise and the quality of the curricula taught are interrelated. This relationship pertains to the relevance of the materials being taught. This is the second element of effective teaching identified above.

Culturally Relevant Curriculum and Pedagogy

We begin with another passage from Darling-Hammond (1998, 1):

> Teacher expertise and curriculum quality are interrelated, because a challenging curriculum requires an expert teacher. Research has found that both students and teachers are tracked: that is, the most expert teachers teach the most demanding courses to the most advantaged students, while lower-track students assigned to less able teachers receive lower-quality teaching and less demanding material. Assignment to tracks is also related to race: even when grades and test scores are comparable, black students are more likely to be assigned to lower-track, nonacademic classes.

I often begin my courses in education and human services by helping my students to see their "shared fate" (Kirk, 1964) with their future students and clients. As future teachers and human service workers, my students

have already been tracked. Like those teachers discussed by Darling-Hammond, my student teachers will be working most often with the less advantaged students and "multiproblem families." They will, like their clientele, frequently find less than favorable work conditions, institutional resources, and social approval (Pinderhughes, 1995). In addition, they will often be misunderstood by the very people they seek to help. This mutual mistrust and shared distress with the system will frequently pit them against each other (Gresson, 2004).

I include this kind of thinking in my students' coursework as a part of my pedagogy; more precisely, I try to share these kinds of thoughts and reflections as part of the "hidden curriculum" that I believe to be relevant to them. If they can see me working to give them things beyond the book, outside the typically spoken classroom ideas, perhaps they can learn additional ways of relating to their students and clients when they get out into the world.

Culturally relevant curriculum and pedagogy means that the teacher recognizes that the learner begins with a worldview—including ways of taking in new information—that reflects the home and community environments. What is taught in the classroom, if it is relevant to this dimension of the student, becomes powerful precisely because it invites or draws the student into developing or adopting more powerful ways of seeing, relating, and working.

Ladson-Billings (1990a) views culturally relevant or sensitive pedagogy as teaching that uses the student's culture to help them achieve success. As I indicated above, all successful teachers must respond at some level to the students' cultural context to help them succeed. As it applies to minorities such as African Americans and Latinos, this means that such pedagogy focuses on teaching the academic subject matter with rigor but in a manner that does not dislodge or alienate the student from her or his culture or personal sense of self or identity.

The critical concern with curriculum that is culturally relevant is captured by Sharon Nelson-Barber and Elise Trumbull Estrin (1995, 174) in their discussion of making mathematics and science culturally relevant to Native American students:

> Many American Indian students have extensive knowledge of mathematics and science-knowledge that is rooted

in naturalist traditions common to Native communities and arrived at through observation and direct experience. Because many Indian communities follow traditional subsistence lifestyles, parents routinely expose their offspring to survival routines, often immersing the children in decision-making situations in which they must interpret new experiences in light of previous ones...Unfortunately, a majority of teachers recognize neither Indian students' knowledge nor their considerable learning strategies.

These authors go on to make a parallel observation regarding the interconnection of culturally relevant content and pedagogy:

American Indian ways of teaching, such as modeling and providing for long periods of observation and practice by children, are quite harmonious with **constructivist** notions of learning. "Mainstream" teachers can look to their American Indian colleagues for such examples of culturally-responsive practice as well as insights into how to interpret student performance on classroom tasks.

Constructivism

This is a philosophy and educational perspective that argues that new knowledge is learned or incorporated into what is already known or understood. From this perspective, the learner is an active participant in constructing new knowledge.

The competent or effective teacher must learn to learn from her or his students, and from their families and communities. The inevitable differences in lived experience among humans mandate that we all engage in a certain degree of intercultural communication if we are to work effectively together. The emphasis on collaborative school communities is one consequence of this perspective. Collaboration thus constitutes a third element in the promotion of effective teaching.

Collaborative School Communities as Pedagogy

Collaboration is a conscious strategy for teaching in diverse, racially mixed communities. This strategy derives, in part, from evidence that teacher interactions and relationships with minorities and their families have often failed to promote quality education (Epstein, 1995). In addition, research on effective collaborative community-school partnerships has strengthened the belief that shared governance is important.

There are at least two important dimensions or forms of collaboration: that among teachers and that between teachers, their schools, and the community at large. The first form of collaboration has particular significance for the ways that instruction in literacy, mathematics, and other subjects might be taught within a given team of teachers. Here, for instance, teachers' pedagogy becomes more

inclusive and pertinent to student interests and needs by a willingness to share decision making. This sharing feature is inclusive of differences; it also assumes or mandates mutual caring and support (Irwin & Farr, 2004; Newmann & Wehlage, 1995). The relevance of such collaboration to issues of race and difference in the classroom and school has been stated in this way by Teachers[21]:

> Within a collaborative culture, educators can work together to ensure that issues of race, class, and achievement are not undiscussable…, but become a central focus of all conversations about student performance. These conversations would have the potential to inform not only individual teacher practice and shared school beliefs, but might also have the power to shape organizational structures. For example, a learning community might examine student achievement patterns (as measured by standardized tests, attendance, disciplinary actions, etc.) to critically evaluate and reform the ways aspects of the school itself might contribute to these patterns.

Working with one's colleagues is very important to the achievement of educational equity. But there is another dimension of collaboration that must also be addressed. This is teacher-student interaction and relationships.

Teacher-Student Relationships

The vast literature on minority student dropouts has been particularly concerned with unproductive teacher-student interactions (Faith, 2007; Miller, 1998). In this context, the overriding observation has been that teachers, especially new and inexperienced ones, frequently fail to develop relationships with minority students that foster **resilience** and a sense of belonging. Resilience and a sense of belonging are two of the most critical factors helping high school completion.

The *failed relationship* is itself pedagogical: it teaches the child that he or she is not valued by the context. Moreover, the child experiences that he or she is not expected to achieve. This has been the critical, repeated finding of research dealing with teaching practices and attitudes. As the educational publishing company ScholarCentric argued on their Web site:

> Not surprisingly, researchers have found strong links between school connections and student resiliency. When researchers compared high-risk Mexican-American students with significantly high grades and those with sig-

Resilience

This term refers simply to the observed capacity to overcome seemingly insurmountable obstacles. Within race and education scholarship and activism, the term has been applied to those minorities who seem to achieve academically and fare well emotionally despite obstacles such as poverty and discrimination.

nificantly low grades, they found that the resilient students reported significantly higher levels of family and peer support, positive ties to school, high levels of teacher feedback, and placed higher value on school. The most significant predictor of success was the student's sense of belonging to the school.

Other studies report similar findings. According to Loyce Caruthers (2006, 1):

"The nature of teacher-student relationships strongly affects student performance, including the decision to drop out of school. A study of high school dropouts among Native American students concluded that dropouts perceived teachers as not caring about them and not providing them sufficient assistance in their work."

These four elements of effective teaching are not discrete in any final sense; they work together to bring about the desired outcome of an effective teacher-pupil exchange that can be described as academic success. But knowing what is needed is one thing, achieving it another. For this reason, in part, there have been many educational reform efforts made in the past twenty-five years (Hampel, 1996; Ravitch, 1983). These have met with varying degrees of success (Stringfield, 2000). Several of these have, nonetheless, commanded considerable attention, both positive and negative.

Some Reform Initiatives in "Race and Pedagogy"

There have been many initiatives aimed at changing the ways schools are structured, teachers are prepared, and curriculum constructed and presented. There have also been broader reform initiatives or positions developed and championed. These initiatives are not always distinguishable from each other or mutually exclusive. Nonetheless, for our purposes, we may divide and consider them in two categories: (1) race-focused initiatives and (2) critical pedagogies. Both categories have social justice and educational equity as important goals. However, they differ in their emphases on achieving these ends.

Some Race-Focused Initiatives

Multiculturalism as Pedagogy. Multicultural education became a major theme and initiative within education in the 1970s (Banks, 2000; Gresson, 2004). Because education

prior to the 1960s emphasized a one-sided, Eurocentric understanding of values, beliefs, and the way things ought to be, some challenged it. The argument was that the nation is pluralistic, made up of diverse groups with multiple perspectives on reality and what is important; accordingly, schools should reflect these various perspectives, particularly with respect to ancestry and cultural traditions. The belief was and is that so much of school success is due to how a person fits into the school culture.

From this view, for example, it was argued that curricular materials in reading that talked only about Dick, Jane, baby Sally, and Spot did more than merely teach one how to read: it also taught one that the world that these fictional children inhabited was the only, the best, and the preferred world. Certainly, I as a child saw the world through their eyes and never even associated myself with having the things and experiences common to them. To be sure, I did learn to read and write despite the common minority experience in segregated schools of the pre-1960s: less learning resources, including the discarded textbooks and materials of White students (Kozol, 1991; 2005).

Multiculturalism, according to some scholars, largely concerns itself with being sure that everyone gets some recognition in the curriculum. From this view, attitudes of "prejudice" due to ignorance must be replaced with tolerance. Tolerance can lead to an intervention or prescription "inclusive knowledge" or curricular enrichment. The goal is cultural pluralism—different cultures living harmoniously side by side in democratic unity.

This view of multiculturalism is simplistic, but it does represent the picture many have of this vast initiative. The reasoning behind the rejection of multiculturalism is complex. It actually has several elements and critics. These include:

- Conservative critics who believe that America's greatness is due to everyone more or less accepting a single, necessarily Euro-American cultural orientation (Bork, 1996; Kirk, 1993; Schlesinger, 1998)
- Radical critics who see multiculturalism as failing to sufficiently characterize and challenge the structural inequities that fuel the political, cultural, and social dominance of the Euro-American and capitalist forces (Kincheloe & Steinberg, 1997)

- Progressive critics who see the assumptions underpinning multiculturalism as flawed (Carter, 2000; Marable, 1992)
- Afrocentric critics who see Eurocentric cultural dominance as deadly to the ultimate forging of a worldview that African peoples (and others) can use to further their collective interests (Asante, 1980/1987)

These various perspectives on multiculturalism seem not to greatly alter the commitment to promote the democratic ideal of cross-educating people about the positives of diversity and pluralism in the United States (Banks, 2000; 2004). They do, nonetheless, point to the perceived need for ways of getting beyond the specifics of race, if not racism, in the effort to further an all-inclusive educational agenda. Recent illustrations of this shift include renewed interest in teaching and modeling social justice and democracy (Ayers, Hunt, & Quinn, 1998). This model has much to commend it, especially the focus on traditional American values regarding liberty, equality, and fair play. But the ultimate viability of such initiatives depends on a critical mass of individuals and groups prepared to undergo the explorations of self, oppression, and the discovery of mutually enhancing experiences (Gresson, 2004).

Afrocentric Education and Culturally Appropriate Pedagogy. Thomas Jefferson said that observers should not return to Africa to judge whether or not enslaved Africans were intellectually equal to Europeans or Asians. His view regarding the Africans has been championed by many since the eighteenth century. It has also been challenged by many, including several African Americans. The movement associated with those who have looked to Africa for evidence of cultural equality or superiority has been called Afrocentrism. This movement emphasizes the contributions of African cultures and a distinctive group or racial identity to the world. It necessarily challenges the attitude expressed by Jefferson and the educational practices traditionally associated with views of European superiority (Eurocentrism). Some of the ideas associated with an Afrocentric worldview—a view that claims African peoples share distinctive, perhaps essential qualities—have generated both opposition (Ginwright, 2004) and support (Allen, 2004).

Afrocentrism begins with Africa, not the United States, to forge a set of images or narratives regarding how African peoples constructed their values and worldview. This strategic return to Africa has been aimed, in part, at offsetting the near total refusal to acknowledge that Blacks had civilizations or compelling cultural traditions prior to the arrival of the White man. Molefi Asante (1980/1987) has viewed the return to places such as Egypt to reclaim a civilized past to construct an "Afrocentric idea" as a necessary corrective to the intentional erasure of historical facts and cultural ways by those oppressing Africans and their descendents.

Nigerian born Afro-Canadian scholar George Dei (1994, 17) offers a related understanding of the theory:

> Afrocentricity as an intellectual paradigm must focus on addressing the structural impediments to the education of the African student by engaging her or him to identify with her or his history, heritage, and culture. To be successful the Afrocentric pedagogue must move away from a manipulation of the "victim status and exploiting white guilt" to work toward finding solutions to pressing problems of educating students of African descent. (Moses, 1991: 88)

From this perspective, African American academic achievement is aided by positive self-esteem; however, this self-affirmation has been truncated by the repeated, mass advertising campaign that presents everything important as the achievement of White men. Without necessarily denying the importance of positive self-esteem for academic achievement, some scholars have called a return to Africa a myth (Mary Lefkowitz, 1996). This dimension of the debate regarding Afrocentrism continues. Still, some have been willing to place African traditions and values in the forefront of curriculum and pedagogy. Dei has described the matter in this way in his essay on Afrocentric education (1994: 17):

> For the Afrocentric educator, Afrocentricity is a commitment to a pedagogy that is political education. It is a form of education intended to equip students and teachers with the requisite cultural capital to work toward the eradication of the structural conditions that marginalize the existence of certain segments of the school population.

A major aspect of the Afrocentric initiative has been to identify traditions, beliefs, values, and styles of survival that were lost to African Americans with enslavement. The

hope has been, in part, to gain a legitimate enhancement of self-esteem. The argument has been that much of the education gap for African Americans is that they have been "miseducated" (Woodson, 1935); they lack knowledge of their past and many of the habits needed to compete in the contemporary world. In such a context, moreover, they are seen to permit maltreatment or misrepresentation by White educationalists—teachers, administrators, policymakers, and researchers.

The rise of Afrocentric pedagogy has been due to this particular perspective on traditional minority educational practice and policy. A wide range of discussion has accompanied the pursuit of a specific set of curricular and pedagogical practices aimed at improving the intellectual (cognitive) and emotional (affective) life of African Americans. For instance, the focus on addressing the language needs of those students who come to school with speaking habits different from the middle-class teacher has led to the so-called Ebonics debate. Ebonics is a term used to describe the dialect associated with many African Americans who have learned a variant of English that has been influenced by traditional African languages. These children, according to mainstream views, merely don't know how to speak proper English. They, like their Latino and Asian peers for whom English is not the first language, are seen as needing to learn English—pure and simple.

But from the Afrocentric view, like that held by many bilingual educators and scholars, knowledge of the non-English, first language is helpful in teaching both English and the other subject matters. Language has been a major theme in discussions of academic achievement. Native Americans were among the first to be "reeducated" about the relative place of English in their lives (Spring, 2004). African Americans, more recently, featured in debates around the role of Ebonics in learning; and there has been a persistent tension around **bilingual education** and its relation to learning among subgroups such as Latinos (Soto, 2001), Native Americans (Garcia, 2002), and Asian Americans (Mouw & Xie, 1999).

Moreover, the Afrocentric focus shares another feature with bilingualism and biculturalism: all reflect the fact that minorities are increasingly less a "deficit" than an "asset" for the United States. More precisely, the student population is increasingly made up of students from bilingual

Bilingual Education

This term refers to providing in-school learning opportunities for children whose first or initial language is not English or who have limited English proficiency. Often misunderstood to mean the valuation of English as the national language, bilingual education builds on the research-based finding that overall academic growth is enhanced when the child's native language is taken into consideration.

and bicultural backgrounds. As Eugene Garcia (2002, 74) wrote in his integrative essay on Native American language recovery:

> Initial signs from efforts by the Navajo and Pueblo cultures in reclaiming indigenous languages are hopeful. Others, including a more optimistic Hinton (1994), conclude that limited progress is being made in retarding the overall phenomenon of language loss among US indigenous people. Clearly, as we address issues of bilingualism and schooling in the US, this issue will continue to require attention. In the US, with the roots of bilingual education in the domain of social justice, attention to the human, particularly education costs, can be related to Native language extinction. At the core of this extinction, Fishman (1991) reminds us, is the issue of "rooted identity." Cesar Chavez also reminded us that in the struggle for education equities in the US, "equities are not about equalities but about dignity." In essence, bilingual educators in the US have come to realize that self-worth is a critical element of educating language-minority students. Crawford (1995) appropriately points out that language and cultural loss is a characteristic of dispersed and disempowered communities; those that may need their language and culture most. It is not a phenomenon of privileged communities.

The emphasis on *self-worth* as a central feature of academic achievement is what has inspired supporters of Afrocentric and other bicultural educational initiatives. The importance of this emphasis seems self-evident to those who recall that race-based oppression has always sought to strip away self-esteem and self-care. Thus, while there are those who point to the apparent "reverse racism" of Afrocentric perspectives on education, this continues to be a preferred strategy among those concerned with helping African American youth to succeed within seemingly hostile environments (Morris, 2004; 2003b).

Culturally appropriate teaching pedagogies for African American males, within such a context, might include hip-hop culture—that is, music, songs, poetry, and videos (Hall, 2007). The goal of this form of **urban pedagogy** is to engage the students by forming a bridge between their lived world and that of the teacher and school. In making her argument for the use of hip-hop as a pedagogy of engagement, Hall (2007, 40) said:

> Several scholars and socially and politically conscious artists are advocating liberatory education and pedagogy

Urban Pedagogy

This term refers to several different and some contradictory school practices. One meaning is the directive teaching style identified by Haberman as characterizing "poverty pedagogy," which operates from the assumption that "urban" means Black, inner-city poor, and violent. Another meaning is a pedagogy that teaches how to understand urban society's "codes" that are used by the powerful to control the lives of urban dwellers.

to educate a new generation of hip hoppers. Liberatory education has its roots in the teachings of Carter G. Woodson, Anna Julia Cooper and W. E. B. Du Bois. Aldridge wrote that Woodson, the father of African American history month, believed that education for African Americans should be realistic, rigorous, and firmly rooted in the culture and historical experiences of African people. This sentiment is shared by socially and politically conscious rappers such as Ishues and KRS-One who believe that "education and schooling as practiced in the United States denies students access to the truth and provides them with illusions rather than an understanding of reality." (Alridge, 2005, 240)

Other emergent instructional approaches share the emphasis on engagement. The idea of **culturally appropriate pedagogy** has been introduced to address this issue. From this perspective, the overall academic program—mathematics, science, and social studies—should attempt to make cultural sense vis-à-vis the background of students from different racial and ethnic groups. Assuming that cultural context strongly impacts learning, this orientation advocates for such practices as the hip-hop curriculum. Among the various ideas associated with culturally appropriate pedagogy is that of **constructivism**. This theory of learning suggests that humans learn or construct knowledge by relating new information to their prior knowledge and experience. As pedagogy, culturally relevant teaching uses the learner's experience to introduce new knowledge.

Many assume that the constructivist approach is merely good commonsense teaching. But the idea of culturally relevant pedagogy, which employs constructivist thinking, has been challenged for its potential inappropriateness. In particular, Guoping Zhao (2007) has noted the potential for overemphasizing differences that are not pertinent to a given instructional task. Zhao cautions against pigeonholing students merely because of an assumed cultural relevance in their learning style. Nonetheless, some scholars have found it useful to explore alternative pedagogical strategies for teaching some minorities. For instance, Sean Coleman (2002) has reported preliminary findings of research employing culturally appropriate teaching pedagogies on specific mathematic exercises with fourth- and sixth-grade at-risk students. Placing students in both individualistic and communal learning situations, he found "that learning and performing fraction problem solving

Culturally Appropriate Pedagogy

This term refers to a broad range of teaching initiatives that share a common concern with applying constructivist principles to teaching learners from diverse cultural backgrounds. The overriding aim of such pedagogy is to build on those parts of the child's culture that are most familiar and relevant to her/his self-esteem, values, and pursuits.

Constructivism

This is a philosophy and educational perspective that argues that new knowledge is learned or incorporated into what is already known or understood. From this perspective, the learner is an active participant in constructing new knowledge.

tasks under a communal condition allows for significant improvement on individual performance of such tasks than in the individual cultural condition."

Prospective teachers can perhaps best view these and related reform initiatives as strategies that can complement their own self-reflective, constructive efforts. The possible temptation to adopt approaches unfamiliar to one, even in the name of cultural sensitivity, can be problematic; so it is best to only adopt new techniques thoughtfully.

Antiracist Education:. Audrey Thompson (1995, 1) has noted:

> To many critics, anti-racist pedagogy has all the earmarks of propaganda. Certainly the popular media portray anti-racist and other progressive pedagogies as extremist, humorless, strident, and biased. The catch phrase "politically correct" has become shorthand for an ideologically mandated equality that violates common sense, a superficial rhetoric thrust upon a sensible populace by out-of-touch academics with a personal ax to grind. To its advocates, on the other hand, anti-oppressive pedagogy represents an important chance to help marginalized students flourish and to engage privileged students in knowledge-seeking that sets aside assumptions allowing them to condescend to, or dismiss, alternative perspectives.

Some might say that all education aimed at achieving social justice will be antiracist. Thus, both multicultural and Afrocentric education and pedagogy are antiracist. But some view the seeming flaws of multiculturalism and Afrocentrism as requiring an alternative reform initiative: antiracist education. This perspective grew chronologically from the failed attempts to bring about social justice by infusing diverse content about groups and their histories, achievements, and contributions to the American mosaic. Racism was and remains the focus of this perspective.

There are problems associated with this approach (Arora, 2005; Thompson, 1995). Perhaps the most notable pertains to the idea of forcing people to be nonracist. Some believe that a democratic value includes the right to be racist and that any effort for schools to try to influence students deemed as racist is undemocratic (Butin, 2001; Kumashiro, 2004).

Nonetheless, efforts continue to introduce policies and practices believed to be nonoppressive to all people (Gresson, 2004). In particular, focus is placed on the structures or institutional arrangements that promote discrimi-

nation and oppression. Expressions of racism by individuals are thus deemphasized; the rationale being that individual behaviors are largely influenced by social arrangements of rules, roles, and relationships. For instance, policies such as zero-tolerance to fighting in schools that seem to disproportionally affect African American or Latino males might be critiqued and eliminated or revised to be more fair (House, 1999; Heckman & Kruger, 2003; Insley, 2001; Wagstaff, 2004).

The primary concern in much antiracist or antioppressive activity at the individual level is largely related to helping willing individuals to explore "power" and "ideology" as factors that tie individuals to systematic arrangements that promote inequality. The goals here are aimed at alerting people to a variety of practices seen as racist in effect. These include

- Use of intelligence test to measure human potential along static "racial" lines
- Acceptance of unequal opportunities along racial lines,
- The creation and dissemination of ideas that normalize—or present as naturally occurring—racially patterned disparities.

These basic goals result in a variety of school-related efforts aimed at changing through challenging the accepted or given social ideas underpinning racism. Of course, as mentioned above, many people believe that their ideas about "race" are the truth and may not want to be a part of an initiative they see as wrong. Many school-based goals of antiracist education are held by most people. Thus, some critics question whether it does enough or is merely hype (Troyna, 1985). Nonetheless, scholars such as Harvard University Professor Mica Pollock (2006) have identified a number of commonplace antiracist practices in education that may seem contradictory but actually complement each:

> These four...[antiracist practices]—rejecting false notions of human difference, engaging lived experiences shaped along racial lines, enjoying versions of such difference, and constantly critiquing and challenging systems of racial inequality built upon these notions of difference—are actually not self-contradictory. Rather, they demonstrate that everyday anti-racism requires doing each situationally on a daily basis. Antiracism requires *not* treating people as race group members when such treatment harms, and

treating people as race group members when such treatment assists. Deciding which move to take when requires thinking hard about everyday life in educational settings as complex, conflict-ridden and deeply consequential.

Audrey Thompson (1995, 1) offers an instructional orientation to the implicit contraction in her illustration of inviting people with different perspectives or lived experience to move toward antiracist perspectives:

> What would this mean for a specific classroom undertaking—say, an inquiry into the debate between Booker T. Washington and W. E. B. Du Bois? It might mean framing the debate as a specific genre within the performance tradition so that particular moves would be identifiable as "playing the game" or "advancing the narrative." What counts as meaningful and persuasive would then be understood in light of the *kind* of public performance that the debate constitutes, including its audiences over time. One way to accomplish that framing would be to enter the debate from an altogether different perspective—that offered by Barbara Fields and James Anderson, for example, or by Toni Morrison or Carter G. Woodson. Taking up the debate in a performance vein also would mean treating each of the sides of the argument as opening up possibilities, rather than as describing "realistic" or "rational" positions. Thus, one would not simply read the positions literally and argue, for example, "Washington was being realistic; there was a very real danger of lynching at the time," or, alternatively, "I agree with Du Bois. The Constitution provides us with our rights; no one is required to earn them." Instead, the classroom project would involve understanding, appreciating, and critiquing each of the positions as a complex move in the attempt to shape race relations against a particular historical backdrop. Developing such an understanding might take any number of directions, but it could not be referred simply to abstract principles or to individuals' experience. Instead, it would involve *creating* an experience in which the elements of the debate were a point of departure rather than themselves setting the limits of the educational experience.

This is a very large passage. It says a great deal. It requires some reading and rereading, but it is a very thoughtful effort to address the enduring, underlying issue of racism as a preferred way of dealing with difference and exercising power in word and deed over others. The prospective teacher, as seen by the above statements from Thompson and Pollock, must be flexible, knowledge, and committed in order to address the moment to moment

actions that give shape to human identity and positive interactions among students.

Partly because antiracist curricula and pedagogy involve so much work by individuals, many doubt whether this kind of initiative is sufficient. Rather, these other critics of race-based policies and practices that reproduce social inequalities call for perspectives that can assist more systemic or large-scale change. A brief review of a few of these will round out our discussion of race-focused reform.

Race and the Critical Perspectives on Education

In Chapter One, I defined *criticality* as an attitude or perspective that forefronts looking at reality—issues, beliefs, values, and behavior—in terms of ideas such as power, ideology, race, gender, and class. These concepts encourage us to see beyond the surface meaning or understanding of a thing. For instance, the term "gender" prompts us to ask how we define "male" and "female" influences development and behavior in ways that we assume are "natural" but really are socially prescribed and created. The earlier noted gender bias in the classroom is one consequence of applying critical ideas to education and schooling.

Several scholarly efforts have emerged to offer other critical insights into education and schooling. Among the theories that have gained attention are

- **Postmodernism**
- Feminism
- Postcolonialism
- **Queer theory**
- Critical pedagogy

These different areas offer both concepts and explanations for understanding issues, including schooling and education. These new concepts do not necessarily claim to have the whole truth or total knowledge regarding an issue; rather, they generally try to challenge perspectives that attempt to talk about issues in non-negotiable terms. That is, they attempt to create a space for alternative voices and perspectives. They are based on the fact that some people have more power than others; and one aspect of this power is the creation and control of knowledge through control of schools, media, and other institutions of finance and governance.

Language, identity, and power can be seen as stable, unchanging and well-defined; they can also be seen as

---

Postmodernism

This term has generated a great deal of controversy regarding its precise meaning. Among the many definitions and scholars associated with this term is a common working meaning: the rejection of a single, comprehensive, essential, and progressive world truth and method of attaining truth however defined.

Queer Theory

This term refers to a school of cultural and literary criticism, that is, analysis of film, literature, and popular culture. Queer Theory has been especially associated with gay and lesbian scholars, but the goal of scholars working from this orientation is to promote greater social justice through undermining the ways that gender norms are used to force humans into predetermined ways of relating to each other as other than fellow humans.

changing, unclear in aspects of their meaning and possible meaning. Change comes, in part, from resistance. When Frederick Douglass resisted enslavement, he was participating in the change in the ideas of the time about the necessary and unchanging nature of "race," "intelligence," and future race relations.

Critical Pedagogy and Constructivism. More radical perspectives have evolved to shape the role of the larger society in creating inequality. Critical Pedagogy is perhaps the most notable of these orientations and initiatives. The term has many meanings because it is not static; its meaning has evolved as different scholars and educators describe and develop their own efforts to make an impact on the way schooling occurs in different times and places. With roots in the 1930s social activism in Europe among the so-called **Frankfurt School** (Kincheloe, 2004) and exemplified in the work of Brazilian educator Paulo Freire, critical pedagogy attempts to achieve educational equity through a variety of strategies.

These strategies aim, in particular, at raising the learner's critical consciousness. As you will recall, we first met this type of thinking in Chapter One. There, I indicated my own critical perspective and commitment through the introduction of the thinking of Kurt Lewin and C. Wright Mills. Both men pursued social justice through ideas or theories aimed at helping us to think more fully about the consequences of human action. Recall, as well, that in Chapter Two, critical theory was introduced as a corrective to some of the oppressive limitations of social theory that would not address issues such as power, ideology, and oppression.

Critical theory and pedagogy are two aspects of a single thrust: to use ideas or analytical tools to influence how learning and teaching are arranged to achieve the enlargement of the individual's perspectives on the world and things occurring around her/him. From this view, of course, critical theory and pedagogy are related to issues facing minorities, women, and other collectivities forced to the margins of society by rules, roles, and relationships that are exclusionary. A major aspect of critical pedagogy, then, is the examination of how communication and language are used to continue domination of some by others.

Critical pedagogy is also a collaborative and democratic form of human action. It seeks to link personal lib-

Frankfurt School

This term refers to a group of early twentieth-century European scholars and activists committed to identifying and using social theories and critical ideas to bring about radical changes in the relations between those who control societies and those who are the workers and ordinary citizens.

eration to collective transformation of the institutions and social arrangements that undermine greater freedom and social justice. It is with respect to social justice, moreover, that critical pedagogy has been most profoundly related to teacher education and the preparation of future teachers who will challenge those practices that lump individuals into categories and essentialize them and their possibilities.

Many scholars and educators have been identified with this initiative (Darder, Torres, and Baltadano, 2002). These include Henry A. Giroux (2006), Peter McLaren (1998), bell hooks (1994), Debbie Britzman (2003), and Joe L. Kincheloe (2004). Kincheloe, for instance, has given sustained attention to the relation of teacher education and critical pedagogy in his primer. He notes, "The dominant culture's conversation about education simply ignores questions of power and justice in the development of educational policy and classroom practice" (2004, 99). Because of this neglect, moreover, Kincheloe emphasizes, as we did in Chapter Two, the important of contextualizing knowledge. That is, it is important to recognize that there are different types of knowledge claiming a voice or hearing and that the teacher must learn to work with the uncertainties that accompany this fact.

Some critical theorists have focused on **"critical race theory"** and education. For instance, Ladson-Billings and Tate (1995) used ideas from critical race theory to clarify aspects of the continuing presence of unequal or unfair treatment for minorities in schooling despite the apparent improvements. They base their discussion on three ideas taken from legal studies, where the idea of critical race theory first arrived (Taylor, 1998). Ladson-Billings and Tate argue that the relevance of critical race theory to education is based on three central propositions:

1. Race continues to be a significant factor in determining inequity in the United States.
2. U.S. society is based on property rights.
3. The intersection of race and property creates an analytic tool through which we can understand social (and, consequently, school) inequity.

From their discussion of these propositions, Ladson-Billings and Tate affirm a general tenet of critical race theory: as long as Whites continue to control the most powerful institutions, they will continue to manipulate cir-

---

Critical Race Theory

Began in the 1970s by legal scholars concerned with the law and race relations, this theoretical orientation considers the failures of full racial justice from a critical perspective. Noting the slow pace of full racial justice in economic, political, and educational contexts as due to continuing racism, these scholars argue that the apparent gains of the civil rights era have been significantly eroded by legal limitations Derrick Bell has been most associated with critical race theory. However, educators have also been associated with the field. In particular, educators have used critical race theory to further understanding of classroom activities and dynamics, curriculum, instructional polices and practices, and testing.

cumstances to their advantage. Thus, a positive shift in the plight of minorities such as African Americans is linked to White self-interests (Bell, 1992). To illustrate this basic assumption of critical race theory and education, they cite a study reported by Kofi Lomotey and John Statley on the education of African Americans in Buffalo Public Schools in the 1980s:

> Lomotey and Statley's examination of Buffalo's "model" desegregation program revealed that Africans American and Latino students continued to be poorly served by the school system. The academic achievement of African-American and Latino students failed to improve while their suspension, expulsion, and dropout rates continued to rise. On the other hand, the desegregation plan provided special magnet programs and extended day care of which whites were able to take advantage. What, then, made Buffalo a model school desegregation program? In short, the benefits that whites derived from school desegregation and their seeming support of the district's desegregation program...Thus, a model desegregation program becomes defined as one that ensures that whites are happy (and do not leave the system altogether) regardless of whether African-American and other students of color achieve or remain.

This interpretation of desegregation efforts is only one lens on the issue. Others see important progress with respect to the success of school integration. Still, the dominant trend, called **resegregation**, does seem to support this tenet of critical race theory, at least for some of the scholars and activists concerned with race in education. Ladson-Billings and Tate (1995, 65) illustrate why this perspective clashes with the more mainstream interest in multiculturalism:

> We argue that the current multicultural **paradigm** functions in a manner similar to civil rights law. Instead of creating radically new paradigms that ensure justice, multicultural reforms are routinely "sucked back into the system" and just as traditional civil rights law is based on a foundation of human rights, the current multicultural paradigm is mired in liberal ideology that offers no radical change in the current order...Thus, critical race theory in education, like its antecedent in legal scholarship, is a radical critique of both the status quo and the purported reforms.

There have been many efforts to address the failures of the nation to act on the promises and expectations of the

---

Resegregation

This term refers to a pattern of increasing segregation within certain schools, especially those schools with predominately minority students. Latino-dominated schools have been among the most segregated in recent years.

Paradigm

Simply, this term refers to a model, or way of framing, characterizing, or viewing reality. In his book, The Structure of Scientific Revolutions, historian of science, Thomas Kuhn, popularized the term. In his work, the term referred to the set of practices and ideas that define or characterize a scholarly discipline during specific periods of time. For instance, traditional medicine focuses on the germ that causes illness, while say, osteopathic medicine, has focused on the skeletal system and its contribution to illness. These are two different paradigms for trying to promote wellness.

Civil Rights Movement, including the Supreme Court decision of 1954. Critical race theory, in general, derived out of the perception that too many things did not change despite the things that have changed. But there are those who caution against too much pessimism regarding the stranglehold of racism. In addition, and perhaps most important, critical race theory assumes that Blacks and Whites are rigidly and essentially different collectivities about which we can theorize easily and accurately. They counter that a balanced perspective recognizes both the need for a critical voice for the oppressed and the consequential presence of Whites pursuing social justice as part of the human family (Taylor, 1998).

Critical race theory reflects a frustration, a fear that things are changing less than many want to claim. It is a way of viewing reality that keeps the pressure on those committed to racial and social equality. Prospective teachers are invited by both critical pedagogy and critical race theory to confront those ways of relating—whether in the classroom or elsewhere—that come down on the side of those who control most of the resources and institutions in society. Teachers may also be encouraged in this invitation by the growing range of globally significant perspectives on attaining social justice and educational equity. One of the most exciting areas for this new thinking and advocacy around race and pedagogy is Whiteness studies and postcolonial pedagogy.

Whiteness Studies and Postcolonial Pedagogies

Whites have always recognized that unequal privileges are built into our society. But what is new, perhaps, is the evolving discourse about "Whiteness" (McIntosh, 1988). Whiteness is an idea foreign to many Whites. But it is, in part, this very unfamiliarity that constitutes an aspect of what is meant by "Whiteness" (Nakayama & Krizek, 1995). Many have attempted to offer a definition for this term that gets at the heart of the issue of privilege based on racial categorization (Hill, 2004; Lipsitz, 1995; McKinney, 2005)

Joe L. Kincheloe (1999, 162) wrote:

> In the emerging sub-discipline of whiteness studies scholars seem better equipped to explain white privilege than to define whiteness itself. Such a dilemma is understandable: the concept is slippery and elusive. Even though no one at this point really knows what whiteness is, most observers agree that it is intimately involved with issues

of power and power differences between white and non-white people. Whiteness cannot be separated from hegemony and is profoundly influenced by demographic changes, political realignments, and economic cycles. Situationally specific, whiteness is always shifting, always reinscribing itself around changing meanings of race in the larger society. As with race in general whiteness holds material/economic implications-indeed, white supremacy has its financial rewards. The Federal Housing Administration, for example, has traditionally favored housing loans for white suburbs instead of "ethnic" inner cities.

Several important ideas are contained in this passage, notably the relation between power and whiteness. The elusiveness of the term is also part of its power. As Kincheloe continues:

Indeed, critical multiculturalists understand that questions of whiteness permeate almost every major issue facing Westerners at the end of the twentieth century: affirmative action, intelligence testing, the deterioration of public space, and the growing disparity of wealth. In this context the study of whiteness becomes a central feature of any critical pedagogy or multicultural education for the twenty-first century. The effort to define and reinvent the amorphous concept becomes the "prime directive" of what is referred to here as a critical pedagogy of whiteness.

The idea of Whiteness has angered or offended many who view "race talk" as inappropriate or out of step with "colorblind" policy (Gresson, 2004). They see such talk as aimed at playing the "race card" or as intended to induce "White guilt" (Steele, 2006; Thernstorm, 2006). Some note that efforts to expose the disingenuous or the "bad faith" among those who speak of any systematic or enduring White racial oppression involve true courage.

However, some see **postcolonial** analysis of Eurocentric pedagogy in other terms. For instance, in their comparative case study of **indigenous** youth in Australia and the United States, Hickling-Hudson and Ahlquist (2003, 67–68) write:

White blindness to the difference race makes in people's lives has a powerful effect on schools and other institutions in white dominant societies. It keeps white people from learning about the role that their privilege plays in personal and institutional racism. If white teachers want to challenge the authority of the white, western worldview, and build an anti-racist, socially just and global

Postcolonialism

Postcolonialism (also called postcolonial theory) is a term used to identify several lines of scholarship and research undertaken by those interested in the development of national and group identities and intergroup relations within geographical areas once dominated by colonial powers.

Indigenous

This term means those who are native to or originally associated with a place or situation. In race and education, the term has been especially used to refer to groups such as Native Americans, Eskimos, and Aborigines.

curriculum, they need to acknowledge their power and privilege. This is the foundation for learning to give up that power and instead working to build anti-racist alliances across ethnic, racial, and cultural differences. A key component of such alliances is the principle of self-determination for indigenous peoples and peoples of color in public schooling. The goal is not to elicit feelings of guilt for white racism but to encourage insight into the racialized nature of oppression, as a foundation for working towards the redistribution of power and resources along more equitable lines.

What is going on within a postcolonial context? The term connotes a time after colonial rule. The specific task is to understand precisely how "Whiteness" works. How do those who have gained power by a variety of methods including enslavement of others organize things to keep their control? This is the question. Since schooling has a pivotal role in this process, the postcolonial perspective considers the curriculum in places across the world that have suffered from colonialism and racism:

> It explores the ways in which the Eurocentric curriculum, which includes the practices and assumptions of "whiteness," is often so accepted as the norm that it is invisible and beyond question for many teachers. It is rarely admitted at any level of the education system that today's curriculum still draws from the white imperialist projects of "fostering a science and geography of race, renaming a good part of the world in homage to its adventurers' homesick sense of place, and imposing languages and literatures on the colonized in an effort to teach them why they were subservient to a born-to-rule civilization"...Poststructural theories offer opportunities to think about how teachers are positioned within discourses of identity. Our research (and others') suggests the need for teachers to interrogate their assumptions about class and culture and how these are played out in their pedagogical relationships with students. (Hickling-Hudson & Ahlquist, 2003, 67–68)

Race, Pedagogy, and Higher Education

Much of the focus thus far has been on issues associated with K-12 settings. But a large part of the race and pedagogy discourse pertains to postsecondary settings (Cabrera et al., 1999; 2002). Historically, minorities, especially African Americans in the South, were not able to pursue higher education. After desegregation in the 1950s, many minorities began attending previously all-White institutions in

the South and elsewhere. Aided by affirmative action policies, the minority population increased significantly.

However, a variety of problems emerged. Ranging from issues of minority student academic readiness to campus climate, these problems have seemed to both ebb and flow over the past several decades. The wide education gap between minorities and majority group students continues. In an incisive article, Anthony Carnevale, vice president at the Educational Testing Service, wrote in the Spring of 2000:

> But the current diversity on U.S. campuses falls short of the diversity we need in our workplaces. Minorities still are underrepresented in higher education. The share of minorities among college students should at least equal their share of the 18- to 24-year-old college-age population. By that measure, there are currently 200,000 African Americans and 430,000 Hispanics missing on today's college campuses. As time passes, the opportunity gap in minority education is likely to widen because our educational policies will not provide sufficient support. Decades, even generations, of equal opportunity in elementary and secondary education will be required to produce equal educational outcomes in postsecondary education. In the meantime, only affirmative action can ensure that those occupying the most elite positions in our society mirror the racial and cultural composition of the United States.

The three important areas of focus in higher education have been teacher education, retention of minorities through pedagogical improvements, and knowledge production by universities. The first of these focuses has been improving teachers' abilities to matriculate minority students, especially those from the most disadvantaged circumstances. The second focus has been on college classroom practices that can either help or hinder minorities performing their best and reaching graduation. The third area of focus is the knowledge production arm of the university itself. With the arrival of area studies—African American, Women's, Gender, Latino, and Asian—the university has been forced to address its own role in the production and reproduction of knowledge that can be a force of either oppression or liberation. A brief comment on each of these initiatives will help clarify the overall concern with race and pedagogy in higher education.

Teacher Education, "Race," and Pedagogy

Ask most prospective teachers if their expectations for students differ, and few will likely say "yes." It is not that they are intentionally denying an awareness of differences. Rather, they truly believe that they treat all students the same. But they don't. This was shown in a now famous study of gender bias in the classroom (Sadker & Sadker, 1994). In this study, female teachers showed preferential treatment toward White male students and were able to believe this only when they were shown on video favoring boys in subtle but important ways. Their behavior reflected often unconscious but very real differences in expectations for the females and males in their classes.

Teacher expectations also differ for racial and ethnic groups. Among findings reported by researchers are:

- White students are expected to achieve higher than African American students (Baron, Tom, & Cooper, 1985).
- Parsons (cited in Weinberg, 1977) reported that teachers praise and encourage White students more, respond to them more, and pay more attention to them than to Mexican American students.

On the other hand, teachers have been found to be incredibly positive influences for disadvantaged students if they are able to care for or support these students (Nettles et al., 2003; Noddings, 1992/2000). This is important to bear in mind because the teaching force is largely made up of White females; hope for overcoming the education gap is dependent partly upon their being successfully connected with certain minority students and their families. The emergent trends in race and pedagogy are premised, in large measure, on evidence of such success in the past and a conviction that it can be improved.

There are two basic objectives of race-related curricula and pedagogy for student teachers. These are:

- providing a set of critical tools or concepts for understanding the contexts of teaching (Kincheloe, Slattery, & Steinberg, 2000)
- encouraging the development of the attitudes and emotions needed for classroom success (Gresson, 2004)

It must be stated from the outset that there are critics of any initiative that seems to point a finger at the dominant group. The above objectives thus are problematic. An excel-

lent illustration of this alternative perspective is offered by Mc Elroy (2005, 1) in a Fox News article where she relates the concept of cultural competence to the notions of "diversity" and "multiculturalism":

> "Cultural competency" advances the same basic goals as those buzz words. Certain groups (such as minorities) and certain ideas (such as gender feminist interpretations of oppression) are to be promoted by institutionalizing policies that encourage them. Of course, this means that other groups and other ideas are de facto penalized or discouraged.

Perspectives such as the above are important for teacher educators to be sensitive when trying to teach about social justice, democracy, and the educational enterprise. The reasons are many, but perhaps the most important is that prospective teachers have a lived experience and a perspective on issues of social justice and oppression that may lead them to resist learning that they may need to disidentify with aspects of their traditions (Gresson, 2004; Kincheloe, 2004). Consequently, much of the race-related literature on teacher education preparation seeks to understand what perspectives a predominately White female teaching force have (Carr & Klassen, 1997; Zembylas, 2003), as well as the impact these perspectives have on their understandings and behaviors regarding issues of educational equity, social justice, and democratic inclusion.

Student Teachers and "Race Pedagogy". The issue of pedagogy is such a complex one, it will be helpful to first contextualize what is being discussed when people talk about "Eurocentric" or "Multiculutral" pedagogy. To do this, let us return once again, briefly, to the case of Frederick Douglass and his master. They had very different needs and intentions. Education did not mean the same thing to them. The master did not fear that Douglass learning to read would in and of itself be the problem; rather he was concerned that the emotional and cognitive growth that comes with such learning would enable Douglass and other slaves to challenge the "facts" and "figures" that the master used to control things.

This is important. It says something about the very idea of education. In this regard, Paulo Freire (1970, 67–68) wrote: "Education as the practice of freedom...denies that [people] are abstract, isolated, independent and unattached to the world; it also denies that the world exists as a reality

apart from people. Authentic reflection considers neither abstract [people] nor the world without people, but people in their relations with the world."

For Freire, becoming educated is becoming a part of the action, a part of the construction of what is and can be. It is liberating. Referring back to slavery, the slave master fears the liberating potential of education. This is what anyone who controls information or knowledge as a means of controlling another person fears. Whether one believes it or not, many feel that "Eurocentric" educational thought and practice have this oppressive potential.

When Frederick Douglass fully understood this fact in relation to his own denial of an education, he had a profound awakening. His education became liberating; he understood not just new information but also ways of relating to the challenging and changing world he inherited. Let me repeat here part of his quotation from Chapter One: "I now understood what had been to me a most perplexing difficulty—to wit, the White man's power to enslave the Black man. It was a grand achievement, and I prized it highly. From that moment, I understood the pathway from slavery to freedom. It was just what I wanted, and I got it at a time when I the least expected it." Here Douglass illustrates **resistance pedagogy**. Moreover, he offers a clue to what is called culturally powerful or relevant pedagogy: that form of teaching and learning that enables one to make one's own decisions. This type of pedagogy has traditionally required that the minority person both accept and resist much of the information present in the dominant society—for instance, to simultaneously learn that "White is pretty" and "Black is ugly," on the one hand, and yet forge for oneself and family, on the other, an image of "Black is Beautiful!" (Gresson, 1982).

This idea, or even talking about it, has often been viewed as offensive by many, especially those who have escaped the lived experience of group oppression due to race, ethnicity, or the like (Gresson, 1995; 2004). It is perhaps less important that the prospective teacher agrees with this implied accusation of the dominant society than it is that she or he is aware that there are those who do feel this way. This awareness is not limited to the majority group teacher, however; as a minority teacher of predominantly White students, I have also had to acknowledge that descriptions of my own experiences with segregated

Resistance Pedagogy

This term has its roots in the work of scholars such as Henry Giroux who have viewed education as often oppressing rather than liberating students from unfavorable circumstances in their lives. While many reject the idea that schools do anything negative, some see a clear and unmistakable downside to education for minorities that does not help prepare them to challenge society's injustices but merely seeks to prepare them to dutifully learn their ABCs.

education and racial oppression can be experienced and interpreted as attacks on how they both see themselves and understand the world (Gresson, 2004).

My own curricula and pedagogy, although approved or sanctioned by some teacher educators as sound, are not acceptable to every scholar. Moreover, my students may resist learning something—however sound or scholarly—that seems to undercut their biographies, histories, and daily life. The same is true for millions of minorities who may experience not only school as oppressive, but aspects of the larger White society as well. With this tension or irony in mind, we can perhaps see why some educators concerned with social oppression have focused on pedagogy. In particular, the teacher-student relationship has been a major concern, since student academic achievement has been often seen as positively affected or influenced by how the teacher feels about her or him.

An excellent summary of the teacher education and "race" is provided by Allard and Santoro (2004, 14) in their study of teacher beliefs and teaching practices in Australia:

> If we accept that identities are constantly in the act of becoming, then how student teachers see themselves, locate themselves within discourses of "difference" e.g.— of social justice, of economic imperatives, of teacher professionalism—depends in part on the experiences, contexts and discourses they are offered. As teacher educators, part of our role is to offer experiences to our students that enable them to understand and examine their own positionings within and through current discourses. While some researchers (e.g., Britzman, 1991; Causey et al., 2000) argue that a way of helping pre-service teacher-education students is to begin from their personal constructs, we recognise that this is an extraordinarily difficult task to undertake, not just for our students, but for anyone. However, while this may serve as a starting point for developing understanding and insights into taken-for-granted beliefs about culture and class, it does not necessarily address the fundamental question: how does one work with difference in classrooms in ways that acknowledge cultural and class values and beliefs without essentialising identities or stereotyping groups?

Minority Retention and Pedagogy

Pedagogy has been especially interesting with respect to minority higher education. The two trajectories that have

evolved are the HBCU and Predominately White Institution models. Each has taken a certain minority constituency and each faces challenges today that reflect the clash between historical and contemporary needs.

Pedagogy and HBCUs. The years immediately following the abolition of slavery saw an almost frenzied effort to achieve an education among the former slaves (Anderson, 1988; Williams, 2005). You will recall that in Chapter Two, G. Stanley Hall described how postwar Blacks were anxious for learning, so much so that presumably Booker T. Washington declared that one of his missions was to lower the sights of his people. Whatever the extent of truth to Hall's observation, it was true that the years immediately following the Civil War were marked by a comprehensive, unrelenting effort to gain an education. The belief then, and to some degree even now, was that "racial uplift" lay at the heart of achieving full equality in America.

The major role of the historically Black colleges and universities was to teach the ex-slaves to read and write. The curriculum was largely precollegiate until after the Civil War. For example, the earliest such institution, Cheyney University in Pennsylvania was organized in 1837 as an Institute for Colored Youth. It taught an elementary and secondary curriculum. Today, more than one hundred HBCUs are in operation (Gasman & Jennings, 2006; Reddick, 2006). Unlike the development of higher education in White private and state postsecondary institutions, the Black schools followed a different path.

The years after the Civil War saw the growth of American colleges and universities; higher education, in general, spread through the passage of the **Morrill Act of 1862.** This act provided the basis for land-grant institutions financed largely by public taxes. In particular, according to James Anderson (undated):

> African American higher education took a different path. From the Reconstruction era through World War II (1939–1945) the majority of Black students were enrolled in private colleges. Northern religious mission societies were primarily responsible for establishing and maintaining the leading Black colleges and universities. African American religious philanthropy also established a significant number.
>
> Given the virtual nonexistence of public education for Blacks in the South, these institutions had to provide preparatory courses at the elementary and high school

Morrill Act of 1862
Named for Vermont congressman Justin Smith Morrill, this act was passed by Congress and signed by Abraham Lincoln in 1862. It called for the setting aside of thousands of acres of land for the establishment of dozens of institutions of higher education.

levels for their students. Often they did not offer college-level courses for years until their students were prepared for them. Nonetheless, the missionary aims of these early schools reflected the ideals of classical liberal education that dominated American higher education in general in that period, with its emphasis on ancient languages, natural sciences, and humanities. Blacks were trained for literacy, but also for teaching and the professions.

The curriculum found in the historically Black post-secondary institutions reflected the complex needs of the newly enfranchised African American group. And as William Watkins (1993) has shown, the curriculum has evolved in different directions to capture needs grounded in the diverse experiences of African Americans. This diverse set of needs continues unto the present. However, the pursuit of fuller participation in the American democracy underlay the shape of much of this curricular focus. In *The Education of Blacks in the South, 1860–1935,* the 1990 recipient of a best book award from the American Educational Research Association, James D. Anderson (1988, 29) explains:

> Black leaders did not view their adoption of the classical liberal curriculum or its philosophical foundations as mere imitation of white schooling. Indeed, they knew many whites who had no education at all. Rather, they saw this curriculum as providing access to the best intellectual traditions of their era and the best means to understanding their own historical development and sociological uniqueness.

These thoughts echo those made in Chapter Two on the relation of race and the curriculum. Throughout African American history, education has been seen as crucial to the argument for full inclusion. It has been the experience of failing to attain inclusion even when academically prepared that has influenced some to question the efficacy of education. This, however, remains a minority perspective among the various minorities. Recent research indicates that education continues to be seen by African Americans, in particular, as very important.

Still, the historical value placed on education by Booker T. Washington and White benefactors of Black Education (Watkins, 2001) was seen as serving both curricular and pedagogical functions. On the pedagogical end, vocational or hands-on instructional practices were seen as facilitating discipline and other qualities some Whites

felt the Africans lacked (Anderson, 1988). Another factor affected the way that schools were designed and instruction carried out in these institutions. Because so many of the students accepted for postsecondary education lacked college preparation, they often needed remedial work. Much like the community college, HBCUs have accepted students needing remedial work as part of the mandate for uplift.

At the same time, partly under the influence of leaders in education such as W. E. B. Du Bois, these schools saw their mission to include the cultivation of the brightest and the best students to assume leadership roles within African American communities.

Pedagogy and Predominately White Institutions.
Minorities outside of the South traditionally attended the private schools up North. Though numerically small, these students typically excelled and returned to African American communities to assume leadership roles. As might be expected, even though their career opportunities were significantly fewer than their White counterparts, they did well. But, interestingly, they did not do as well as students attending historically Black institutions. However, things have changed. According to Fryer and Greenstone (2007), economists at Harvard and MIT respectively:

> Until the 1960s, Historically Black Colleges and Universities (HBCUs) were practically the only institutions of higher learning open to Blacks in the US. Using nationally representative data files from 1970s and 1990s college attendees, we find that in the 1970s HBCU matriculation was associated with higher wages and an increased probability of graduation, relative to attending a Traditionally White Institution (TWI). By the 1990s, however, there is a wage penalty, resulting in a 20% decline in the relative wages of HBCU graduates between the two decades.... The data provide modest support for the possibility that HBCUs' relative decline in wages is partially due to improvements in TWI effectiveness at educating blacks.

These results do not necessarily tell the full story regarding the curricular and pedagogical functions traditionally assumed by the HBCUs. That is, the greatest dropout rates for minorities are at the predominately White institutions. Moreover, there is considerable evidence that the various minorities do not necessarily achieve wage parity with Whites as a result of attending predominately White institutions (Darity & Myers, 1998).

There have been a wide range of issues associated with minority higher education in predominately White institutions. These include:

- Preferential treatment—fairness and affirmative action policies
- Effective mentoring of diverse students
- Racial intolerance on campus
- Retention of minority students
- Diversity and cultural autonomy of campus Minority faculty at predominately White institutions

These are just some of the areas of concern that have been prevalent in minority higher education. They all touch on issues of school climate and organizational structure. The more precise issue of pedagogy and race has also been an enduring one. Perhaps the one area in which it has been most notable is with respect to minority underachievement in mathematics and science. It is here that important differences between HBCUs and HWCUs might be seen (Inniss & Perry, 2003). Ebony McGee (2005, 1) has framed the challenge in this way:

> The disturbingly low rates of math achievement by students of color (African Americans, Latinos, Native Americans), women, and low-income students have gained increasing attention in the education community.... Although African Americans, Latino/as, and Native Americans made up 28 percent of the college-age population in 1995, they received only 9 percent of the bachelor's degrees and 2 percent of the doctorates in engineering. On the other hand in that same year, 50 percent of high school Asian graduate students took advanced mathematics, while 31 percent of African-American and 24 percent of Hispanic graduates took remedial mathematics courses compared to 15 percent of white and Asian students. (National Science Foundation, 2000)

This higher education racial gap has been the rationale for advocating for new pedagogies. For instance, Annie Howell and Frank Tuitt (2003) have advocated for the need to adjust modes of instruction or pedagogy. The traditional modes of pedagogy, including lectures, have potentially harmful consequences. Chief among these is the potential creation of a variant of hostility that turns students away from engagement.

Traditional forms of classroom teaching include such things as lectures and independent laboratory work. This form of pedagogy is considered teacher-centered; information is decontextualized (that is, isolated from a specific relevant situation). In addition, the textbooks that are used are routinely treated as the truth rather than partial truth or knowledge. Emphasis is on memorization and giving it back to the instructor (regurgitation). Recitation, multiple-choice test items, and selecting the one "right" or correct answer are emphasized.

This type of pedagogy is familiar to most of us. And it works reasonably well, or so it seems. Where and when it does not, we accept this as evidence that the learner has some flaw, individual or group. We have already discussed the consequence of this type of teaching elsewhere, noting that this form of teaching is one way of tracking youth into prescribed positions within society (Clark, 1960).

Of course, elite institutions do not necessarily follow this precise model of teaching. There is evidence that elite schools, both K-12 and postsecondary, do vary their pedagogies (Anyon, 1981; Bartlett, 2005). In particular, elite institutions tend to provide a wide range of instructional or learning opportunities for their students. Interestingly, within the predominately White institutions, emphasis on minority-related pedagogy found a special expression and focus within the newly emerging area studies programs.

Area Studies: Curricula and Pedagogy. In Chapter Two, we noted that institutionalized education such as found in universities and colleges was promoted by those who believed that a unified, cumulative knowledge base would promote civilization. As a consequence, certain people became the official producers of knowledge and shared beliefs that were considered "the truth." Of course, humans have probably always competed to determine whose vision or version of truth was the accepted one. The term "canon" has been used to refer to knowledge we have come to accept as true and worthy of passing on from generation to generation.

In the 1960s, with the arrival of the various liberation movements—Black, women's, gay and lesbian, and so forth—there were parallel efforts to influence the knowledge accepted as the truth. Within the academy, one form this new effort took was the creation of departments and programs that focused on histories of the minorities and the disenfranchised. In addition, new information or research studies were initiated to correct or update what was traditionally thought and taught about minorities.

Two aspects of area studies might be mentioned just briefly. The first pertains to the very idea of an area studies as a field of inquiry. According to James B. Stewart (2006):

> As disciplines evolve sub-disciplines develop enabling researchers to pursue specialized inquiries. However, sub-disciplines subscribe to a set of shared values and interests that provide a coherent macro-level disciplinary identity. Distinctive schools of thought typically develop within disciplines as a result of differing interpretations of some aspects of the discipline's mandate, for example, disagreements regarding the relative merits of quantitative and qualitative research. Different schools of thought can also exist within individual sub-disciplines. In several disciplines there are disagreements within sub-disciplines regarding the relative importance of race and class in perpetuating disparities.
>
> Africana Studies can be appropriately characterized as an "academic discipline" with distinctive intellectual assumptions and values. Afro-American Studies, Critical Race Studies, Diaspora Studies, African Studies, Afro-Latino/a Studies, and Africana Women's Studies can be treated as sub-disciplines within the discipline of Africana Studies and rational judgments can be made about whether a school of thought within each sub-discipline is best identified with Africana Studies, per se, or some other intellectual tradition. (See Stewart, 1992; 2004)

From the pedagogical side, Tunde Adeleke (2002, 1) has noted:

> History has shown that oppressed and subordinated groups often invoke "liberation pedagogy." This pedagogy has come in the form of revisionist critique of prevailing body of thought—as was the case in the United States, with the struggles for Black Studies—and for the intellectual recognition and legitimacy of the historical and cultural heritage of blacks.... In both the United States and Africa, the emergent intellectual tradition served to correct the misconceptions and fallacies of a dominant tradition, and moved toward creating a holistic body of knowledge that more accurately depicts and represents marginalized and indigenous people's historical experiences.

Together, Stewart and Adeleke address the emerging race-based questions stimulated by an ever-evolving vision of the possible and how it affects what is traditionally viewed as essential and unchanging. More specifically, the notion of "race" and its relation to education and pedagogy is in

constant flux. Where we go in the realms of both research and pedagogy depends in large measure on what choices are made on the global stage. In the next and final chapter, we will return to some of the themes introduced in previous chapters, but with a difference. We shall ask how the issue of globalism impacts on the notion of "race" in education.

GLOSSARY

Bilingual Education: This term refers to providing in-school learning opportunities for children whose first or initial language is not English or who have limited English proficiency. Often misunderstood to mean the valuation of English as the national language, bilingual education builds on the research-based finding that overall academic growth is enhanced when the child's native language is taken into consideration.

Constructivism: This is a philosophy and educational perspective that argues that new knowledge is learned or incorporated into what is already known or understood. From this perspective, the learner is an active participant in constructing new knowledge.

Critical Race Theory: Began in the 1970s by legal scholars concerned with the law and race relations, this theoretical orientation considers the failures of full racial justice from a critical perspective. Noting the slow pace of full racial justice in economic, political, and educational contexts as due to continuing racism, these scholars argue that the apparent gains of the civil rights era have been significantly eroded. legal limitations Derrick Bell has been most associated with critical race theory. However, educators have also been associated with the field. In particular, educators have used critical race theory to further understanding of classroom activities and dynamics, curriculum, instructional polices and practices, and testing.

Culturally Appropriate Pedagogy: This term refers to a broad range of teaching initiatives that share a common concern with applying constructivist principles to teaching learners from diverse cultural backgrounds. The overriding aim of such pedagogy is to build on those parts of the child's culture that are most familiar and relevant to her/his self-esteem, values, and pursuits.

Frankfurt School: This term refers to a group of early twentieth-century European scholars and activists committed to identifying and using social theories and critical ideas to bring

about radical changes in the relations between those who control societies and those who are the workers and ordinary citizens. A major focus of these scholars from philosophy, sociology, political science, and related fields was power or, more specifically, the social ills they associated with capitalism.

Indigenous: This term means those who are native to or originally associated with a place or situation. In race and education, the term has been especially used to refer to groups such as Native Americans, Eskimos, and Aborigines.

Morrill Act of 1862: Named for Vermont congressman Justin Smith Morrill, this act was passed by Congress and signed by Abraham Lincoln in 1862. It was a controversial bill and was once vetoed before Lincoln became president. It called for the setting aside of thousands of acres of land for the establishment of dozens of institutions of higher education. Despite the importance of this leadership role by the federal government with respect to higher education in the United States, Native American peoples suffered additional land losses as a result of this move.

Paradigm: Simply, this term refers to a model, or way of framing, characterizing, or viewing reality. In his book, The Structure of Scientific Revolutions, historian of science, Thomas Kuhn, popularized the term. In his work, the term referred to the set of practices and ideas that define or characterize a scholarly discipline during specific periods of time. For instance, traditional medicine focuses on the germ that causes illness, while say, osteopathic medicine, has focused on the skeletal system and its contribution to illness. These are two different paradigms for trying to promote wellness.

Postcolonialism: Postcolonialism (also called postcolonial theory) is a term used to identify several lines of scholarship and research undertaken by those interested in the development of national and group identities and intergroup relations within geographical areas once dominated by colonial powers. Scholars writing in this tradition are concerned with the legacy of colonialism—what is life like for those who have been both brutalized and constructed or shaped by those whose primary goal was the exploitation of resources.

Postmodernism: This term has generated a great deal of controversy regarding its precise meaning. Among the many definitions and scholars associated with this term is a common working meaning: the rejection of a single, comprehensive, essential, and progressive world truth and method of attaining truth however defined. This view of the term

indicates the concern of those associated with it to indicate a flight from confidence in "reason" and "civilization" as constructed by those ruling much of the world at the start of the twentieth century.

Queer Theory: This term refers to a school of cultural and literary criticism, that is, analysis of film, literature, and popular culture. Dating from the 1980s, this orientation grew out of feminist theory, which was concerned with challenging many of the given assumptions about the necessary relation between the sexes and the ways in which gender is socially constructed to appear as God-ordained rather than as arbitrary preferences of humans. Queer Theory has been especially associated with gay and lesbian scholars, but the goal of scholars working from this orientation is to promote greater social justice through undermining the ways that gender norms are used to force humans into predetermined ways of relating to each other as other than fellow humans. Scholars feel that they achieve their goal through helping to reveal the strategies—often invisible-like—that regulate sexual behavior and sometimes aid sexual oppression of those who break various sex taboos.

Resegregation: This term refers to a pattern of increasing segregation within certain schools, especially those schools with predominately minority students. Latino-dominated schools have been among the most segregated in recent years.

Resilience: This term refers simply to the observed capacity to overcome seemingly insurmountable obstacles. Within race and education scholarship and activism, the term has been applied to those minorities who seem to achieve academically and fare well emotionally despite obstacles such as poverty and discrimination. Many scholars have begun to look at students identified as resilient to gain insights into how others can be helped to overcome similar obstacles.

Resistance Pedagogy: This term has its roots in the work of scholars such as Henry Giroux who have viewed education as often oppressing rather than liberating students from unfavorable circumstances in their lives. While many reject the idea that schools do anything negative, some see a clear and unmistakable downside to education for minorities that does not help prepare them to challenge society's injustices but merely seeks to prepare them to dutifully learn their ABCs. Critical pedagogy is considered a resistance pedagogy because it tries to get learners to think in uncommon ways about some of the things we are taught and the views that we accept without reflection. "Resistance" in this context

pertains merely to the human capacity to act as our own agent with respect to the ways we see, understand, and experience things. One important context in which this term has been recently applied is teacher education, where the goal has been to help future teachers learn to go beyond merely teaching the assigned curriculum or defining students, their families, and communities in familiar but unsupportive and limiting terms. Sometime student nonlearning is related to resistance to the feeling that what is being taught or the manner in which it is being taught are alienating and threatening. Resistance pedagogy ultimately means that all learners, including prospective teachers of minority students, can benefit from liberating teaching practices.

Urban Pedagogy: This term refers to several different and some contradictory school practices. One meaning is the directive teaching style identified by Haberman (undated) as characterizing "poverty pedagogy," which operates from the assumption that "urban" means Black, inner-city poor, and violent. Another meaning of the term is that it is a pedagogy that teaches how to understand urban society's "codes" that are used by the powerful to control the lives of urban dwellers (See Dobson, 2002; Haymes, 1995; Rowley, 1998).

"Race and Education" in Global Perspective

The contemporary context of all school knowledge and experiences is profoundly shaped by *globalization* and the ever-expanding pattern of integration of local realities into more global dynamics and vice versa.

—*McCarthy et al. (2003, 461)*

A recent surprise visit to my daughter's MySpace site revealed her to be an "18-year-old female of African, Native American, and European ancestry." I had been told to expect the unexpected. So I was largely tickled to learn that she had added a few years to her age. But her "**hybrid identity**" was not expected. While it was true enough, reference to her mixed origins reminded me that my daughter belongs to another generation and another world. Moreover, the Internet and sites such as MySpace are an essential part of that world.

By placing her photo and hybrid biography on MySpace, my daughter was participating in the globalization process. I do not know if this international Web site was the source of or a mere vehicle for my daughter's decision to adopt a hybrid identity. But it is certain that her

Hybrid Identity
An identity constructed through taking bits and pieces of what has been accepted as distinct group identities, for example, Tiger Woods calling himself a "cablinasian" to acknowledge his mixed ancestry: Caucasian, Asian, African, and Native American.

Global Education

Education has been defined as a life-span encounter and engagement with knowledge about the world community. Emphasis is on interdependency of the earth's people, notably the ecological, social, economic, and technological interconnections.

behavior participates in the **global education** movement enabled by technologies such as the Internet and cell phones. MySpace, then, is part of that worldwide information technology phenomenon that helps shape school experience and knowledge. Susan McLester's (2007, 1) description of her daughter as student is suggestive of the global educational impact of such technology:

> On a typical day after school, you'll find Hannah in her bedroom, iPod charging on the desk, headphones in ears, cell phone in one hand, paperback book in the other, television tuned to a *Gilmore Girls* rerun, and computer with display divided among iTunes, YouTube, a *Pride and Prejudice* DVD, and, of course, MySpace, which she constantly checks for messages from friends.

Global Education has been gaining an increasingly central place in the school knowledge of today's generation. Information technology leaders have recognized the importance of increasing technology literacy on a global scale; as a result, they have fostered a variety of projects to engage youth such as my daughter. But the implications go far beyond tech savvy (Chandler-Olcott & Mahar, 2003; Lam, 2006a).

What youth's engagement with MySpace implies for prospective teachers is a radically new way of thinking about "race" in education in general, and global education, in particular. How my daughter and millions of other youth are fashioning their identities across time and space points to the critical place of globalization in the twenty-first century.

The world is much larger than the United States, and through globalization, it has become more interconnected than ever before. As a result, scholars on race and education have increasingly realized that "to study race, identity or culture and to intervene in their fields of effects, one must be prepared to live with extraordinary complexity and variability" (McCarthy, 2005, 413).

The topic of "race and education" comes full circle with the emerging emphasis on the relation of global developments to race and education (Hilliard, 1999). As citizens, teachers benefit from and stand in jeopardy because of the global changes occurring socially, politically, economically, and culturally. As educators, they participate in what is taught and learned about the human condition, its pitfalls and possibilities (McCarthy et al., 2003).

In this chapter, we revisit the topic of race and education from this global perspective. Three areas require particular emphasis. These are (1) the relation of globalism to race and education; (2) the importance of diasporic knowledge to the interplay of race and education on global scales; and (3) some of the practical and theoretical implications of these changes for the core concepts within race and education, including "race," "identity," and "culture."

Globalism: Some Pitfalls and Possibilities

Globalism and Globalization

According to Joseph Nye, former dean of the Kennedy School at Harvard University, "Globalism seeks to explain nothing more than a world which is characterized by networks of connections that span multicontinental distances. It attempts to understand all the interconnections of the modern world—and to highlight patterns that underlie (and explain) them" (2002, 1). A *world interconnected* is the core meaning of the term globalism. From this view, Christopher Columbus's sharing of resources from far off lands such as "America" with Spain and Europe was a form of global interconnection, or globalism.

Travel with ships aided Columbus's global reach. The term globalization refers to the speed and scope of the global reach, and to its increase through technology such as the Internet and cell phones. These and related technological advances have aided interconnectedness among nations, especially with respect to markets and ideas.

Nye (2002, 1) relates the two concepts in this way: "consider globalism as the underlying basic network, while globalization refers to the dynamic shrinking of distance on a large scale." According to Nye, there are four dimensions or forms of globalism:

- Economic—long-distance flows of goods, services, and markets, multinational organizations.
- Military—long-distance networks in which force, and the threat or promise of force, are deployed.
- Environmental—long-distance transport of materials in the atmosphere or oceans or of biological substances.

- Social/Cultural—the movement of ideas, information, and images across space, such as the diffusion of religions or scientific knowledge.

These different forms of globalism tend to operate simultaneously or close together. Thus, traditionally, religion and other cultural ideas might follow one nation that has invaded and conquered another militarily and economically. But the Internet has changed this tradition because as a result of the relative inexpensiveness of cell phone and computer-based communications, it is possible to spread ideas without military conquest preceding it.

The four dimensions also reflect patterns of interconnectedness that increase or decrease in different ways and at different times. What the student or educator needs to understand are the potential dangers that accompany these interconnections. Consider economic globalism, which relates to the interconnectedness of markets. Markets are defined broadly not only as places where goods are bought and sold, but also as sites where information is shared that enables this exchange of goods and services. In this context, for instance, economic globalization "has led to low-wage production in Asia for the United States and European markets" (Nye, 2002, 1).

These various globalizing processes have many consequences and possibilities. Some of these outcomes and tendencies are hurtful and others are very positive. Both are important for teachers and others educators to understand if they are to be advocates for themselves and their students in a global educational context.

Globalization—Some Problems

The negative possibilities of globalization are associated with inequality, poverty, and gender gaps in education. For instance, young females in developing countries are being left behind. The question being raised by some is contained in a recent study done by the National Research Council titled "Growing Up Global: Can Education Reduce Gender Inequality and Poverty?" (Lloyd, Grant, & Ritchie, 2008). These scholars document the scope of female adolescent work in relation to males in their rural homelands; they also seek to identify how improved global development can help girls gain a greater share in formal, higher education. Globalization has too often been a detriment to this desired improvement.

There are a number of problems associated with globalization. First among these is the possibility of misusing people, or playing them off against each other in ways that continue the social and economic inequalities within and between nations. Another pertains to something that is also a positive consequence of globalization: Telecommunications, the Internet, and advances in air travel have meant that people can "be on the same page" with respect to business, politics, and entertainment. How people go about their daily lives, how they think about issues and events, and how they react to the challenges they consider important can all become part of a "global" process. Frank Lechner (2001) has spoken of this as a "consolidation of world society."

Others refer to it as the McDonaldization effect— everything is the same everywhere. But McDonald's has been seen as both good and bad: at the simplest level, for instance, the Big Mac has, until recently, been not only a quick burger fix but also a contributor to poor eating habits. But the criticism goes beyond making "bad burgers" to the corporation's role in reeducating people around the world to certain questionable values, beliefs, and practices (Kincheloe, 2004).

Perhaps the greatest potential negative associated with globalization relates to the issue of racism and the role of education in its perpetuation. We are all familiar with the idea of "outsourcing" American jobs to countries such as Haiti, Honduras, Pakistan, and Vietnam where people are forced to work for horrible wages in sweatshops creating products to be sold back to us here in the United States. Another outcome of this outsourcing has been the loss of American jobs for millions, especially poor minorities and poor Whites.

How should teachers think about global dynamics such as these? What are the pragmatic and social justice implications of participating in teaching curricula and maintaining institutional practices that do not address these and related issues? These are some of the questions that have been raised as part of the global race and education discourse (McCarthy et al., 2003; Rizvi, 2003). Educators have, in some instances, tried to address these issues through focusing on racism in the global context.

Racism and the Global Context. Bigelow and Peterson (2002, 1) wrote in the introduction to their edited volume,

Rethinking Globalization:

> As we teach and organize around these matters, it's vital that we emphasize the centrality of race. The development of European colonialism was sheathed in theories of white supremacy which sought to justify the slaughter of indigenous peoples, the theft of their lands, and the enslavement of millions of Africans.

Educational policy and ideas regarding curriculum and pedagogy within the global context are significantly influenced by the more powerful Western countries. This is true both with respect to ideas transported to the less developed nations (Tomlinson, 2003) and with respect to the meanings of ideas such as "global citizenship" for developed nations such as Canada and the United States. One interesting possibility has been reported by Leslie Roman (2003) who found that Canadian nation building and nationalism were strengthened rather than weakened by certain kinds of scholarship and teaching practices.

That is, although globalization has been deemed capable of fostering greater sharing of the power and resources, it can work in the reverse manner if curricular and educational policy conversations continue to use ideas of "we/they" with "we" being stronger and "they" being weaker. Roman (2003, 269) described the tension in this way:

> Dominant conceptions of globalization from "above" emphasize discourses of national and global competitiveness, efficiency, consumption, and productive citizenship. Yet, other contending but less prevalent **counter-hegemonic** conceptions from "below," focus on and employ the discourses, among others, of values of civic global responsibility, service to community, respect for the environment, and a shared sense of belonging to a common human community across national borders.

Counter-hegemonic

This term refers to the active resistance against the controlling influence of those with control over information, resources, and understanding, including one's understanding of one's own circumstances. Another way of seeing this is as a resistance to institutionalized power such as school rules and policies that seem unfair or discriminatory.

Leslie Roman here identifies how globalization can lead to discourses or conversations that cut short the fullness of human potential as well as those that take the human race toward greater sharing and caring. At a very personal level, her reflection reminds the educator that how she or he teaches affects how students see not only themselves but others throughout the world community. But so much of education in the United States continues to overemphasize competition and rugged individualism. It is difficult for the individual teacher to address this challenge, but she must.

This kind of tension has led Sally Tomlinson (2003, 215) to conclude:

> Globalization is affecting the education and economic placement of minorities world-wide. Policy-makers around the world have assigned education a major role in improving the competitiveness of national economies in the global market and encourage individuals to develop their human capital, without acknowledgement of social and racial disadvantages.... The economic advancement of developing countries is impeded as skilled workers and professionals migrate...and capital moves to where workers have the lowest wages. The economic migration of unskilled workers to "global cities" leads to the creation of even more intensive immigrant underclasses...It is becoming clear that in the globalized world order the struggle for educational and economic equity and justice for ethnic and racial minorities has taken on new dimensions.

Both Roman and Tomlinson are sensitive to the possibility that "race" can be reenergized and employed to aid the deepening of the gaps between classes of people. Roman is also concerned that our language may seem more democratic and caring than our tendencies; and we may thus claim "color-blindness" or "race-nonconsciousness" even as we engage in practices that lead to racialized ends. Tomlinson is concerned that the structures put into place in the market also push people to experience themselves and each other in ways that often accompany the practice of racism.

Asa Hilliard (2001) pinpointed the broader educational issue: power operating at the global level can continue traditional patterns of dividing people into "racial" categories as a means of controlling relations across various areas of social life. Although migration and immigration may contribute to these undesirable ends, there are other possibilities. One of these possibilities is the expansion of diasporic knowledge.

Popular Culture

This is simply the culture of the people or the masses. The significance of the concept is due to the historical bias shown by some intellectuals to deny as important the things that ordinary people valued, such as comic books, playing cards, love stories, and westerns.

Globalization and Its Possibilities: Diasporic Knowledge

Globalization has many positive possibilities. Among these is the influence of **popular culture** on youth identity (McCarthy et al., 2003). Through global processes, young people around the world share cultural values and practices through Internet options such as my daughter's Web page on MySpace. Thousands of youth from diverse ethnic backgrounds living in the United States are engaged

Semiotics

This is the science for studying signs and symbols, including what they mean and how they are used to convey meanings.

---

in this sharing across nations. As Wan Shun Eva Lam (2006b, 171) argues, "networked electronic communications have given rise to new social spaces, linguistic and **semiotic** practices, and ways of fashioning the self beyond the national context for immigrant youths in the United States."

When immigrant and nationalist students interact with youth from around the world through global media, they create new, nonlocal or traditional perspectives. These new perspectives offer the possibility for the creation of nontraditional knowledge. This cross-fertilization of ideas, artifacts, and traditions is a boon for the world community, especially where it enables a greater attentiveness to the need for global social justice (Rikowski, 2002; Spring, 2004).

Diaspora Identities and Knowledge. What is diaspora? Simply, it means the dispersal or a breaking up and scattering of a group of people. Typically, the diaspora refers to people settled far from their ancestral homeland or the communities to which they belong. Identity is a core issue associated with life in the diaspora. Relations with both the ancestral home and the host nation impact on individuals' sense of belonging, loyalties, and movement back and forth between countries.

Collective Memory

This term refers to several different kinds of shared memories. Here the reference is simply to the collection of memories shared by a group of people through either a shared experience of something or hearing about it from others.

The diversity of diasporic groups—from African to Asian and Irish—means a wide range of diasporas: people share different **collective memories** of forced dispersion. As you will recall from John Ogbu's theories of minority achievement behavior, some groups have been *forced* and some have *chosen* to find new homes. Differences such as these can and do play a major role in the kinds of collective memories—actual and fictive—that a diasporic group might have.

Sally Tomlinson (2003, 213) offers one understanding of the dispersal:

> The second half of the twentieth century saw unprecedented mass movement of peoples around the world. This movement included forced migrations as attempts were made to separate ethnic and cultural groups; voluntary migrations as groups embraced political and religious freedoms; economic migrations from "old" to "new" worlds and from former colonial countries in Africa, the Caribbean, and Asia to fill Europe's labour markets; and increasing numbers of political refugees and asylum seekers from war and conflicts.

As people move around, they bring ideas and information with them. They also send ideas and information back home. The information or knowledge that occurs as a result of being people in motion has been called *diaspora knowledge* (Yang, 2002).

The ongoing "War against Terror" playing out in Iraq illustrates this. The information was not as we said it was and everyday we gather "new intelligence" that foretells an American military presence for several years more in that region. But what of the millions of people forced to leave the Middle East and elsewhere? What do they know? What knowledge will they now construct in their new homelands? We are accustomed to think of migrants simply as Mexicans stealing across the borders to work in the fields of "greedy Anglos." Education for their children, granted all too often begrudgingly, is seen as simply teaching them English so they can learn to read, write, and do mathematics.

Thus, there are millions of people living in the United States and elsewhere who not only learn what we choose to teach, they also participate in constructing knowledge. Today there are many *disaporic* intellectual traditions—Asian, African, Caribbean, Latin. These produce alternative knowledge about what has been and are their achievements, interests, and priorities.

The combined impact of globalization and disasporic knowledge on race and education is both exciting and challenging. In the previous chapters, we have explored the traditional narrative of race and education. This narrative has been largely simple and straightforward: there is a dominant group whose power has included first denying and then allowing minimal educational opportunity to those defined as inferior. Race has been the overriding force employed in this process. But there have been many changes over the past several decades, including globalization and increasing dispersals that require us to reimage aspects of race in education (Carter, 2000). In the final pages, we consider a few of the more significant implications of this revision of thinking about race in education.

Emergent Themes: Reframing "Race" and Other Core Concepts

In our view it is crucial to break with these habits of thought. The effort must be made to understand race as

an unstable and "decentered" complex of social meanings constantly being transformed by political struggle."
—Omi & Winant (1986, 66)

In class, one of my White female students was discussing the naturalness of her being "White." For her, she was "White" and self-evidently so. Affirming that her skin color was proof she was "White," she pursued her argument by pointing to the difference between herself and a darker skin female. She recognized this classmate as White "but less fair than me because she is Italian and I am Irish." The Italian female responded that she had always been White, "although they [the Irish] didn't consider my ancestors as so."

This conversation was part of a larger one on "race" in education that turned up a number of other interesting and common viewpoints. For instance, one White male student declared his disappointment that race had to be mentioned in an education course. He felt that "we are color-blind." The belief that "race" is essential and unchanging goes well with the first of these developments. The nation has always seen different groups as fixed in their character and culture and sought to conform them to the Euro-American images and versions of truth, including the desirable things in life and the ways to get them (McCarthy et al., 2003).

Melting Pot

A term introduced to present the idea—rejected as untrue by many—that the United States is a "melting pot" of cultural traditions. The term is a metaphor that seeks to say that "American" means that we are culturally mixed into one shared unity. Given various discordant realities such as prejudice or racism, this "melting pot" idea has been disclaimed by many; seeing the nation as essentially pluralistic, some have argued that we must practice and teach multiculturalism as a corrective to the monoculturalism they feel has characterized the nation historically.

The idea of the **melting pot** has been jettisoned; even the idea of the "salad bowl" has its limitations for describing the new energies associated with the coming of both race and ethnicity. Both social and political life in the United States, and increasingly elsewhere, are intertwined with race. The "White-Black" formulation is not, however, the sole expression of race. Asian Americans, Latinos, and other ethnic groups also have been constructed; and they have responded by both accepting and rejecting certain attributions regarding them. In addition, they have insisted upon due recognition of their historical constructions and the need for fuller inclusion of their histories, cultures, and group-related concerns.

"Race" has evolved. So has the notion of racism. The former is considered unstable and negotiable. The second is realized as less the state or quality of a person than the relation between a given person and those institutions within society that a person may join to perform a racist action. Perhaps one of the most critical developments taking place today is the forced necessity of social science

researchers to "wrestle" with the fact that "race" is not only unstable or changeable but also a source of struggle that takes place all the time (Pollock, 2004). This is not a new fact; recall that the slave struggling for freedom and education was resisting the notion of race laid upon her and him. What is different now is that some scholars have argued that researchers can both learn from and positively influence the struggles over race taking place daily.

Some ask if we can change the face of racism by changing the use and perpetuation of racialized identities. Race is real in its consequences, regardless of its constructed nature. These realities include things racial groups do with and toward each other as well as between the dominant race and the others.

Prejudice and the Pursuit of Social Justice

In Chapter One, Thomas Jefferson is quoted as saying that *prejudice* and *discrimination* were wrongs experienced by enslaved Africans that would affect future relations: Whites would continue to be hurtful toward Blacks and the latter would not forget the wrongs inflicted against them. This somewhat pessimistic attitude has been partially borne out by race relations over the centuries; but it is not the whole story. Important changes in beliefs and behavior have occurred among many who were originally raised in racist societies. This includes the arrival of Barack Obama as a 2008 presidential candidate. Still, the ongoing task is to understand, monitor, and manage those situations or conditions that encourage prejudging others unfairly or engaging in systematic and official practices that deny social justice to some humans, whether in housing, employment, or education (Enns & Sinacore, 2005; Michelli & Keiser, 2005).

Students often struggle with the question of whether or not they are racist or prejudiced by the mere fact that they hold a particular opinion regarding a particular individual or group. Social scientists largely agree that bias or prejudgments are both common and not altogether undesirable attitudes. What is seen as wrong or unhealthy are hurtful attitudes that resist new information or alternative facts. Many negative ideas toward a particular group are the result of negative experiences with them; such experiences may or may not be something that is inevitable or unchangeable. Moreover, many negative experiences are

self-fulfilling prophecies; that is, we create or help bring about the conditions that elicit what we have been prepared to believe.

Whether hurtful or not, prejudice and bias seem to be pretty common human adaptations that, at times, seem adaptive; that is, useful for the context. The importance of this observation by some social scientists is intended to alert us to the need to be sensitive in our attempts to impact on issues such as racism. The idealistic student teacher, for instance, often finds her or himself struggling with one of these qualities in a family member or friend; the resulting disillusionment can be detrimental to both the family member or friend and the student teacher (Gresson, 2004).

A more useful focus has been on racism—a belief that essential differences exist with respect to race and accepts or promotes hurtful or discriminatory behaviors toward those identified as racially different. When this racist belief or behavior is built into systems or organizations, it is considered as *structural racism*. Institutional racism is the name given to this form of collective racism. Prejudice and discrimination are generally not perceived as more pernicious or damaging than structural racism.

Racism is a belief or ideology that too many understand as residing within a person in a total or complete way; likewise, it is often felt that it does not exist within one if one rejects certain odious ideas about others. But racism can pertain to a wide variety of behaviors that result in people feeling inferior, marginalized, threatened, or less than human. This remains a continuing challenge for those committed to bringing social justice into education and democratic society.

It has been recognized that racism no longer exists in ways that it once did; some of the most blatant examples of discrimination and abuse have disappeared. Yet, some have maintained that never has there been more racism than today. People who take this position recognize that having made this claim, it can be difficult to precisely pinpoint it or to formulate strategies that can effectively counter it (Balibar, 1991).

Racism is the mechanism through which power is able to maintain its hold on the lives of the oppressed. Teachers who see no issues of racism are often more likely to miss opportunities for transforming the classroom and the school as an organization in ways that promote their commitment to educational excellence among those defined as marginalized and "at risk" (Kailin, 1999). While race as a concept has come under increasing challenge, racism as a reality has been much less questioned, especially outside of the United States (Arora, 2005; Gresson, 1995; 2004). Racism within contemporary America is often denied by many nonminority and conservative group members (Gresson, 2004). But it remains a centerpiece for understanding and sustaining social inequality in the United States. Both individual and institutional racism are persisting problems that many recognize as the primary sources of the continuing education gap (Arora, 2005).

Racism is a form of *hegemony*—control of the less powerful or strong through ideas, social institutions, and practices that bind them to the will and interests of the strong. Wijeyesinghe, Griffin, and Love (1997, 88) define racism as "the systematic subordination of members of targeted racial groups who have relatively more social power." Jerry Diller (1999, 27) has added: "It is supported simultaneously by individuals, the institutional practices of society, and dominant cultural values and norms."

Racism, thus understood, breeds inequality and sustains it through the ways that people see, experience, and relate to each other on a daily basis. But racism is a complex, volatile, and highly contested concept: some people believe that it doesn't exist except as an individual idiosyncrasy (Wilson, 1980; 1987); others think it is at the heart of life in most places in the world. Of particular note, nonetheless, is the observation made by Melvin Thomas (2000, 1): "Since the Civil Rights movement, theories identifying other explanations [of racial inequality] have been growing increasingly popular. They have in common the view that the sources of black disadvantage are characteristics of blacks themselves."

This observation by Melvin Thomas reminds us of one crucial foundation or beginning of the emergence and the ongoing importance of "race" in education: The idea that racial differences are real, necessary, and only minimally changeable has endured despite the many strides made by millions of racial and ethnic group members. Because schools are traditionally expected to overcome the historical events, misfortunes, and realities that created a pecking order according to racial and ethnic status, many

sidestep the enduring belief that the education gap cannot be breached or eliminated. Thus, one pivotal meaning of "race and education" is the recognition of and commitment to eliminate the educational gap. But the persistence of this gap—even across nations—continues to raise two types of questions that constitute the twin pillars of the various themes within the field. These two questions are: (1) Are racial/ethnic differences measured by intelligence and achievement tests signs of real, essential differences? (2) Do racist and discriminatory practices and policies continue to produce social inequality despite various reform efforts? In response to these two issues, scholars have offered a number of opinions. Writing on race and teacher education in Canada, Carr and Klassen (1996, 68) argue: "A number of factors can explain the low educational outcomes or underperformance of some groups in schools: the formal—as well as the hidden—curriculum, involvement of parents, teacher effectiveness, beliefs of minority groups, and school culture. Teachers are, undoubtedly, an important factor, and the influence of the lived experiences of predominantly White teachers and administrators working with an increasingly racially diverse student body needs to be understood."

Culture, Identity, and Schooling

Who am I? What can I be? Recall (from Chapter Three) that Alice asked these questions when she was in the rabbit's hole. These questions pertain to identity. At the core of all of the changes that have taken place within the realm of race relations, identity is possibly the most challenging and critical to be mindful of. People can change who they are in so many ways: physical appearance, geography, career, hobbies, and friends are some of the factors that help us locate or "know" ourselves. As these change, so can we; moreover, we can change who we are by actively (agency) changing these factors.

Culture has been seen at the heart of much of the inequality in schooling and society. The assumptions or beliefs underpinning this cultural perspective imply that culture is a stable, concrete entity that can be poured into the individual to yield precise, predictable results. That is, give children knowledge of their cultural group's achievements and they will necessarily achieve.

Culture has been often seen as a cluster of beliefs, values, and practices that not only resist change but also defy it. But this is not so. People and cultures do change, both from within as well as without. Established habits, ways of living and loving, hating and co-habilitating, can and do change. With changes in ways of seeing and living come changes in "identity."

Identity Shifting

As seen in the hybrid identity situation, one's identity is not fixed; it can be negotiated. That is, one may emphasize one or more aspects of a socially constructed identity.

In recent times, **identity shifting** has been identified as a normal part of daily life. This concept speaks to something that many minorities have always had to do in order to be accepted by the mainstream society (Goffman, 1959; 1963). Increasingly, given the rise in diversity, everyone may need to know how to deal with others, to get along, and to make shifts in the ideas and behaviors *forefronted* in any given exchange with others. The importance of this challenge for prospective teachers has been emphasized by scholars doing research in schools.

Ethnography and Understanding Human Possibility

Among some of the scholars of ethnography are Mica Pollock and Stanley Wortham, two anthropologists whose classroom research has been very helpful in charting some of the identity negotiations taking place. Mica Pollock (2006, 1) has written:

> I have found that anthropology and its methodological tool, ethnography, offer some key components for moving dialogue in education beyond oversimplified notions of "racial" difference and oversimplified explanations for racial inequality. For rather than simply asking respondents to restate these common sense notions, ethnography can show educators the ways in which they and their students struggle daily *with* race. By focusing attention on *everyday struggles* over race categories and racial inequality, ethnography can facilitate what I call "race wrestling": people struggling self-consciously with normalized ideas about "racial" difference and about how racial inequality is produced.

Ethnography is an especially powerful and popular tool today because it allows for both observation of behaviors and immediate exploration as to the meaning of behavior for the actors. The relevance of ethnography for educators is due partly to this quality. In addition, Pollock (2006, 3) believes that educators "need tools for analyzing the consequences of their everyday behaviors because they are often unsure which ordinary moves, in an already racialized

world, are racist and which antiracist." Indeed, antiracist educators must constantly negotiate between two *antiracist* impulses in deciding their everyday behaviors toward students. Moment to moment, they must choose between the antiracist impulse to treat all people as human beings *rather* than "race" group members, and the antiracist impulse to recognize people's real experiences as race group members in order to assist them and treat them equitably.

Amy Best (2003) extends this discussion in her study of how researchers help themselves and others create "Whiteness" through the taken-for-granted assumptions that get played out in everyday interactions, thereby creating something that is not really all that clear or determined. This orientation toward "race" has become increasingly exciting for those committed to creating new human possibilities.

In the 1960s, many important changes were taking place both in the everyday lives of people and in the scholarship aimed at understanding and explaining their everyday lives and world. It wasn't that people changed in some dramatic way all at once, but certain things made the changes or things that were less visible or acknowledged more evident and important. For instance, the ideas of both culture and identity had begun to be seen as less certain, less stable—always there and unchanging—than before.

Conclusion: A Global Multiculturalism?

In Chapter Two, we saw that multiculturalism has been adopted by various countries forced to consider the limits of an assimilationist education policy (Arora, 2005; Banks, 2002). While many see the inclusion of historical materials on minorities and their culture in the K-16 curriculum as a positive move, others have criticized this strategy as flawed. This has been true for those who think that what has traditionally been offered in the curriculum—reading, writing, and arithmetic, and taught in English—was sufficient to get all Americans on the same page and achieve their best in school and society (Bork, 1996; Kirk, 1993).

Others have challenged the multicultural emphasis on curriculum content as a mere bandage on a serious wound—the racist, sexist, and classist structure of schools and society. In this regard, Yon (1999, 6) has offered:

> In countries such as Canada, the United States, Britain, and Australia, where cultural pluralism is embraced as

official state policy, multicultural and inclusive education were initially premised on the belief that learning about one's own and other cultures, ethnic roots, and heritage boosts self-esteem, improves the performance of minority students and reduces prejudice toward groups different from one's own. However, a preoccupation with cultural differences that disconnects them from the social and economic inequalities in which they are located can have the effect of perpetuating racism.

From this perspective, a radical change is required in the way life is organized in schools. The need for greater inclusion and democratic practices across curriculum and pedagogy has been called for (Goldberg, 1993; Kanpol, 1995; Kincheloe & Steinberg, 1997; May, 1999)

"Global Multiculturalism" is one attempt to find a new way of thinking about the relation of symbolic identity struggles to the global context, particularly the struggle against global policies that pit humans against each other (Cornwell & Stoddard, 2001). One motive pushing the effort to think beyond the national boundaries of nation-states such as the United States, Canada, or Cuba is the recognition of *heterogeneity*. We have always recognized difference, to be sure; but now there are pressures from individuals and groups to deal with the pragmatic implications of difference. If we can integrate only so far, then we need to accept and work with divisions of various types.

The tensions created by multiculturalism were introduced above, notably the challenge that mere acknowledgement of group diversity does not eliminate inequality in society and schooling. The new focus takes up and goes beyond this tension caused by internal division. As Cornwell and Stoddard note, the struggle is now between "cementing a national identity" and "recognizing...identities that can cross national boundaries" (2001, 14–15).

> Some countries have accepted diversity in a proactive or planned rather than reactive way; they seek to consciously reflect on the situation and work toward broadly satisfying ways of accommodating difference. Many countries have diverse populations although we in the United States seldom think about this. For example, there are Chinese in Thailand, Koreans in Japan, East Indians in Tanzania, Muslims in France, and West Indians in Canada.

The international music industry can be used to support or breakdown "racial solidarity" as a constructed reality. That is, some will pick up on and follow through on the

Hip-hop Culture

An outgrowth of the Civil Rights and Black Power Movements, the hip-hop movement represents the African American youth's initiative to define itself and construct an urban pedagogy, a way of understanding and renegotiating how life in the urban communities could and should be lived.

Rastafarian Music

Popularized by the late Bob Marley, this Jamaican form of music has roots in the revolutionary 1960s when music from this once colonial nation was used to convey resistance pedagogy or messages of racial self-love and commitment to liberation from all forms of oppression.

idea of, say, "Pan-African identity" or "diasporic Identities" as fostered by **hip-hop culture** or **Rastafarian music** (Whiteley et al., 2004). The flow of multiculturalism themes back and forth across borders, say, between the United States and Canada, is a good example of the globalizing of multiculturalism. Similarly, the African continent has offered an opportunity for globalizing processes (Abdi, 2006). The struggle between African knowledge systems and cultures as portrayed by Europeans and the efforts of Africans themselves offers a view of an emerging postcolonial struggle.

Finally, there needs to be a greater consideration of "global social justice." As Roberto Flores (2003, 1) wrote regarding the global focus of James Banks's multiculturalism:

> Banks' lack of connection to the global setting and the role of the U.S. can lead to a separation of the goal for internal educational equality and the goal for global equality…Banks does not contextualize the U.S. within the current economic globalization project and its impact on social justice curriculum. Banks' U.S. multicultural pedagogy is ultimately not (at this point) within the agenda of global social justice and is not within the present political economic realities of the U.S.

Barack Obama is the first major Black American candidate for president. Some see in his rise the end of Jesse Jackson and Al Sharpton, two well-known, traditional African American leaders (George Will, on ABC Sunday, November 25, 2007). Others see this multiracial politician, the son of an African father and a Euro-American mother, as a signal to the world of a new America. Visions such as ascribed to James Banks seem sanguine with the current shift in U.S. racial politics despite the wisdom of Roberto Flores's critique.

At the beginning of this primer, I identified race and education as perspective, policy, and practice. This is true enough; but in this final chapter, we have see that many traditional concerns and guiding concepts have been challenged by globalism and the changing character of the world community. It has become increasingly difficult to interpret challenges in simplistic "race" terms. Still, "race" continues to be the "elephant in the china shop." More precisely, racism continues to frustrate many initiatives intended to overcome educational gaps; and thus undermines the fuller inclusion of all in the prosperity promised by achievements in technology. The challenge for future discourse on race and education is twofold: to acknowledge the persistence of "racial" interests that undermine the progressive efforts to realize greater global social justice; yet recognize the gains made and their implications. It is my hope that the prospective teacher will be able to see her or himself as part of this discourse; and that this primer has aided a more informed participation in it.

GLOSSARY

Collective Memory: This term refers to several different kinds of shared memories. Here the reference is simply to the collection of memories shared by a group of people through either a shared experience of something or hearing about it from others.

Counter-hegemonic: This term refers to the active resistance against the controlling influence of those with control over information, resources, and understanding, including one's understanding of one's own circumstances. Another way of seeing this is as a resistance to institutionalized power such as school rules and policies that seem unfair or discriminatory.

Global Education: Education has been defined as a life-span encounter and engagement with knowledge about the world community. Emphasis is on interdependency of the earth's people, notably the ecological, social, economic, and technological interconnections.

Hip-hop Culture: An outgrowth of the Civil Rights and Black Power Movements, the hip-hop movement represents the African American youth initiative to define itself and construct an urban pedagogy, a way of understanding and renegotiating how life in the urban communities could and should be lived. As a culture, hip-hop deals with music, language, dress style, and politics. Through mass media, moreover, it has interpenetrated the global context and has been mutually influencing and influenced by the world at large. Rap music is perhaps the best known aspect of hip-hop culture, although leading spokespersons of hip-hop have emphasized the social and political nature of its mission.

Hybrid Identity: An identity constructed through taking bits and pieces of what has been accepted as distinct group identities, for example, Tiger Woods calling himself a "cablinasian" to acknowledge his mixed ancestry: Caucasian, Asian, African, and Native American.

Identity Shifting: As seen in the hybrid identity situation, one's identity is not fixed; it can be negotiated. That is, one may emphasize one or more aspects of a socially constructed identity: hence, some see Tiger Woods as physically gifted because of his Black father and mentally strong because of his Asian mother. However, Tiger might argue that his strong genes are from his Asian mother and his strong mental strength from his military officer father.

Melting Pot: A term introduced to present the idea—rejected as untrue by many—that the United States is a "melting pot" of cultural traditions. The term is a metaphor that seeks to say that "American" means that we are culturally mixed into one shared unity. Given various discordant realities such as prejudice or racism, this "melting pot" idea has been disclaimed by many; seeing the nation as essentially pluralistic, some have argued that we must practice and teach multiculturalism as a corrective to the monoculturalism they feel has characterized the nation historically.

Popular Culture: This is simply the culture of the people or the masses. The significance of the concept is due to the historical bias shown by some intellectuals to deny as important the things that ordinary people valued, such as comic books, playing cards, love stories, and westerns. Critical scholars have led the way in breaking down the class-based distinction between these pastimes and the so-called high-brow activities such as opera, the ballet, and bridge (the card game).

Rastafarian Music: Popularized by the late Bob Marley, this Jamaican form of music has roots in the revolutionary 1960s when music from this once colonial nation was used to convey resistance pedagogy or messages of racial self-love and commitment to liberation from all forms of oppression. The global appeal of Reggae music lies, in part, in its ability to carry a diaspora message of global struggle against all forms of oppression (see Rasta Music—Global Struggle at http://www.jahworks.org/music/features/rasta_music/mar_15_01.html).

Semiotics: This is the science for studying signs and symbols, including what they mean and how they are used to convey meanings.

Bibliography

References and Resources

Related Primer-Oriented Materials

There are a number of Web sites and a few books and articles that contain primers on race and education topics. Some of the more useful ones are included below:

Diller, J. V., & Moule, J. (2005). *Cultural Competence: A Primer for Educators* New York: Wadsworth.

Edward Taylor (1998, Spring) A Primer on Critical Race Theory. *The Journal of Blacks in Higher Education,* 19, 122–124.

New York Times. (1996). Primer: Race and Opportunity http://www. nytimes.com/specials/issues/ihome/race.html

Primer on Discrimination in Education http://www.humanrights.state. mn.us/rsonline/edu_over.html

References

Abdelhamid, R., & Choudhury, K. (1998). Minorities Share Dissatisfaction with Social Scene on Prospect. *The Daily Princetonian*. Retrieved November 11, 1997, from http://www.dailyprincetonian.com/ archives/1998/02/03/news/5833.shtml.

Abdi, Ali A. (2006). African Education and Globalization: An Introduction. In A. Abdi, K. P. Puplampu, & G. J. S. Dei (Eds.), *African Education and Globalization: Critical Perspectives*. Lanham, MD: Rowman & Littlefield.

Achievement Trap: How America Is Failing Millions of High-Achieving Students from Lower-Income Families. (2007). Jack Kent Cooke Foundation and Civic Enterprises. Retrieved March 7, 2008, from http://www.jackkentcookefoundation.org/jkcf_web/Documents/ Achievement%20 Trap.pdf.

Adams, D. W. (2004). Book Reviews. *History of Education Quarterly*, 44(2), 271–326.

Adams, D. W. (1995). *Education for Extinction: American Indians and the Boarding School Experience, 1875–1928*. Lawrence: University Press of Kansas.

Adeleke, T. (2002). Globalization and the Challenges of Race-Based Pedagogy. Retrieved January 9, 2008, from http://globalization. icaap.org/content/v2.2/adeleke.html

Ainsworth-Darnell, J. W., & Downey, D. B. (1998). Assessing the Oppositional Culture Explanation for Racial/Ethnic Differences in School Performance. *American Sociological Review*, 63, 536–553.

Alladin, M. I. (Ed.). (1996). *Racism in Canadian Schools*. Toronto: Harcourt Brace.

Allard, A., & Santoro, N. (2004). Making Sense of Difference? Teaching Identities in Postmodern Contexts. Retrieved February 17, 2008, from http://www.aare.edu.au/04pap/all04561.pdf.

Allen, T. D. (2004, December). *Review of* Black in School: Afrocentric Reform, Urban Reform, and the Promise of Hip-Hop Culture. *E-Journal of Teaching and Learning in Diversity Settings*, 2(1), 177–181. Retrieved February 15, 2008, from http://www.subr.edu/ coeducation/ejournal/Allen%20Book%20Review.htm.

Allen, W. (1993). A Response to a White Discourse on White Racism. *Educational Researcher*, 22, 11–13.

Allison, C. B. (1995). *Present and Past: Essays for Teachers in the History of Education*. New York: Peter Lang.

Alridge, D. (2006). The Limits of Master Narratives in History Textbooks: An Analysis of Representations of Martin Luther King, Jr. *Teachers College Record*, 108(4), 662–686.

Alridge, D. (2005, Summer). From Civil Rights to Hip-Hop: Toward a Nexus of Ideas. *Journal of African American History*, 90(2), 226–252.

Alridge, D. (2003). The Dilemmas, Challenges, and Duality of an African American Educational Historian. *Educational Researcher*, 32(9), 25–34.

Alridge, D. (1999). Guiding Philosophical Principles for a Du Boisian-Based African-American Educational Model. *Journal of Negro Education*, 68(2), 182–199.

Alridge, D. P., & Stewart, J. B. (2005, Summer). Introduction: Hip Hop in History: Past, Present, and Future. *Journal of African American History,* 90(3), 190–195.

Alvarez, Jr., R. R. (1986, Spring). The Lemon Grove Incident: The Nation's First Successful Desegregation Court Case. *The Journal of San Diego History,* 32(2). Retrieved January 20, 2008, from http://www.sandiegohistory.org/journal/86spring/lemongrove.htm.

American Educational Research Association. (2004, Fall). Closing the Gap: High Achievement for Students of Color. *AERA Research Points,* 2(3). Retrieved November 1, 2007, from http://www.aera.net/uploadedFiles/Journals_and_Publications/Research_Points/RP_Fall-04.pdf.

Anderson, J. D. (undated). Colleges and Universities, Historically Black, in the United States. Retrieved February 15, 2008, from www.pbs.org/itvs/fromswastikatojimcrow/blackcolleges_2.html.

Anderson, J. (1988). *The Education of Blacks in the South: 1865–1935.* Chapel Hill: University of North Carolina Press.

Andrade, S. (2007, August). Tensions and Possibilities in Applying Freirean Critical Pedagogy towards Fostering Critical Literacy in India's Education System. Unpublished Master's thesis, Queen's University, Kingston, Ontario, Canada.

Anyon, J. (2005). *Radical Possibilities: Public Policy, Urban Education, and a New Social Movement.* New York: Routledge.

Anyon, J. (1985, Summer). Social Class and School Knowledge Revisited: A Reply to Ramsay. *Curriculum Inquiry,* 15(2), 207–214.

Anyon, J. (1981). Social Class and School Knowledge. *Curriculum Inquiry,* 11(1), 3–42.

Apple, M. W. (2000). *Official Knowledge: Democratic Education in a Conservative Age,* 2nd edition. New York: Routledge.

Apple, M. W. (1999). *Power, Meaning, and Identity: Essays in Critical Educational Studies.* New York: Peter Lang.

Apple, M. W. (1990). *Ideology and Curriculum,* 2nd edition. New York: Routledge.

Archuleta, M., Child, B., & Lomawaima, K. (Eds.). (2000). *Away from Home: American Indian Boarding School Experiences.* Phoenix, AZ: Heard Museum.

Arora, R. K. (2005). *Race and Ethnicity in Education.* Burlington, VT: Ashgate.

ASA (2002, September/October). ASA Issues Official Statement on Importance of Collecting Data on Race. *Footnotes.* Retrieved March 2, 2008, from http://www2.asanet.org/footnotes/septoct02/index-two.html.

Asakawa, K., & Csikszentmihalyi, M. (2000). Feelings of Connectedness and Internalization of Values in Asian American Adolescents. *Journal of Youth and Adolescence,* 29, 121–145.

Asante, M. (1991). The Afrocentric Idea in Education. *Journal of Negro Education,* 60(1), 170–179.

Asante, M. (1980/1987). *The Afrocentric Idea.* Philadelphia: Temple University Press.

Asato, Noriko (2003). Mandating Americanization: Japanese Language Schools and the Federal Survey of Education in Hawaii, 1916–1920. *History of Education Quarterly,* 43(1), 10–38.

ATS (1997). Leading African-American Scholar Kicks Off Series of All-Campus Convocations. *Around the Square.* Retrieved March 2, 2008, from http://www.oberlin.edu/wwwcomm/ats/atspast/ats0197/ats0197_west.html.

Ayers, W., Hunt, J. A., & Quinn, T. (Eds.). (1998). *Teaching for Social Justice: A Democracy and Education Reader.* New York: New Press.

Baldwin, D. (2005). Black Belts and Ivory Towers: The Place of Race in U.S. Social Thought, 1892–1948. In Boston College Editorial Collective (Ed.), *Culture, Power, and History: Studies in Critical Sociology,* 309–364. Boston: Brill.

Balfanz, R., & Legters, N. (2004). *Locating the Dropout Crisis.* Baltimore, MD: Johns Hopkins University Center for Social Organization of Schools. Retrieved December 13, 2007, from http://www.csos.jhu.edu/crespar/techReports/Report70.pdf.

Balibar, Etienne. (1991). *Race, Nation, Class: Ambiguous Identities.* London: Verso.

Banks, J. A. (Ed.). (2004). *Diversity and Citizenship Education: Global Perspectives.* San Francisco, CA: Jossey-Bass.

Banks, J. A. (2002). Race, Knowledge Construction, and Education in the USA: Lessons from History. *Race, Ethnicity & Education,* 5(1), 7–27.

Banks, J. A. (2000). *An Introduction to Multicultural Education,* 3rd edition. Boston: Allyn & Bacon.

Banks, J.A. (1997). Multicultural education: Dimensions of. In C. A. Grant & G. Ladson-Billings (Eds.), *Dictionary of multicultural education* (pp. 177–182). Phoenix, AZ: The Oryx Press.

Banks, J. A. (1995). The Historical Reconstruction of Knowledge about Race: Implications for Transformative Teaching. *Educational Researcher,* 24, 15–25.

Banks, J. A. (1991). *Teaching Strategies for Ethnic Studies,* 5th edition. Boston: Allyn & Bacon.

Banks, J. A., & McGee Banks, C. A. (Eds.). (2004). *Handbook of Research on Multicultural Education,* 2nd edition. San Francisco, CA: Jossey-Bass.

Banton, M. (2003, May). Teaching Ethnic and Racial Studies. *Ethnic and Racial Studies,* 26(3), 488–502.

Bard, J. C. (1997). Ethnographic/Contact Period (Lewis and Clark 1805–Hanford Engineer Works 1943) of the Hanford Site,

Washington. *National Register of Historic Places Multiple Property Documentation Form—Historic, Archaeological and Traditional Cultural Properties of the Hanford Site, Washington.* DOE/RL-97–02, U.S. Department of Energy, Richland Operations Office, Richland, Washington. Retrieved January 20, 2008, from http://www.hanford.gov/doe/history/mpd/sec3.htm.

Barnes, S. L. (2003, September). The Ebonics Enigma: An Analysis of Attitudes on an Urban College Campus. *Race, Ethnicity & Education,* 6(3), 247–264.

Baron, R. M., Tom, D. Y. H., & Cooper, H. M. (1985). Social Class, Race and Teacher Expectations. In J. B. Dusek (Ed.), *Teacher Expectancies,* 251–269. Hillsdale, NJ: Lawrence Erlbaum Associates.

Bartlett, L. (2005, August). Dialogue, Knowledge, and Teacher-Student Relations: Freirean Pedagogy in Theory and Practice. *Comparative Education Review,* 49(3), 344–364.

Beaulieu, D. L. (2000). Comprehensive Reform and American Indian Education. *Journal of American Indian Education,* 39(2), 29–38.

Becker, E. (1971). *The Birth and Death of Meaning,* 2nd edition. New York: Free Press.

Bederman, G. (1995). *Manliness & Civilization: A Cultural History of Gender and Race in the United States, 1880–1917.* Chicago: University of Chicago Press.

Bell, D. (1992). *Faces at the Bottom of the Well: The Permanence of Racism.* New York: Basic Books.

Bempechat, J. Boulay, B. A., Piergross, S. C., & Wenk, K. A. (2008, January). Beyond the Rhetoric: Understanding Achievement and Motivation in Catholic School Students. *Education and Urban Society,* 40(2), 167–178.

Bengal, M. (1989). *Black Athena: The Fabrication of Ancient Greece 1785–1985.* New Brunswick, NJ: Rutgers University Press.

Benson-Hale, J. (1986). *Black Children, Their Roots, Culture, and Learning Styles.* Baltimore, MD: Johns Hopkins University Press.

Berg, A. (2002). *Mothering the Race: Women's Narratives of Reproduction, 1890–1930.* Urbana: University of Illinois Press.

Berlak, A., & Berlak, H. (1983). Toward a Nonhierarchical Approach to School Inquiry and Leadership. *Curriculum Inquiry,* 13(3), 267–294.

Berlak, H. (2001, Summer). Race and the Achievement Gap. *Rethinking Schools Online,* 15(4). Retrieved January 9, 2008, from http://www.rethinkingschools.org/archive/15_04/Race154.shtml

Berry, J. W. (1980). Social and Cultural Change. In H. C. Triandis & R. Brislin (Eds.), *Handbook of Cross-cultural Psychology,* 5, 211–275. Boston: Allyn & Bacon.

Best, A. L. (2003). Doing Race in the Context of Feminist Interviewing: Constructing Whiteness through Talk. *Qualitative Inquiry,* 9(6), 895–914.

Bigelow, B., & Peterson, B. (Eds.). (2002). *Rethinking Globalization: Teaching for Justice in an Unjust World*. Milwaukee, WI: Rethinking Schools Press.

Borhek, J. T. (1995). Ethnic Group Cohesion. *American Journal of Sociology*, 9(40), 1–16.

Bork, R. H. (1996). *Slouching towards Gomorrah: Modern Liberalism and American Decline*. New York: Regan Books/HarperCollins.

Bourdieu, P. (1993). Cultural Reproduction and Social Reproduction. In Brown, R. (Ed.), *Knowledge, Education and Cultural Change*, 71–112. London: Willmer.

Bowen, W., & Bok, D. (2000). *The Shape of the River: Long-Term Consequences of Considering Race in College and University Admissions*, 1st edition. Princeton, NJ: Princeton University Press, 1998.

Bowles, S., & Gintis, H. (1976). *Schooling in Capitalist America: Education Reform and the Contradictions of Economic Life*. London: Routledge & Kegan Paul.

Britzman, D. (2003). *Practice Makes Practice: A Critical Study of Learning to Teach*, revised edition. Albany, NY: SUNY Press.

Britzman, D. (1992). The Terrible Problem of Knowing Thyself: Toward a Poststructural Account of Teacher Identity. *Journal of Curriculum Theorizing*, 9(3), 23–46.

Britzman, D. (1991). *Practice Makes Practice: A Critical Study of Learning to Teach*. Albany, NY: SUNY Press.

Brayboy, B. M. J. (2004, Summer). Hiding in the Ivy: American Indian Students and Visibility in Elite Educational Settings. *Harvard Educational Review*, 74(2), 125–153.

Brophy, J. (1983). Research on the Self-fulfilling Prophecy and Teacher Expectations. *Journal of Education Psychology*, 75(5), 631–661.

Brophy, J. E., & Good, T. L. (1986). Teacher Behavior and Student Achievement. In M. C. Wittrock (Ed.), *Handbook of Research on Teaching*, 3rd edition, 328–375. New York: Macmillan.

Brophy, J. E., & Good, T. L. (1974). *Teacher-Student Relationships: Causes and Consequences*. New York: Holt, Rinehart and Winston.

Browne, K. (2005, November 1). Placing the Personal in Pedagogy: Engaged Pedagogy in "Feminist" Geographical Teaching. *Journal of Geography in Higher Education*, 29(3), 339–354.

Bullock, H.A. (1967). *A History of Negro Education in the South: From 1619 to the Present*. New York: Simon & Schuster.

Bush, M. E. L. (2005). *Breaking the Code of Good Intentions: Everyday Forms of Whiteness*. Lanham, MD: Rowman & Littlefield.

Butin, D. W. (2002). This Ain't Talk Therapy: Problematizing and Extending Anti-oppressive Education. *Educational Researcher*, 31(3), 14–16.

Butin, D. W. (2001). If This Is Resistance I Would Hate to See Domination: Retrieving Foucault's Notion of Resistance within Educational Research. *Educational Studies, 32*(2), 157–176.

Cabrera, A. F., Crissman, J. L., Bernal, E. M., Nora, A. P. T., & Pascarella, E. T. (2002). Collaborative Learning: Its Impact on College Students' Development and Diversity. *Journal of College Student Development, 43*(2), 20–34.

Cabrera, A. F., Nora, A., Terenzini, P. T., Pascarella, E., & Hagedorn, L. S. (1999). Campus Racial Climate and the Adjustment of Students to College: A Comparison between White Students and African-American Students. *The Journal of Higher Education, 70*(2), 134–160.

Cairney, T. H. (2000). The Construction of Literacy and Literacy Learners. *Language Arts, 77*(6), 496–504.

Caldwell, P. (1995). A Hair Piece: Perspectives on the Intersection of Race and Gender. In R. Delgado (Ed.), *Critical Race Theory: The Cutting Edge,* 267–277. Philadelphia: Temple University Press.

Carnevale, A. (2000, Spring). The Opportunity Gap: Campus diversity and the New Economy. *National Crosstalk.* Retrieved February 17, 2008, from http://www.highereducation.org/crosstalk/ct0500/voices0500-carnevale.shtml.

Carpenter-Song, E., Schwallie, M. N., & Longhofer, J. (2007, October). Cultural Competence Reexamined: Critique and Directions for the Future. *Psychiatric Services, 58*(10), 1362–1365.

Carson, C. (1981). In Struggle: SNCC and the Black Awakening of the 1960s. Harvard University Press.

Carr, P. R., & Klassen, T. R. (1997). Different Perceptions of Race in Education: Racial Minority and White Teachers. *Canadian Journal of Education, 22*(1), 67–81.

Carr, P. R., & Klassen, T. R. (1996). The Role of Racial Minority Teachers in Anti-racist Education. *Canadian Ethnic Studies, 28*(2), 126–138.

Carter, L. (2006). Postcolonial Interventions within Science Education: Using Postcolonial Ideas to Reconsider Cultural Diversity Scholarship. *Educational Philosophy and Theory, 38*(5), 677–691

Carter, R. T. (2000). Reimaging Race in Education: A New Paradigm from Psychology. *Teachers College Record, 102*(5), 864–897.

Caruthers, L. (2006, Fall). Using Storytelling to Break the Silence That Binds Us to Sameness in Our Schools. *Journal of Negro Education, 75*(4), 661–676.

Causey, V., Thomas, C., & Armento, B. (2000). Cultural Diversity is Basically a Foreign Term to Me: The Challenges of Diversity for Preservice Teacher Education. *Teaching and Teacher Education, 16,* 33–45.

Chandler-Olcott, K., & Mahar, D. (2003). Adolescents' Anime-Inspired "Fanfictions": An Exploration of Multiliteracies. *Journal of Adolescent and Adult Literacy, 46*(7), 556–566.

Chavez, Linda. (1992). *Out of the Barrio: Toward a New Politics of Hispanic Assimilation*. New York: Basic Books.

Civil Rights Project Harvard University (2000). Opportunities Suspended: The Devastating Consequences of Zero-Tolerance Expulsion Policies and School Discipline (Conference Report) 2000.

Clark, B. (1960). The Cooling Out Function in Higher Education. *American Journal of Sociology, 65*, 569–576.

Clark, L. S. (undated). Critical Theory and Constructivism: Theory and Methods for the Teens and the New Media @ Home Project. Retrieved March 2, 2008, from http://www.colorado.edu/ Journalism/mcm/qmr-crit-theory.htm.

Clifton, R. A. (1994). Race and Ethnicity in Education. In H. Torstein & T. N. Postlethwaite (Eds.), *The International Encyclopedia of Education,* 2nd edition (4891–4896). New York: Pergamon Press.

Clowes, G. (2003, October 1). Race and Education: An Exclusive Interview with Abigail Thernstrom. *School Reform News*. Retrieved February 16, 2008, from http://www.heartland.org/Article. cfm?artId=12959.

Coben, D. (2002, November). Use Value and Exchange Value in Discursive Domains of Adult Numeracy Teaching. *Literacy and Numeracy Studies: An International Journal in the Education and Training of Adults, 11*(2), 25–35.

Cochran-Smith, M., & Lytle, S. L. (1999). Relationships of Knowledge and Practice: Teacher Learning in Communities. *Review of Research in Education, 24*, 249–305.

Coladarci, T. (1983). High School Dropout among Native Americans. *Journal of American Indian Education, 23*(1), 15–22.

Coleman, J. S. (2002, Spring). From Kindergarten to College (K-16): Preparing Students to Meet the Academic, Social, Technological, and Professional Challenges in the 21st Century. *SIG Newsletter,* 3(1). Retrieved March 5, 2008, from http://www.geocities.com/ talentdevelopment/newsletter/newsle tter.html

Coleman, J. S. (1988). Social Capital in the Creation of Human Capital. *American Journal of Sociology, 94*, S95–S120.

Coleman, J. S. (1985, April). Schools and the Communities They Serve. *Phi Delta Kappa, 66*(8), 527–532.

Coleman, J. S. (1981). Quality and Equality in American Education. Public and Catholic Schools. *Phi Delta Kappa, 63*, 159–164.

Coleman, J. S. Campbell, E. Q., Hobson, C. J., McPartland, J., Mood, A. M., Weinfeld, F. D., & York, R. L. (1966). *Equality of Educational Opportunity*. Washington, DC: U. S. Government Printing Office.

Coloma, R. S. (2006, March). Disorienting Race and Education: Changing Paradigms on the Schooling of Asian Americans and Pacific Islanders. *Race Ethnicity and Education, 9*(1), 1–15.

Coontz, S. (1993). *The Way We Never Were: American Families and the Nostalgia Trap*. New York: Basic Books.

Cooper, R. S. (2005, January). Race and IQ: Molecular Genetics as Deus ex Machina. *American Psychologist,* 60(1), 71–76.

Cornwell, G. H., & Stoddard, E. V. (Eds.). (2001). *Global Multiculturalism: Comparative Perspectives on Ethnicity, Race, and Nation.* Lanham, MD: Rowman & Littlefield.

Counts, G. S. (1927, September). The Subject Matter of the Curriculum and Sociology. *Journal of Educational Sociology,* 1(1), 11–17.

Crawford, J. (2000). Anatomy of the English-Only Movement. Retrieved March 6, 2008, from http://ourworld.compuserve.com/homepages/jWCRAWFORD/anatomy.htm.

Crawford, J. (1995). Endangered Native American languages: What Is to Be Done and Why? *Bilingual Research Journal,* 19(1), 17–38.

Crenshaw, K. (1993). Mapping the Margins: Intersectionality, Identity Politics and the Violence against Women of Color. *Stanford Law Review,* 43, 1241–1299.

Crenshaw, K., Delgado, R., Lawrence, C., & Matsuda, M. (1993). *Words That Wound: Critical Race Theory, Assaultive Speech, and the First Amendment.* Boulder, CO: Westview Press.

Croninger, R. G., & Lee, V. E. (2001). Social Capital and Dropping out of High School: Benefits to At-Risk Students of Teachers' Support and Guidance. *Teachers College Record,* 103, 548–581.

Cross, W. E., Strauss, L., & 1999). African American Identity across the Life Span: Educational implications. In R. Hernandez Sheets & E. R. Hollins (Eds.), *Racial and Ethnic Identity in School Practices,* 29–47. Mahwah, NJ: Lawrence Erlbaum Associates.

Curti, M. E. (1966). *The Social Ideas of American Educators.* Lanham, MD: Littlefield, Adams.

D'Ambrosio, U. (1985). Ethnomathematics and Its Place in the History and Pedagogy of Mathematics. *For the Learning of Mathematics,* 5(1), 44–48.

D'Souza, D. (1995). *The End of Racism—Principles for a Multiracial Society.* New York: Free Press.

Darder, A., Torres, R. D., & Baltodano, M. (Eds.). (2002). *The Critical Pedagogy Reader.* New York: RoutledgeFalmer.

Darity, W. A., & Myers, S. L. (1998). *Persistent Disparity: Race and Economic Inequality in the United States since 1945.* Northampton, MA: Edward Elgar.

Darling-Hammond, L. (2006). *Powerful Teacher Education: Lesson from Exemplary Programs.* San Francisco, CA: Jossey-Bass.

Darling-Hammond, L. (1998, Spring). Unequal Opportunity: Race and Education. *The Brookings Review,* 16(2), 28–32. Retrieved September 29, 2007, from http://www.brookings.edu/press/review/spring98/darling.htm.

Davis, A. (1971). *Lectures on Liberation.* Los Angeles: National United Committee to Free Angela Davis.

Dei, G. J. S. (1996–97, Winter). Beware of False Dichotomies: Revisiting the Idea of "Black-Focused" Schools in Canadian Contexts. *Journal of Canadian Studies, 31*(4), 58–79.

Dei, G. J. S. (1994, March). Afrocentricity: A Cornerstone of Pedagogy. *Anthropology & Education Quarterly, 25*(1), 3–28.

Dei, G. J. S., & Calliste, A. (Eds.). (2000). *Power, Knowledge and Anti-racism Education: A Critical Reader.* Toronto: Fernwood.

Dei, G. J. S., Karumanchery, L. L., & Karumanchery-Luik, N. (2004). *Playing the Race Card: Exposing White Power and Privilege.* New York: Peter Lang.

Delgado, R. (1996). *The Coming Race War? And Other Apocalyptic Tales of America after Affirmative Action and Welfare.* New York: New York University Press.

Del Pilar, J. A., & Udasco, J. O. (2004). Deculturation: Its Lack of Validity. *Cultural Diversity and Ethnic Minority Psychology, 10,* 169–176.

Delpit, L. (1995). *Other People's Children: Cultural Conflict in the Classroom.* New York: New Press.

Delpit, L. (1988). The Silenced Dialogue: Power and Pedagogy in Educating Other People's Children. *Harvard Educational Review, 58,* 280–298.

Diller, J. V. (1999). *Cultural Diversity: A Primer for the Human Services.* Belmont, CA: Thomson.

Dobson, S. (2002). The Urban Pedagogy of Walter Benjamin. Lessons for the 21st Century, Part 1. Retrieved March 10, 2008, from http://www.goldsmiths.ac.uk/cucr/pdf/benjamin1.pdf.

Donaldson, M. (2007, March 21). Responses to Racism and Strategies for Building Diversity. Eliminating Racism: Valuing Diversity Conference. The Human Rights and Equal Opportunity Commission. Retrieved March 5, 2008, from http://www.hreoc.gov.au/about/media/speeches/race/2007/Eliminating_racism210 307.html.

Dorfman, R. (1997). The Culture Wars and the Great Conversation: An Idiosyncratic Web Essay. Retrieved March 8, 2008, from http://www.pbs.org/shattering/culture.html.

Douglas, A. (1978/1988). *The Feminization of American Culture.* New York: Anchor/Doubleday.

Douglass, F. (1845). Narrative of the Life of Frederick Douglass, an American Slave. Retrieved January 20, 2007, from http://sunsite.berkeley.edu/Literature/Douglass/Autobiography/.

Dunn, F. (1993, Winter). The Educational Philosophies of Washington, Du Bois, and Houston: Laying the Foundations for Afrocentrism and Multiculturalism. *Journal of Negro Education, 62*(1), 24–34.

Dyer, T. G. (1980). *Theodore Roosevelt and the Idea of Race.* Baton Rouge: Louisiana State University Press.

Ellison, Ralph (1964). *Shadow and Act.* New York: Random House.

Ellwood, C. A. (1927, September). What Is Educational Sociology? *Journal of Educational Sociology, 1*(1), 25–30.

Endres, B. J. (1997). Ethics and the Critical Theory of Education. Retrieved March 3, 2008, from http://www.ed.uiuc.edu/EPS/PES-Yearbook/97_docs/endres.html.

Enns, C. Z., & Sinacore, A. L. (2005). *Multicultural and Feminist Literatures: Themes, Dimensions, and Variations*. In C. Z. Enns & A. L. Sinacore (Eds.), *Teaching and Social Justice: Integrating Multicultural and Feminist Theories in the Classroom,* 99–108. Washington, DC: American Psychological Association Press.

Epstein, J. (1995). School, Family, Community Partnerships. *Phi Delta Kappa,* 76(9), 701–712.

Espino, R., & Franz, M. M. (2002). Latino Phenotypic Discrimination Revisited: The Impact of Skin Color on Occupational Status. *Social Science Quarterly,* 83(2), 612–623.

Faith, E. (2007). Finding Healing and Balance in Learning and Teaching at the First Nations University of Canada. *First Peoples Child & Family Review,* 4(3), 8–12. Retrieved February 10, 2008, from http://www.fncfcs.com/pubs/vol3num4/Faith_pp8.pdf.

Fanon, F. (1963). *The Wretched of the Earth.* New York: Grove.

Farrow, A., Lang, J., & Frank, J. (2005). *Complicity: How the North Promoted, Prolonged and Profited from Slavery.* New York: Ballantine Books.

Ferg-Cadima, J. (2004, May). Black, White, and Brown: Latino School Desegregation Efforts in the Pre–and Post–Brown v. Board of Education era. Washington, DC: Mexican-American Legal Defense and Education Fund.

Ferguson, A. A. (2000). *Bad Boys: Public Schools and the Making of Black Masculinity.* Ann Arbor: University of Michigan Press.

Ferguson, R. (2006, November/December). Recent Research on the Achievement Gap—An Interview. *Harvard Education Letter.* Retrieved November 26, 2007, from http://www.edletter.org/current/ferguson.shtml.

Fishman, J. (1991). What Is Reversing Language Shift (RLS) and How Can It Succeed? *Journal of Multilingual and Multicultural Development,* 11(1–2), 5–36.

Flores, R. (2003). From U.S.-Centered Multiculturalism to Global Intercultural Educational Equality: The Role of Reforms and Autonomy. *Motion Magazine.* Retrieved March 5, 2008, from http://www.inmotionmagazine.com/auto/multi_3.html.

Foner, E. (2002). Race in America: From the Naturalization Act of 1790 to the Civil War. *The Fathom Knowledge Network.* Retrieved March 3, 2008, from http://www.fathom.com/feature/121862/index.html.

Ford, D. Y. (1996). *Reversing Underachievement among Gifted Black Students: Promising Practices and Programs.* New York: Teachers College Press.

Ford, D. Y. (1992). The American Achievement Ideology as Perceived by Urban African American Students. *Urban Education,* 27, 196–211.

Ford, D. Y., & Harris, J. J. (1994). Promoting Achievement among Gifted Black Students: The Efficacy of New Definitions and Identification Practices. *Urban Education,* 29(2), 202–229.

Ford, D. Y., Harris, J. J., & Schuerger, J. M. (1993). Racial Identity Development among Gifted Black Students: Counseling Issues and Concerns. *Journal of Counseling and Development,* 71, 409–417.

Fordham, S. (1991). Racelessness in Private Schools: Should We Deconstruct the Racial and Cultural Identity of African-American Adolescents? *Teachers College Record,* 92, 470–484.

Fordham, S. (1982). Racelessness as a Strategy in Black Students' School Success: Pragmatic Strategy or Pyrrhic Victory? *Harvard Educational Review,* 58(1), 54–84.

Foster, M. (1996). *Black Teachers on Teaching.* New York: New Press.

Frankenberg, E., Lee, C., & Orfield, G. (2003, January). *A Multiracial Society with Segregated Schools: Are We Losing the Dream?* Cambridge, MA: Civil Rights Project, Harvard University.

Frankenberg, R. (1993). *The Social Construction of Whiteness: White Women, Race Matters.* London & New York: Routledge.

Franklin, V. P. (1979). *The Education of Black Philadelphia: The Social and Educational History of a Minority Community, 1900–1950.* Philadelphia: University of Pennsylvania Press.

Franklin, V. P. (1978, February). *Review of* A Chance to Learn. *The School Review,* 86(2), 287–289.

Freedman, J. (2000). *The Temple of Culture: Assimilation and Anti-Semitism in Literary Anglo-America.* New York: Oxford University Press.

Freire, P. (1970). *Pedagogy of the Oppressed.* Trans. Myra Bergman Ramos. New York: Continuum Press.

Fryer, R. G. (2006, Winter). Acting White. *Education Next,* 53–59.

Fryer, R. G., & Greenstone, M. (2007, April). The Causes and Consequences of Attending Historically Black Colleges and Universities. NBER Working Paper No. 13036] [under review]. Retrieved February 15, 2008, from http://www.nber.org/papers/w13036.pdf.

Gabe, J. (1991). Explaining "Race"-Education. *British Journal of Sociology of Education,* 12, 347–376.

García, E. (2002). Bilingualism and Schooling in the United States. *International Journal of the Sociology of Language,* 155/156(1), 1–92.

García, M. C. (1996). *Havana USA: Cuban Exiles and Cuban Americans in South Florida, 1959–1994.* Berkeley, CA: University of California Press.

Gasman, M., & Jennings, M. (2006). New Research, New Questions: Social Foundations Scholarship on Historically Black Colleges and Universities. *Educational Foundations,* 20(1–2), 3–8.

Gay, G. (2004). Multicultural Curriculum Theory and Multicultural Education. In J. A. Banks & C. M. Banks (Eds.), *Handbook*

of Research in Multicultural Education, 2nd edition, 30–49. San Francisco, CA: Jossey-Bass.

Gay, G. (2000). *Culturally Responsive Teaching: Theory, Research & Practice.* New York: Teachers College Press.

Gay, G. (1993). Building Cultural Bridges: A Bold Proposal for Teacher Education. *Education and Urban Society,* 25(3), 285–299.

Ghosh, R. (2004, Winter). Globalization in the North American Region: Toward Renegotiation of Cultural Space. *McGill Journal of Education,* 39(1), 87–101.

Ghosh, R., & Abdi, A. (2004). *Education and the Politics of Difference: Canadian Perspectives.* Toronto: Canadian Press.

Ginorio, A. B., & Martinez, L. J. (1998). Where Are the Latinas? Ethno-Race and Gender in Psychology Courses. *Psychology of Women Quarterly,* 22, 53–68.

Ginsburg, M. (1988). *Contradictions in Teacher Education and Society: A Critical Analysis.* New York: Falmer Press.

Ginwright, S. A. (2004). *Black in School: Afrocentric Reform, Urban Reform, and the Promise of Hip-Hop Culture.* New York: Teachers College Press.

Giroux, H. A. (2006). The Giroux Reader *(Cultural Politics and the Promise of Democracy),* Nick Couldry (series ed.). Boulder, CO: Paradigm.

Giroux, H. A. (2003). *The Abandoned Generation: Democracy beyond the Culture of Fear.* New York: Palgrave Macmillan.

Giroux, H. A. (1996a). *Fugitive Cultures: Race, Violence, and Youth.* New York: Routledge.

Giroux, H. A. (1996b). *Living Dangerously: Multiculturalism and the Politics of Difference.* New York: Peter Lang.

Giroux, H. A. (1994, Fall). Doing Cultural Studies: Youth and the Challenge of Pedagogy. *Harvard Educational Review,* 64(3) 278–308.

Giroux, H. A. (1981) *Ideology, culture & the process of schooling.* Philadelphia London: Temple University Press.

Goffman, E. (1959). The Presentation of self in everyday life. Doubleday Anchor. New York: Anchor/Doubleday.

Goffman, E. (1963). Stigma: Notes on the Management of Spoiled Identity. New Jersey: Prentice Hall.

Goldberg, D. (1993). *Racist Culture: Philosophy and the Politics of Meaning.* Oxford: Blackwell.

Gonäs , L., & Karlsson, J. (2006). Gender Segregation: Divisions of Work in Post-Industrial Welfare States. Ashgate: Aldershot.

Good, T. L. (1981). Teacher Expectations and Student Perceptions: A Decade of Research. *Educational Leadership,* 38(5), 415–422.

Goodchild, L. F., & Wechsler, H. S. (Eds.). (1997). *The History of Higher Education.* ASHE Reader Series. Boston: Pearson.

Goodrich, J. (2002). "Curriculum," Retrieved November 7, 2007, from http://www.yale.edu/ynhti/brochures/A3/2002/programnh.htm. Yale-New Haven Teacher Institute.

Gordon, M. M. (1964). *Assimilation in American Life: The Role of Race, Religion and National Origins.* New York: Oxford University Press.

Goyette, K., & Xie, Y. (1999). Educational Expectations of Asian American Youths: Determinants and Ethnic Differences. *Sociology of Education, 72,* 22–36.

Grant, C., & Wieczorek, K. (2000). Teacher Education and Knowledge in "the Knowledge Society": The Need for Social Moorings in Our Multicultural Schools. *Teachers College Record, 102*(5), 913–935.

Gresson, A. D. (2007). My Daughter, Myself: Class Reflections through the Parent-Race-Gender Lens. In Joe L. Kincheloe & Shirley L. Steinberg (Eds.), *Cutting Class: Essays on School and Social Class,* 211–222. Lanham, MD: Rowman & Littlefield.

Gresson, A. D. (2006). Doing Critical Research in Mainstream Disciplines: Reflections on a Study of Black Female Individuation. In K. Tobin & J. L. Kincheloe (Eds.), *Doing Educational Research,* 191–209. Rotterdam: Sense.

Gresson, A. D. (2004). *America's Atonement: Racial Pain, Recovery Rhetoric and the Pedagogy of Healing.* New York: Peter Lang Press.

Gresson, A. D. (1997). Identity, Class and Teacher Education: The Persistence of Class Effects in the Classroom, *The Review of Education Pedagogy Cultural Studies, 19*(3), 335–348.

Gresson, A. D. (1996, Winter). Postmodern America and the Multiculturalism Crisis: Reading Forrest Gump as the "Call Back to Whiteness." *Taboo,* 2(4), 11–33.

Gresson, A. D. (1995). *The Recovery of Race in America.* Minneapolis: University of Minnesota Press.

Gresson, A. D. (1985, Spring). Langston Hughes' Style and the Psychology of Black Selfhood. *The Langston Hughes Review,* 4(1), 47–54.

Gresson, A.D. (1982). The Dialectics of Betrayal: Sacrifice, Violation and the Oppressed. Norwood, N.J.: Ablex.

Gresson, A. D. (1980). The Black Special Educator as Educational Pathologist. *Journal of Negro Education,* 49(1), 31–41.

Gresson, A. D. (1978a). The Sociology of Social Pathology: Focus on Black Education. *The Black Sociologist,* 6(2), 25–39.

Gresson, A. D. (1978b). Phenomenology and the Rhetoric of Identification: A Neglected Dimension of Coalition Communication. *Communication Quarterly,* 26(4), 14–23.

Gresson, A. D. (1977). Minority Epistemology and the Rhetoric of Creation. *Philosophy and Rhetoric,* 10(4), 244–262.

Gresson, A. D., & Carter, D. G. (1978). Equal Educational Opportunity for the Gifted: In Search of a Legal Standard. *NOLPE School Law Journal,* 6(2), 145–154.

Gresson, A. D., & Carter, D. G. (1976). In Search of the Potentially Gifted: Suggestions for the School Administrator. *The Clearing House,* 50(8), 369–371.

Guess, R. (1981). The Idea of Critical Theory: Habermas and the Frankfurt School. Cambridge University Press, Cambridge

Guglielmo, J., & Salerno, S. (Eds.). (2003). *Are Italians White?: How Race Is Made in America.* New York: Routledge.

Guinier, L., & Torres, G. (2002). *The Miner's Canary: Enlisting Race, Resisting Power, Transforming Democracy.* Cambridge, MA: Harvard University Press.

Guy, T. (2004, Spring). Gangsta Rap and Adult Education. *New Directions for Adult and Continuing Education,* 101, 43–55.

Haberman, M. (undated). The Pedagogy of Poverty Versus Good Teaching. Retrieved March 9, 2008, from http://www.wmich.edu/coe/tles/urban/Haberman.pdf.

Haberman, M. (1995). *Star Teachers of Children in Poverty.* West Lafayette, IN: Kappa Delta Pi.

Hale-Benson, J. (1986). *Black Children: Their Roots, Culture and Learning Styles.* Baltimore, MD: Johns Hopkins University Press.

Hall, G. S. (1901, December). How Far is the Present High School and Early College Training Adapted to the Nature and Needs of Adolescents? *School Review,* 9, 649–665.

Hall, T. D. (2007). A Pedagogy of Freedom: Using Hip Hop in the Classroom to Engage African-American Students. Unpublished doctoral dissertation, University of Missouri-Columbia. Retrieved March 1, 2008, from http://edt.missouri.edu/Fall2007/Dissertation/HallT-120507-D8654/short.pdf.

Hampel, R. (1996, Winter). Forum: History and Education Reform. *History of Education Quarterly,* 36, 473–502.

Hartmann, D., Croll, P. R., & Guenther, K. (2003, September). The Race Relations "Problematic" in American Sociology: Revisiting Niemonen's Case Study and Critique. *American Sociologist,* 34(3), 20–55.

Haymes, S. N. (1995). *Race, Culture, and the City: A Pedagogy for Black Urban Struggle.* Albany, NY: SUNY Press.

Heckman, J. J., & Kruger, A. B. (2003). *Inequity in America: What Role for Human Capital Policies?* Cambridge, MA: MIT Press.

Henderson, C. B. (2000). The History of Japanese Immigration. *The Brown Quarterly.* Retrieved on June 23, 2004, from http://brownvboard.org/brwnqurt/03–4/03–4a.htm

Herring, C. (2002). *Bleaching Out the Color Line?: The Skin Color Continuum and the Tripartite Model of Race. Race and Society,* 5(1), 17–31.

Herrnstein, R. J., & Murray, C. (1995). *The Bell Curve: Intelligence and Class Structure American Life.* New York: Free Press.

Hickling-Hudson, A., & Ahlquist, R. (2003). Contesting the Curriculum in the Schooling of Indigenous Children in Australian and the United States: From Eurocentrism to Culturally Powerful Pedagogies. *Comparative Education Review, 47,* 64–91.

Hill, M. (2004). *After Whiteness: Unmaking an American Majority.* New York: NYU Press.

Hilliard, A. (2001). "Race," Identity, Hegemony, and Education: What Do We Need to Know Now? In W. H. Watkins, J. H. Lewis, & V. Chou (Eds.), *Race and Education: The Roles of History and Society in Educating African American Students.* Boston: Allyn & Bacon.

Hilliard, A. (1999). What Do We Need to Know Now? "Race," Identity, Hegemony, and Education. *Rethinking Schools Online, 14*(2). Retrieved December 12, 2007, from http://www.rethinkingschools. org/archive/14_02/race142.shtml.

Hinton, L. (1994). *Flutes of Fire: Essays on California Indian Languages.* Berkeley, CA: Heyday.

Hirsch, E. D., Jr. (1987). *Cultural Literacy: What Every American Needs to Know.* Boston: Houghton Mifflin.

hooks, b. (2003). *Teaching Community: A Pedagogy of Hope.* New York: Routledge.

hooks, b. (1994). *Teaching to Transgress: Education as the Practice of Freedom.* New York: Routledge.

hooks, b. (1990). *Yearning: Race, Gender and Cultural Politics.* Boston: South End.

hooks, b. (1981). *Ain't I a Woman?: Black Women and Feminism.* Boston: South End Press.

Hopson, R. (2003, September). The Problem of the Language Line: Cultural and Social Reproduction of Hegemonic Linguistic Structures for Learners of African Descent in the USA. *Race, Ethnicity & Education, 6*(3), 227–246.

House, E. (1999, April). Race and Policy. *Education Policy Analysis Archives, 7*(16). Retrieved on January 11, 2008, from http://epaa. asu.edu/epaa/v7n16.html.

Howard, T. C. (2003, Summer). Culturally Relevant Pedagogy: Ingredients for Critical Teacher Reflection. *Theory Into Practice, 42*(3), 195–202.

Howell, A., & Tuitt, F. (Eds.). (2003). *Race and Higher Education: Rethinking Pedagogy in Diverse College Classrooms.* Cambridge, MA: Harvard University Press.

Ilg, T. J., & Massucci, J. D. (2003, November). Comprehensive Urban High School. *Education & Urban Society, 36*(1), 63–78.

Inniss, L., & Perry, R. (2003, November). A Retrospective Profile of Electrical Engineering Graduates from the FAMU-FSU College of Engineering. *Frontiers in Education Annual, 1*(5–8), T2A-5–10.

Insley, A. C. (2001). Suspending and Expelling Children from Educational Opportunities: Time to Reevaluate Zero Tolerance Policies. *American University Review,* 50, 1039–1074.

Irwin, J. W., & Farr, W. (2004, October). Collaborative School Communities That Support Teaching and Learning. *Reading and Writing Quarterly,* 20(4), 343–363.

Isaacs, H. R. (1975). *Idols of the Tribe: Group Identity and Political Change.* New York: Harper & Row.

Jackson, P.W. (1968). Life in Classrooms. New York: Holt, Rinehart and Winston.

Jacoby, R. (1994). *Dogmatic Wisdom: How the Culture Wars Divert Education and Distract America.* New York: Doubleday.

James, T. (1987). *Exile Within: The Schooling of Japanese Americans, 1941–1945.* Cambridge, MA: Harvard University Press.

Jencks, C., & Phillips, M. (Eds.). (1998). *The Black-White Test Score Gap.* Washington, DC: Brookings Institution.

Jenifer, F. G. (2005, October 6). Minorities and Women in Higher Education and the Role of Mentoring in Their Advancement. Prepared for the Office of Academic Affairs, University of Texas System. Retrieved February 17, 2008, from http://www.utsystem.edu/aca/files/Mentorship.pdf

Jensen, A. R. (1981). *Straight Talk about Mental Tests.* New York: Free Press.

Jerald, C. (2007). *Keeping Kids in School: What Research Says about Preventing Dropouts.* Alexandria, VA: Center for Public Education.

Jones, C. P. (2001, August 15). Invited Commentary: "Race," Racism, and the Practice of Epidemiology. *Am. J. Epidemiol,* 154(4), 299–304.

Kailin, J. (1999). How White Teachers Perceive the Problem of Racism in Their Schools: A Case Study in "Liberal" Lakeview. *Teachers College Record,* 100, 724–750.

Kanpol, B. (1995). Outcomes-Based Education and Democratic Commitment Hopes and Possibilities. *Educational Policy,* 9(4), 359–374.

Karabel, J. (2005). *The Chosen: The Hidden History of Admission and Exclusion at Harvard, Yale and Princeton.* New York: Houghton Mifflin.

Karier, Clarence. (1967). *Man, Society, and Education: A History of American Educational Ideals.* Glenview, IL: Scott, Foresman.

Kaufman, J. S., & Cooper, R. S. (2001). Considerations for Use of Racial/Ethnic Classification in Etiologic Research. *American Journal of Epidemiology,* 154, 291–298.

Kellner, D. (1998). Multiple Literacies and Critical Pedagogy in a Multicultural Society. *Educational Theory,* 48(1): 103–122.

Kincheloe, J. L. (2004). *Critical Pedagogy: A Primer.* New York: Peter Lang.

Kincheloe, J. L. (1999). The Struggle to Define and Reinvent Whiteness: A Pedagogical Analysis. *College Literature,* 26(3), 162–195.

Kincheloe, J. L., & McLaren, P. (2000). Rethinking Critical Theory and Qualitative Research. In N. K. Denzin & Y. S. Lincoln (Eds.), *Handbook of Qualitative Research,* 2nd edition, 279–313. Thousand Oaks, CA: Sage.

Kincheloe, J. L., & Steinberg, S. R. (1997). *Changing Multiculturalism.* Buckingham: Open University Press.

Kincheloe, J. L., Slattery, P., & Steinberg, S. R. (2000). *Contextualizing Teaching: Introduction to Education and Educational Foundations.* Boston: Allyn & Bacon.

Kincheloe, J. L., Steinberg, S. R., Rodriguez, N. M., & Chennault, R. E. (Eds.). (1998). *White Reign: Deploying Whiteness in America.* New York: St. Martins Press.

Kincheloe, J. L., Steinberg, S. R., & Gresson, A. (1996). *Measured Lies: The Bell Curve Examined.* New York: St. Martins Press.

Kilson, M. (1981). Black Social Classes and Intergenerational Poverty. *The Public Interest,* 64, 58–78.

Kirk, H. D. (1964). *Shared Fate: A Theory of Adoption and Mental Health.* New York: Free Press.

Kirk, R. (1993). *America's British Culture.* New Brunswick, NJ: Transaction.

Kiviat, Barbara J. (2000). The Social Side of Schooling. *Pioneers of Advocacy. Johns Hopkins Magazine.* Retrieved November 20, 2007, from http://www.jhu.edu/~jhumag/0400web/18.html.

Kliebard, H. M. (1987). *The Struggle for the American Curriculum, 1893–1958.* Boston: Routledge & Kegan Paul.

Kober, N. (2001). It Takes More than Testing: Closing the Achievement Gap. Center on Education Policy. Retrieved November 12, 2007, from http://www.learningpt.org/gaplibrary/text/whatcontributes.php.

Kowalczewski, P. S. (1982). Race and Education: Racism, Diversity and Inequality, Implications for Multicultural Education. *Oxford Review of Education,* 8(2), 145–161.

Kozol, J. (2005). *The Shame of the Nation: The Restoration of Apartheid Schooling in America.* New York: Crown Publishing.

Kozol, J. (1991). *Savage Inequalities: Children in America's Schools.* New York: Crown.

Kumashiro, K. (2004). *Against Common Sense: Teaching and Learning toward Social Justice.* New York: RoutledgeFalmer.

Kumashiro, K. (2002). *Troubling Education: Queer Activism and Anti-oppressive Pedagogy.* New York: RoutledgeFalmer.

Kurland, P. B., & Lerner, R. (Eds.). (1987). *The Founders' Constitution.* Chicago: University of Chicago Press.

Kusimo, P. (1999). *Rural African Americans and Education: The Legacy of the Brown Decision.* ERIC Clearinghouse on Rural Education and Small Schools. Retrieved January 20, 2008, from http://www.eric-digests.org/1999–3/brown.htm.

Ladson-Billings, G. (2006). Presidential Address—from the Achievement Gap to the Education Debt: Understanding Achievement in U.S. Schools. *Educational Researcher,* 35(7), 3–12.

Ladson-Billings, G. (1994). *The Dreamkeepers: Successful Teachers of African American Children.* San Francisco, CA: Jossey-Bass.

Ladson-Billings, G. (1990a). Culturally Relevant Teaching: Effective Instruction for Black Students. *The College Board Review,* 155, 20–25.

Ladson-Billings, G. (1990b). Like Lightening in a Bottle: Attempting to Capture the Pedagogical Excellence of Successful Teachers of Black Students. *Qualitative Studies in Education,* 3, 335–344.

Ladson-Billings, G., & Gillborn, D. (2004). *The RoutledgeFalmer Reader in Multicultural Education.* London: RoutledgeFalmer.

Ladson-Billings, G., & Tate, W. F. (1995). Toward a Critical Race Theory of Education, *Teachers College Record,* 97, 47–68.

LaGrand, J. B. (2002). *Indian Metropolis: Native Americans in Chicago, 1945–75.* Urbana: University of Illinois Press, 2002.

Lam, Wan Shun Eva (2006a). Re-envisioning Language, Literacy, and the Immigrant Subject in New Mediascapes. *Pedagogies: An International Journal,* 1(3): 171–195.

Lam, Wan Shun Eva (2006b). Culture and Learning in the Context of Globalization: Research Directions. *Review of Research in Education,* 30, 213–237.

Landrine, H., & Klonoff, E. A. (1996, May). The Schedule of Racist Events: A Measure of Racial Discrimination and a Study of Its Negative Physical and Mental Health Consequences. *Journal of Black Psychology,* 22(2), 144–168.

Lauer, C. (2003). Family Background, Cohort and Education: A French-German Comparison Based on a Multivariate Ordered Probit Model of Educational Attainment. *Labour Economics,* 10, 231–251.

Lawrence, C. (2003). Still Blaming the Victim: A Review of *Young, Gifted, and Black: Promoting High Achievement among African-American Students.* Retrieved July 3, 2007, from http://bostonreview.net/BR28.3/lawrence.html.

Lechner, F. (2001). Globalization Issues. The Globalization Website. Retrieved March 5, 2008, from http://www.sociology.emory.edu/globalization/issues01.html.

Lee, J. (2002). *Civility in the City: Blacks, Jews, and Koreans in Urban America.* Cambridge, MA: Harvard University Press.

Lefkowitz, M. (1996). *Not Out of Africa: How Afrocentrism Became an Excuse to Teach Myth as History.* New York: Basic Books.

Lemert, C. (1999). *Social Theory: The Multicultural and Classic Readings.* New York: Westview Press.

Levesque, D. M. (1994). Cultural and Parental Influences on Achievement among Native American Students in Barstow Unified School District. Paper presented at the National Meeting of the Comparative and

International Educational Society. San Diego, CA. Cited in Research on the Closing the Achievement Gap for Native American Students. Retrieved January 20, 2008, from http://www.swcompcenter.org/pdf/Native_American_Overview.pdf

Lewin, K. (1948). *Resolving Social Conflicts*. New York: Harper & Row.

Lewis, J., & D'Orso, M. *Walking with the Wind*. New York: Simon & Schuster.

Lewis, J. L., & Kim, E. (2008). A Desire to Learn: African American Children's Positive Attitudes toward Learning within School Cultures of Low Expectations. *Teachers College Record*, 110(6). Retrieved February 12, 2008, from http://www.tcrecord.org.

Lipsitz, G. (1995, September). The Possessive Investment in Whiteness. *American Quarterly*, 47(3), 369–386.

Lloyd, C. B., Grant, M. J., & Ritchie, A. (2008). Gender Differences in Time Use among Adolescents in Developing Countries: Implications of Rising School Enrollment Rates. *Journal of Research on Adolescence*, 18(1), 99–120.

Lloyd, C.B., Mete, C., & Grant, M. (2007). "Rural girls in Pakistan: Constraints of policy and culture," in Maureen Lewis and Marlaine Lockheed (Eds.) *Exclusion, Gender and Schooling: Case Studies from the Developing World*, 99–118. Washington DC: Center for Global Development.

Lomotey, K., & Statley, J. (1990). The Education of African Americans in Buffalo Public Schools. Paper presented at the annual meeting of the American Educational Research Association, Boston.

Louis, K., & Kruse, S. (Eds.). (1995). *Professionalism & Community*. Thousand Oaks, CA: Corwin Press.

Lowden, F. Y. (1996, Summer). Review: *Star Teachers of Children in Poverty. Journal of Negro Education*, 65(3), 394–395.

Lutz, F., & Gresson, A. D. (1980). Local School Boards as Political Councils. *Educational Studies*, 11(2), 125–144.

Lynch, F. R. (1989). *Invisible Victims: White Males and the Crisis of Affirmative Action*. New York: Greenwood.

Marable, M. (1992). *Black America*. Westfield, NJ: Open Media.

Marden, C. F., & Meyer, G. (1968). *Minorities in American Society*, 3rd edition. New York: Van Nostrand Reinhold Company.

Marinucci, J. (2001, Summer). Literacy in Native American Education. University of New Mexico Summer Institute. Retrieved December 10, 2007, from http://si.unm.edu/Web%20Journals/articles2001/jmarinucci_jrn.htm.

Marker, P. M. (2003). Another Brick in the Wall: High Stakes Testing in Teacher Education—The California Teacher Performance Assessment. *Workplace*. Retrieved on February 3, 2008, from http://www.louisville.edu/journal/workplace/issue5p2/marker.html

Marone, J. A. (2003). *Hellfire Nation: The Politics of Sin in American History*. New Haven, CT: Yale University Press.

Marshall, J. D., Sears, J. T., & Schubert, W. H. (2000). *Turning Points in Curriculum: A Contemporary American Memoir.* Upper Saddle River, NJ: Merrill.

Mathews, J. (2004, October 12). Should Colleges Have Quotas for Asian Americans. Retrieved April 3, 2007, from http://www.Washingtopost.com.

May, S. (1999). *Critical Multiculturalism: Rethinking Multicultural and Antiracist Education.* London: Falmer Press.

McCarthy, C. (2005). English Rustic in Black Skin: Post-colonial Education, Cultural Hybridity and Racial Identity in the New Century. *Policy Futures in Education,* 3(4), 413–422.

McCarthy, C. (1990a). *Race and Curriculum: Social Inequality and Theories and Politics of Difference in Contemporary Research on Schooling.* London: Falmer Press.

McCarthy, C. (1990b). Multicultural Education, Minority Identities, Textbooks, and the Challenge of Curriculum Reform. *Journal of Education,* 172(2), 118–129.

McCarthy, C. (1988). Reconsidering Liberal and Radical Perspectives on Racial Inequality in Schooling: Making the Case for Nonsynchrony. *Harvard Educational Review,* 58(2), 265–279.

McCarthy, C., Crichlow, W., Dimitriadis, G., & Dolby, N. (2005). *Race, Identity and Representation in Education,* 2nd edition. New York: Taylor & Francis.

McCarthy, C., Giardina, M. D., Harewood, S. J., & Park, J.-K. (2003). Contested Culture: Identity and Curriculum Dilemmas in the Age of Globalization, Postcolonialism, and Multiplicity. *Harvard Educational Review,* 73(3), 449–465.

McElroy, W. (2005, October 19). Cultural Competence: Coming to a School Near You? Retrieved November 15, 2007, from Fox News Online: http://www.foxnews.com/story/0,2933,172816,00.html.

McGee, E. (2005). Chronicles of Success: Black College Students Achieving in Mathematics and Engineering. Retrieved February 17, 2008, from http://www.blacksuccessfoundation.org/Achieving%20in%20Math%20and%20Engineering.htm.

McIntosh, P. (1988). White Privilege and Male Privilege. Wellesley College, Centre for Research on Women. Working Paper No. 189.

McKee, J. (1993). *Sociology and the Race Problem: The Failure of a Perspective.* Urbana: University of Illinois Press.

McKinney, K. (2005). *Being White: Stories of Race and Racism.* New York: Routledge.

McLaren, P. (1998). *Life in Schools: An Introduction to Critical Pedagogy in the Foundations of Education,* 3rd edition. New York: Longman.

McLaren, P., & Dantley, M. (1990). Leadership and a Critical Pedagogy of Race: Cornel West, Stuart Hall and the Prophetic Tradition. *Journal of Negro Education,* 59(1), 29–43.

McLester, S. (2007, March 15). Technology Literacy and the MySpace Generation. *Tech Learning*. Retrieved February 18, 2008, from http://www.techlearning.com/showArticle.php?articleID=196604312.

McWhorter, J. (2000). *Losing the Race: Self-sabotage in Black America*. New York: Free Press.

Meighan, R. (1981). *A Sociology of Educating*. London: Holt, Rinehart & Winston.

Michelli, N., & Keiser, D. L. (2005). *Teacher Education for Democracy and Social Justice*. Boston: RoutledgeFalmer.

Michigan Daily (March 6, 2001). Retrieved September 1, 2007, from http://media.www.michigandaily.com.

Mickelson, R. A. (1990). The Attitude-Achievement Paradox among Black Adolescents. *Sociology of Education, 63*, 44–61.

Miller, L. S. (2005). Exploring High Academic Performance: The Case of Latinos in Higher Education. *Journal of Hispanic Higher Education, 4*(3), 252–271.

Miller, R. E. (1998, September). The Arts of Complicity: Pragmatism and the Culture of Schooling. *College English, 61*(1), 10–28.

Milliken, B. (2007). *The Last Drop-Out. Stop the Epidemic!* Carlsbad, CA: Hay House.

Mills, C. W. (1959). *The Sociological Imagination*. London & New York: Oxford University Press.

Milner, R. (2003). Teacher Reflection and Race in Cultural Contexts: History, Meanings, and Methods in Teaching. *Theory into Practice, 42*(3), 173–180.

Minh-ha, T. (1989). *Woman, Native, Other. Writing Postcoloniality and Feminism*. Bloomington & Indianapolis: Indiana University Press.

Min, P. G. (1992, Spring). A Comparison of the Korean Minorities in China and Japan. *International Migration Review, 26*(1), 4–21.

Miron, L. F. (1996). *The Social Construction of Urban Schooling: Situating the Crisis*. Cresskill, NJ: Hampton Press.

Montalvo, F. F. (2004). Surviving Race Skin Color and the Socialization and Acculturation of Latinas. *Journal of Ethnic & Cultural Diversity in Social Work, 13*(3), 25–43.

Moroney, J. R. (1979, September). Do Women Earn Less Under Capitalism? *The Economic Journal, 89*(355), 601–613.

Morris, J. E. (2004). Can Anything Good Come from Nazareth? Race, Class, and African-American Schooling and Community in the Urban South and Midwest. *American Educational Research Journal, 41(1)*, 69–112.

Morris, J. E. (2003a). Race, Ethnicity and Culture: Cultural Expectations and Student Learning In J. W. Guthrie (Ed.), *Encyclopedia of Education*, 2nd edition, volume 6, 1961–1966. New York: Macmillan.

Morris, J. E. (2003b). What Does Africa Have to Do with Being African-American: A Micro-ethnographic Analysis of a Middle School Inquiry Unit on Africa. *Anthropology & Education Quarterly, 34*(3) 255–276.

Morris, J. E. (2002a). A Communally Bonded School for African-American Students, Families, and a Community. *Phi Delta Kappa, 84(3), 230–234.*

Morris, J. E. (2002b). African-American Students and Gifted Education: The Politics of Race and Culture. *Roeper Review, 24*(2), 59–62.

Morris, J. E. (2001). Forgotten Voices of African-American Educators: Critical Race Perspectives on the Implementation of a Desegregation Plan. *Educational Policy, 15*(4), 575–600.

Morrison, Toni. (1992). *Playing in the Dark: Whiteness and the Literary Imagination.* Cambridge, MA: Harvard University Press.

Moses, W. J. (1991). Eurocentrism, Afrocentrism, and William Ferris's *The African Abroad,* 1911. *Journal of Education,* 173(1), 76–90.

Mouw, T., & Xie, Y. (1999, April). Bilingualism and the Academic Achievement of First- and Second-Generation Asian Americans: Accommodation with or without Assimilation? *American Sociological Review,* 64(2), 232–252.

Nakayama, T., & Krizek, R. (1995). Whiteness: A Strategic Rhetoric. *Quarterly Journal of Speech,* 81, 291–309.

Nash, R. (1990). Bourdieu on Education and Social and Cultural Reproduction. *British Journal of Sociology of Education,* 11(4), 431–448.

National Science Foundation. (2000). *Science and Engineering Indicators.* Washington DC.

Neal, D. (1997). The Effect of Catholic Secondary Schooling on Educational Attainment. *Journal of Labor Economics,* 15, 98–123.

Nelson-Barber, S., & Estrin, E. T. (1995, Summer). Bringing Native American Perspectives to Mathematics and Science Teaching. *Theory into Practice,* 34(3), 174–185.

Nettles, M.T., Millett, C.M., & Ready, D.D. (2003). Attacking the African American-White Achievement Gap on College Admissions Tests Brookings Papers on Education Policy, 215–238.

Newmann, F., & Wehlage, G. (1995). *Successful School Restructuring.* Madison, WI: Center on Organization and Restructuring of Schools.

Ng, R., Staton, P., & Scane, J. (Eds.). (1995). *Anti-racism, Feminism, and Critical Approaches to Education.* Toronto: OISE Press.

Nieto, S. (2004). *Affirming Diversity: The Sociopolitical Context of Multicultural Education,* 4th edition. New York: Allyn & Bacon.

Nieto, S. (2003). *What Keeps Teachers Going?* New York: Teachers College Press.

Nieto, S. (1999). *The Light in Their Eyes: Creating Multicultural Learning Communities.* New York: Teachers College Press.

Nieto, S. (1998). Fact and Fiction: Stories of Puerto Ricans in U.S. Schools. *Harvard Educational Review,* 68(2), 133–163.

Nobles, W. W. (1990). The Infusion of African and African American Content: A Question of Content and Intent. In A. G. Hilliard III, L. Payton-Steart, & L. O. Williams (Eds.), *Infusion of African and African American Content in the School Curriculum: Proceedings of the First National Conference,* October, 1989 (5–24). Morristown, NJ: Aaron Press.

Noddings, N. (1992/2000). The Challenge of Care in Schools: An Alternative Approach to Education. In R. Reed & T. Johnson (Eds.), *Philosophical Documents in Education,* 2nd edition, 247–257. New York: Longman (Reprinted from *The Challenge to Care in Schools: An Alternative Approach to Education,* by Noddings, 1992, New York: Teachers College Press).

Noguera, P., & Akom, A. (2000, June 19). The Significance of Race in the Racial Gap in Academic Achievement. Retrieved September 21, 2007, from *Motion Magazine,* http://www.inmotionmagazine.com/pnaa.html.

Noguera, P. A. (2002). Understanding the Link Between Racial Identity and Academic Achievement and Creating Schools Where that Link Can be Broken, *Sage Race Relations Abstracts,* Institute of Race Relations, Vol. 27(3):5–15

Nye, J. (2002, August 12). Globalism versus Globalization. *The Globalist.* Retrieved March 5, 2008, from http://www.theglobalist.com/StoryId.aspx?StoryId=2392.

O'Connor, A. (2001). *Poverty Knowledge: Social Science, Social Policy, and the Poor in Twentieth-Century U.S. History.* Princeton, NJ: Princeton University Press.

O'Connor A., C., Horvat, E., & Lewis, A. (2006). Framing the Field: Past and Future Research on the Historic Underachievement of Black Students. In E. McNamara, E. Horvat, & C. O'Connor (Eds.), *Beyond Acting White: Reframing the Debate on Black Student Achievement,* 1–24. Lanham, MD: Rowman & Littlefield.

Ogbu, J. (2002). Black-American Students and the Academic Achievement Gap: What Else You Need to Know. *Journal of Thought,* 37(4), 9–33.

Ogbu, J. (1992). Understanding Cultural Diversity and Learning. *Educational Researcher,* 21(8), 5–14.

Ogbu, J. (1991). Minority Coping Responses and School Experience. *Journal of Psychohistory,* 18, 433–456.

Ogbu, J. (1978). *Minority Education and Caste.* New York: Academic Press.

Ogbu, J., & Fordham, S. (1986). Black Students' School Success: Coping with the "Burden of 'Acting White.'" *The Urban Review,* 18, 176–206.

Olsen, L. (1997). *Made in America: Immigrant Students in Our Public Schools.* New York: New Press.

Omi, M., & Winant, H. (1986). *Racial Formation in the United States: From the 1960s to the 1980s.* New York: Routledge.

Orfield, G., & Lee, C. (2006, January). *Racial Transformation and the Changing Nature of Segregation.* Cambridge, MA: Civil Rights Project, Harvard University.

Orfield, G., & McArdle, N. (2006, August). The Vicious Cycle: Segregated Housing, Schools and Intergenerational Inequality. Cambridge, MA: Civil Rights Project, Harvard University. Retrieved on January 11, 2008, from http://www.jchs.harvard.edu/publications/communitydevelopment/w06-4_orfield.pdf.

Ornstein, A. C., & Hunkins, F. P. (1998). *Curriculum Foundations, Principles, and Issues,* 3rd edition. Boston: Allyn & Bacon.

Oswald, D., Coutinho, M., & Best, A. (2000). Community and School Predictors of Overrepresentation of Minority Students in Special Education. Paper presented at the Harvard University Civil Rights Project Conference on Minority Issues in Special Education, Cambridge, MA.

Oswald, D., Coutinho, M., Singh, N., & Best, A. (1999). Ethnicity in Special Education and Relationships with School-Related Economic and Educational Variables. *Journal of Special Education,* 32(4), 194–206.

Park, R. E. (1928). Human Migration and the Marginal Man. *American Journal of Sociology,* 3, 881–893.

Parkay, F. W., & Hass, G. (2000). *Curriculum Planning: A Contemporary Approach.* Boston: Allyn & Bacon.

Patterson, O. (2001, May/June). The American View of Freedom: What We Say, What We Mean. *Society* 38(4), 37–45.

Pennachio, D. L. (2004, July 9). Cultural Competence: Caring for Chinese, Japanese, and Korean Patients. Retrieved November 15, 2007, from *Medical Economics* http://www.memag.com/memag/article/articleDetail.jsp?id=10897.

Perry, T., C. Steele, & A. Hilliard (Eds.). (2003). *Young, Gifted, and Black: Promoting High Achievement among African American Students.* Boston: Beacon Press.

Peterson, P. E., & Llaudet, E. (2006, August). On the Public-Private School Achievement Debate. Unpublished Paper prepared for the annual meetings of the American Political Science Association, Philadelphia, PA. Retrieved June 27, 2008, from http://www.hks.harvard.edu/pepg/PDF/Papers/PEPG06–02-PetersonLlaudet.pdf.

Pew Hispanic Center. (2004). Kaiser Family Foundation National Survey of Latinos: Education. Retrieved October 12, 2007, from http://pewhispanic.org/factsheets/factsheet.php?FactsheetID=3.

Pfohl, S. (1985, February). Toward a Sociological Deconstruction of Social Problems. *Social Problems,* 32(3), 228–232.

Pinar, W. F. (Ed.). (2003). *International Handbook of Curriculum Research.* Mahwah, NJ: Lawrence Erlbaum Associates.

Pinar, W. F., & Bowers, C. A. (1992). Politics of Curriculum: Origins, Controversies and Significance of Critical Perspectives. *Review of Research in Education,* 18(2), 163–191.

Pinar, W. F., Reynolds, W. M., Slattery, P., & Taubman, P. M. (1995). *Understanding Curriculum.* New York: Peter Lang.

Pinderhughes, E. (1995). Empowering Diverse Populations: Family Practice in the 21st Century. *Families in Society: The Journal of Contemporary Human Services,* 76, 131–139.

Pinderhughes, E. (1989). *Understanding Race, Ethnicity, and Power: The Key to Efficacy in Clinical Practice.* New York: Free Press.

Pinderhughes, E. (1983). Empowerment for Our Clients and for Ourselves. *Social Casework: The Journal of Contemporary Social Work,* 64(6), 331–338.

Pollock, M. (2006). Everyday Antiracism in Education. Retrieved November 23, 2007, from http://www.understandingrace.org/resources/pdf/rethinking/pollock.pdf

Pollock, M. (2005). *Colormute: Race Talk Dilemmas in an American School.* Princeton, NJ: Princeton University Press.

Pollock, M. (2004). Race Wrestling: Struggling Strategically with Race in Educational Practice and Research. *American Journal of Education,* 111, 25–67.

Portilio, B., & McClary, G. (2004, Spring). Future Teachers Confront Globalization: A Critical Approach to "Good Citizenship" in Social Studies Education. *Electronic Magazine of Multicultural Education,* 6(6). Retrieved February 15, 2008, from http://www.eastern.edu/publications/emme/2004spring/porfilio_mcclary.html.

Portelli, J. P. (1993). Exposing the Hidden Curriculum. *Journal of Curriculum Studies,* 25(4), 343–358.

Puriefoy, W. D. (2001). Education and Race: School Boards Have Critical Roles to Play. National School Board Association. Retrieved November 11, 2007, from http://www.nsba.org/site/doc.

Putney, C. (2001). *Muscular Christianity: Manhood and Sports in Protestant America, 1880–1920.* Cambridge, MA: Harvard University Press.

Pyong, G. M. (1992, Spring). A Comparison of the Korean Minorities in China and Japan. *International Migration Review,* 26(1), 4–21.

Ravitch, D. (2000). *Left Back: A Century of Failed School Reforms.* New York: Simon & Schuster.

Ravitch, D. (1983). *The Troubled Crusade: American Education, 1945–1980.* New York: Basic Books.

Reardon, S. F., & Yun, J. T. (2005). Integrating Neighborhoods, Segregating Schools: The Retreat from School Desegregation in the South, 1990–2000. In Jack Boger & Gary Orfield (Eds.), *School Resegregation: Must the South Turn Back?* 51–69. Chapel Hill: University of North Carolina Press.

Reddick, R. J. (2006). The Gift That Keeps Giving: Historically Black College and University-Educated Scholars and Their Mentoring

at Predominantly White Institutions. *Educational Foundations,* 20(1–2), 61–84.

Reder, S., & Wikelund, K. (1993). Literacy, Development and Ethnicity: An Alaskan Example. In B. Street (Ed.), *Cross-cultural Approaches to Literacy.* Cambridge: Cambridge University Press, 176–197.

Rex, John. (1994, September). Review Article. *Contemporary Sociology,* 23(5), 646–648.

Rikowski, G. (2002, January 22). Globalisation and Education. Paper prepared for the House of Lords Select Committee on Economic Affairs, Inquiry into the Global Economy. Retrieved March 5, 2008, from http://firgoa.usc.es/drupal/node/4280/print.

Rist, R. (1970). Student Social Class and Teacher Expectations. *Harvard Educational Review,* 40, 411–451.

Rizvi, F. (2003, September). Globalization and the Cultural Politics of Race and Educational Reform. *Journal of Educational Change,* 4(3), 209–211.

Roberts, R. H. (2002). *Religion, Theology and the Human Sciences,* Cambridge: Cambridge University Press.

Rodriquez, N. M., & Villaverde, L. E. (Eds.). (2000). *Dismantling White Privilege: Pedagogy, Politics, and Whiteness. New York: Peter Lang.*

Roediger, D. L. (1999). *The Wages of Whiteness: Race and the Making of the American Working Class,* 2nd edition. New York: Routledge.

Rolo, M. A. (2007, March 9). Current News: Cherokee Nation Votes to Oust Freedmen from Tribal Rolls. *Diverse Issues in Higher Education.* Retrieved March 5, 2008, from http://www.diverseeducation.com/artman/publish/article_7102.shtml.

Roman, L. (2003, September). Education and the Contested Meanings of "Global Citizenship." *Journal of Educational Change,* 4(3), 269–293.

Roman, L. (1993). White Is a Color!: White Defensiveness, Postmodernism and Antiracist Pedagogy. In C. McCarthy & W. Critchlow (Eds.), *Race Identity and Representation in Education,* 71–88. New York: Routledge.

Roscigno, V. J. (1998). Race and the Reproduction of Educational Disadvantage. *Social Forces,* 76, 1033–1060.

Roscigno, V. J., & Ainsworth, D. (1999). Race, Cultural Capital, and Educational Resources: Persistent Inequalities and Achievement Returns. *Sociology of Education,* 72(3), 158–178.

Ross, W. W., & Pang, V. O. (2006). *Race, Ethnicity & Education.* Westport, CT: Praeger.

Rowley, L. L. (1998). Review of *Race, Culture, and the City: A Pedagogy for Black Urban Struggle* by Stephen Nathan Haymes. *The Journal of Negro Education,* 65(4), 477–479.

Rowley, L. L. (1997). Review of *The Future of the Race,* by Henry Louis Gates, Jr. and Cornel West. *The Journal of Negro Education,* 64(4), 486–488.

Rowley, S. J., Sellers, R. M., Chavous, T. M., & Smith, M. A. (1998). The Relationship Between Racial Identity and Self-esteem in African American College and High School Students. *Journal of Personality and Social Psychology,* 74, 715–724.

Ruby, R.H., & Brown, J.A. (1988). Indians of the Pacific Northwest. University of Oklahoma Press, Norman.

Sadker, M., & Sadker, D. (1994). *Failing at Fairness: How America's Schools Cheat Girls.* New York: Charles Scribners Sons, Macmillan Publishing Co.

Sadker, M., Sadker, D., & Steindam, S. (1989). Gender Equity and Educational Reform. *Educational Leadership,* 46(6), 44–47.

Sansone, L. (2003). *Blackness without Ethnicity: Constructing Race in Brazil.* New York: Palgrave Macmillan.

Saphier, J. (1997). *The Skillful Teacher: Building Your Teaching Skills.* Acton, MA: Research for Better Teaching.

Schlesinger, A. M. (1998). *The Disuniting of America: Reflections on a Multicultural Society,* revised edition. New York: W. W. Norton & Company.

Schmid, C. (2001). Educational Achievement, Language Minority Students, and the New Second Generation. *Sociology of Education,* 74, 71–87.

ScholarCentric. (undated). Success Highways. Retrieved November 21, 2007, from http://www.scholarcentric.com.

Schubert, W. (1986). *The Curriculum: Perspective, Paradigm, and Possibility.* New York: Macmillan.

Sellers, R. M., & Shelton, J. N. (2003). The Role of Racial Identity in Perceived Racial Discrimination. *Journal of Personality and Social Psychology,* 84, 1079–1092.

Sellers, R. M., Smith, M. A., Shelton, J. N., Rowley, S. J., & Chavous, T. M. (1998). Multidimensional Model of Racial Identity: A Reconceptualization of African American Racial Identity. *Personality and Social Psychology Review,* 2, 18–36.

Sherman, L. (2002). From Division to Vision: Achievement Climbs at a Reservation School High in the Rocky Mountains. *Northwest Education,* 8(1), 22–27.

Shimbori, M. (1979). Sociology of Education. *International Review of Education,* 25(2–3), 393–413.

Shulman, L. (1990). *Research in Teaching and Learning: A Project of the American Educational Research Association.* New York: Macmillan.

Singleton, G. (2005). *Courageous Conversations about Race: A Field Guide for Achieving Equity in Schools.* Thousand Oaks, CA: Sage Publications.

Sleeter, C. E. (2001). *Culture, Difference and Power*. New York: Teachers College Press.

Sleeter, C. E. (1996). *Multicultural Education as Social Activism*. Albany, NY: SUNY Press.

Slotkin, R. (1973). *Regeneration through Violence: The Mythology of the American Frontier, 1600–1860*. Middletown, CT: Wesleyan University Press.

Snavely, L., & Cooper, N. (1997). Competing Agendas in Higher Education: Finding a Place for Information Literacy. *Reference & User Services Quarterly, 37*(1), 53–62.

Sobel, M. (1989). *The World They Made Together: Black and White Values in Eighteenth-Century Virginia*. Princeton, NJ: Princeton University Press.

Soto, L. D. (2001). *Making a Difference in the Lives of Bilingual/Bicultural Children*. New York: Peter Lang.

Soto, L. D. (Ed.). (2000). *The Politics of Early Childhood Education*. New York: Peter Lang.

Soto, L. D. (1997). *Language, Culture, and Power. Bilingual Families and the Struggle for Quality Education*. Albany, NY: SUNY Press.

Spack, R. (2000). *America's Second Tongue: American Indian Education and the Ownership of English, 1860–1900*. Lincoln: University of Nebraska Press.

Spencer, M. B. (2006). Phenomenology and Ecological Systems Theory: Development of Diverse Groups. In W. Damon & R. Lerner (Eds.), *Handbook of Child Psychology,* 6th edition, volume 1, 829–893. New York: Wiley.

Spivey, D. (1978). *Schooling for the New Slavery: Black Industrial Education, 1868–1915*. Westport, CT: Greenwood.

Spring, J. (2004). *How Educational Ideologies are Shaping Global Society*. Mahwah, NJ: Lawrence Erlbaum Associates.

Spring, J. (1994). *Deculturalization and the Struggle for Equality: A Brief History of the Education of Dominated Cultures in the United States*. New York: McGraw-Hill.

Steele, C. M. (1999, August). Thin Ice: "Stereotype Threat" and Black College Students. *Atlantic Monthly, 284*, 44–47, 50–54.

Steele, C. M. (1992). Race and the Schooling of Black Americans. *Atlantic Monthly, 4*, 68–78.

Steele, C. M., & Aronson, J. (1995). Stereotype Threat and the Intellectual Test Performance of African Americans. *Journal of Personality and Social Psychology, 69*, 797–811.

Steele, S. (2006). *White Guilt: How Blacks and Whites Together Destroyed the Promise of the Civil Rights Era*. New York: HarperCollins.

Stepick, A. (2002). Becoming American, Constructing Ethnicity: Immigrant Youth and Civic Engagement. *Applied Developmental Science, 6*(4), 246–257.

Stewart, J. B. (2006, April). Sub-disciplinary Specializations and Disciplinary Maturation: Relationships among Afro-American Studies, Critical Race Studies, Diaspora Studies, African Studies, Afro-Latino/a Studies, and Africana Women's Studies at the Conversations for Sustaining Black Studies in the 21st Century. Ford Foundation Conference, New York City.

Stewart, J. B. (2004). *Flight in Search of Vision*. Trenton, NJ: Africa World Press.

Stewart, J. B. (1992). Reaching for Higher Ground: Toward an Understanding of Black/Africana Studies. *The Afrocentric scholar,* 1(1), 1–63.

Stoler, A. L. (1989, January). Rethinking Colonial Categories: European Communities and the Boundaries of Rule. *Comparative Studies in Society and History,* 31(1), 134–161.

Stoler, A. L. (1995). *Race and the Education of Desire: Foucault's History of Sexuality and the Colonial Order of Things*. Durham, NC: Duke University Press.

Stringfield, S. (2000, June). A Synthesis and Critique of Four Recent Reviews of Whole-School Reform in the United States. *School Effectiveness and School Improvement,* 11(2), 259–269.

Sunderman, G. L., & Orfield, G. (2006). The Unraveling of No Child Left Behind: How Negotiated Changes Transfer the Law. Retrieved May 20, 2006, from http://www.civilrightsproject.harvard.edu/ research/esea/NCLB_Unravel.pdf.

Taggart, L. A., & Kao, G. (2003, August). Effects of Social Capital on Minority and Immigrant Students' School Achievement. Paper presented at the annual meeting of the American Sociological Association, Atlanta Hilton Hotel, Atlanta, GA. Online Retrieved February 24, 2008, from http://www.allacademic.com/meta/ p107112_index.html.

Takaki, R. (2000). *Iron Cages: Race and Culture in 19th-Century America*. New York: Oxford University Press.

Tate, W. F. (1995, Summer). Returning to the Root: A Culturally Relevant Approach to Mathematics Pedagogy. *Theory into Practice,* 34(3), 166–173.

Tatum, B. (1992, Spring). Talking about Race, Learning about Racism. *Harvard Educational Review,* 62(1).

Taylor, E. (1998, Spring). A Primer on Critical Race Theory. *The Journal of Blacks in Higher Education,* 19, 122–124

Teachers21 (undated). Critical Actions for Promoting Educational Equity. Retrieved February 10, 2008, from http://www.teachers21.org/ documents/EquityPaper.doc.

Thelin, J. R. (2004). *A History of American Higher Education*. Baltimore, MD: Johns Hopkins University Press.

Thernstrom, A. (2006, May 10). Steele Sense: From White Racism to White Guilt, America Still Struggles with Race. *National Review*

Online. Retrieved February 16, 2008, from http://www.thernstrom. com/pdf/National%20Review%20Online_May10_2006.pdf.

Thernstrom, S., & Thernstrom, A. (2003). *No Excuses: Closing the Racial Gap in Learning.* New York: Simon & Schuster, 2003.

Thernstrom, S., & Thernstrom, A. (1997). *America in Black and White: One Nation, Indivisible.* New York: Simon & Schuster.

Thomas, L. A. (2000). On the Study of Race, Racism, and Health: A Shift from Description to Explanation. *International Journal of Health Services, 30*(1), 217–219.

Thomas, M. (2000). Anything but Race: The Social Science Retreat from Racism. Retrieved March 5, 2008, from http://www.rcgd.isr.umich. edu/prba/perspectives/winter2000/mthomas.pdf.

Thompson, A. (1995). Anti-racist Pedagogy—Art or Propaganda? Retrieved February 12, 2008, from http://www.ed.uiuc.edu/eps/ PES-Yearbook/95_docs/thompson.html.

Thompson, L. (1995, April). Teaching about Ethnic Minority Families Using a Pedagogy of Care. *Family Relations, 44,* 2129–2135.

Tierney, W. G. (1993). The College Experience of Native Americans: A Critical Analysis. In L. Weis & M. Fine (Eds.), *Beyond Silenced Voices,* 309–324. Albany, NY: SUNY Press.

Tomlinson, S. (2003, September). Globalization, Race and Education: Continuity and Change. *Journal of Educational Change, 4*(3), 213–230.

Toth, E. (1997). *Ms. Mentor's Impeccable Advice for Women in Academia.* Philadelphia: University of Pennsylvania Press.

Trifonas, P. P. (Ed.). (2005). *Communities of Difference: Culture, Language, Technology.* New York: Palgrave Macmillan.

Troyna, B. (1985). The Great Divide: Policies and Practices in Multicultural Education. *British Journal of Sociology of Education, 6*(2), 209–224.

Tyson, K., Darity, W., & Castellino, D. (2005). It's Not "a Black Thing": Understanding the Burden of Acting White and Other Dilemmas of High Achievement. *American Sociological Review, 70,* 582–605.

Varenne, H. (2000). An Introduction to Anthropology of Education: Culture—Possibilities and Consequences. Retrieved March 4, 2008, from http://varenne.tc.columbia.edu/hv/edu/anthredu/anthredu-first.html.

Vasquez, J. (1988). Contexts of Learning for Minority Students. *The Educational Forum, 52*(3), 243–253.

Wagstaff, L. H. (2004). *Zero-Tolerance Discipline: The Effect of Teacher Discretionary Removal on Urban Minority Students.* Unpublished dissertation, University of Texas, Austin.

Walker, E. (2003). Race, Class, and Cultural Reproduction: Critical Theories in Urban Education. *REDIE, 5*(2). Retrieved January 20, 2008, from http://redie.uabc.mx/vol5no2/contents-walker.html

Walker, V. S. (1996). *Their Highest Potential: An African American School Community in the Segregated South*. Chapel Hill: University of North Carolina Press.

Wallerstein, I. (1987). The Construction of Peoplehood: Racism, Nationalism, Ethnicity. *Sociological Forum, 2*(2), 373–388.

Wang, L. L. (1988). Meritocracy and Diversity in Higher Education: Discrimination against Asian. Americans in the Post-Bakke Era. *Urban Review, 20*, 189–209.

Wardekker, W. L. (1995). Identity, Plurality, and Education. *Philosophy of Education*. Retrieved on January 12, 2008, from http://www.ed.uiuc.edu/EPS/PES-Yearbook/95_docs/wardekker.html

Warren, E., & A. W. Tyagi, A. W. (2003). *The Two-Income Trap: Why Middle-Class Mothers and Fathers are Going Broke*. New York: Basic Books.

Washington, B. T. (1901/1963). *Up from Slavery*. New York: Doubleday.

Watkins, W. H. (2005). *Black Protest Thought and Education*. New York: Peter Lang.

Watkins, W. H. (2001). *The White Architects of Black Education: Ideology and Power in America, 1865–1954*. New York: Teachers College Press

Watkins, W. H. (1993, Fall). Black Curriculum Orientations: A Preliminary Inquiry. *Harvard Education Review, 63*(3), 321–338.

Watkins, W. H., Lewis, J. H., & Chou, V. (2001). *Race and Education: The Roles of History and Society in Educating African American Students*. Boston: Allyn & Bacon.

Weinberg, M. (1977). *A Chance to Learn: The History of Race and Education in the United States*. Cambridge: Cambridge University Press.

Weiss, S. (2003). *Lagging Achievement of Disadvantaged Students Remain a Critical Problem*. Denver, CO: Education Commission of the States.

Wexler, P. (1992). *Becoming Somebody: Toward a Social Psychology of School*. Washington, DC: Falmer Press.

Whiteley, S., Bennett, A., & Hawkins, S. (Eds.). (2004). *Music, Space and Place: Popular Music and Cultural Identity*. Burlington, VT: Ashgate.

Wiggins, G., & McTighe, J. (1998). *Understanding by Design*. Arlington, VA: Association for Supervision and Curriculum Development.

Wijeyesinghe, C., Griffin, P., & Love, B. (1997). Racism curriculum Design. In M. Adams, L. A. Bell, & P. Griffin (Eds.), *Teaching for Diversity and Social Justice: A Sourcebook*, 82–109. New York: Routledge.

Williams, H. A. (2005). *Self-taught African American Education in Slavery and Freedom*. Chapel Hill: University of North Carolina Press.

Williams, P. (1991). *The Alchemy of Race and Rights: Diary of a Law Professor*. Cambridge, MA: Harvard University Press.

Willie, C. V. (1978). *The Sociology of Urban Education: Desegregation and Integration.* Boston: Lexington Books.

Willie, C. V., & Edmonds, R. R. (1978). *Black Colleges in America.* New York: Teachers College Press.

Willinsky, J. (1998). *Learning to Divide the World: Education at Empire's End.* Minneapolis: London.

Wilson, W. J. (1987). *The Truly Disadvantaged: The Inner City, the Underclass, and Public Policy.* Chicago: University of Chicago Press.

Wilson, W. J. (1980). *The Declining Significance of Race—Blacks and Changing American Institutions.* Chicago: University of Chicago Press.

Winfield, L. (1986). Teacher Beliefs toward At-Risk Students in Inner-Urban Schools. *The Urban Review,* 18, 253–267.

Woodson, C. G. (1935/2000). *The Mis-education of the Negro.* Chicago: African-American Images.

Wortham, S. E. (2006). *Learning Identity: The Joint Emergence of Social Identification and Academic Learning.* New York: Cambridge University Press.

Yang, L. (2002, June). Theorizing Asian America: On Asian American and Postcolonial Asian Diasporic Women. *Intellectuals Journal of Asian American Studies,* 5(2), 139–178.

Yinger, J. M., & Simpson, G. E. (1978). The Integration of Americans of Indian Descent. *Annals of the American Academy,* 436, 136–151.

Yon, D. A. (2000). *Elusive Culture: Schooling, Race and Identity in Global Times.* Albany, NY: SUNY Press.

Yon, D. A. (1999). Pedagogy and the "Problem" of Difference: On Reading Community. *The Darker Side of Black. Qualitative Studies in Education,* 12(6), 623–641.

Young, J., & Braziel, J. E. (Eds.). (2006). *Race and the Foundations of Knowledge: Cultural Amnesia in the Academy.* Urbana: University of Illinois Press.

Zembylas, M. (2003, March). Interrogating "Teacher Identity": Emotion, Resistance, and Self-formation. *Educational Theory,* 53, 107–127.

Zhao, G. (2007, February). The Making of the Modern Subject: A Cross-cultural Analysis. *Educational Theory,* 57(1), 75–88.

Zwick, T. T., & Miller, K. W. (1996). A Comparison of Integrated Outdoor Education Activities and Traditional Science Learning with American Indian Students. *Journal of American Indian Education,* 35(2), 1–9.

Nonprint Resources and Journals

Columbia University Directory of Anti-bias Education Resources and Services—http://www.racematters.org/colunivdirantibiasedress-vcs.htm

Commission on Research in Black Education (CORIBE) http://www.coribe.org/homePage.html

Council for Basic Education—http://www.cbe.org

Council for Exceptional Children—http://www.cec.sped.org/

Electronic Guide for African Resources on the Internet—http://www.sas.upenn.edu/African_Studies/Home_Page/other.html

ERIC (Educational Research Information Center)—http://www.eric.ed.gov/

Ethnic Majority—http://www.ethnicmajority.com/Education.htm

Global School Net Foundation (GSN)—http://www.globalschoolnet.org/index.cfm

Multicultural Review—http://www.mcreview.com

The National Center for Culturally Responsive Educational Systems—http://www.nccrest.org/

National Center for Education Statistics—http://www.ed.gov/NCES/

National Women's History Project—http://www.nwhp.org

Native American Rights Fund—http://www.narf.org

Native American Teaching Project—http://www.cradleboard.org

Native American Tribes—http://www.afn.org/~native/tribesl.htm

NETWORK Education Program—www.networklobby.org/nep

Office for Civil Rights, U.S. Dept of Education—http://www.ed.gov/about/offices/list/ocr/know.html

Office of Bilingual and Minority Language Affairs (OBEMLA)—http://www.ed.gov/about/offices/list/oela/index.html?src=mr

Poverty & Race Research Action Council: Education—http://prrac.org/topic.php?topic_id=6

"Race" and Difference—Developing Practice in Lifelong Learning http://www.infed.org/lifelonglearning/b-race.htm

Race: A Teacher's guide—http://www.understandingrace.org/resources/for_teachers.html

Race Equity Project—http://lsnc.net/equity/education-race-resources

Rethinking Schools—http://www.rethinkingschools.org

Suggested Readings

Race and Education is a comprehensive and complex area of scholarship and practice. The previous chapters introduce some of the most important themes in the field. The following materials are intended to point you to other, more detailed readings and resources for specific themes and issues. They serve also as an introduction to both scholars and some of the more important books and journals that deal with aspects of the field.

Suggested Readings for Chapter One

Three important themes are introduced in Chapter One. The first of these is the meanings and scope of the field. Several important essays and books are mentioned in the chapter related to this theme. Let me mention a few of them here and indicate precisely what each offers for further reflection. First, the essay by the late Asa Hilliard cannot be emphasized enough as a starting point. While it represents only one way of thinking about race and education, it is a forthright and honest statement: it does not claim to be "neutral" or "disinterested" like so many other works. Since I share Hilliard's view that there is no value-neutral way of thinking about this topic, I prefer to direct you to him and authors who are up front about where they are coming from.

Another author who is clear about her position on this topic is Diane Ravitch (1983), author of *The Troubled Crusade: American Education, 1945–1980*. New York: Basic Books. In this volume, two chapters are particularly helpful: Chapter Five on "Race and Education: The Brown Decision" and Chapter Six: "Race and Education: Social Science and Law." Ravitch, a self-identified conservative educational historian, belongs to a group of scholars who emphasize a "liberal progressive" view of race and education. From this view, major strides have been made against blatant racist laws and policies of the past. According to some conservative critics, the new problems in education are due largely to problems of "radical" agitators who confuse the issues facing minorities, notably African Americans and Latinos.

From the conservative view, the important needed reforms include the cultural traditions of minorities that undermine efforts to bring them into the mainstream. Challenges to this perspective are numerous, including the work of Stanley Aronowitz and Henry Giroux (1985), *Education Under Siege: The Conservative, Liberal, and Radical Debate over Schooling*. South Hadley, MA: Bergin and Garvey.

The second major theme covered in Chapter One pertains to teacher education and the topic of race and education. A powerful essay on this topic is Peter S. Kowalczewski's (1982) "Race and Education: Racism, Diversity and Inequality, Implications for Multicultural Education." *Oxford Review of Education*, 8(2), 145–161. As indicated in Chapter One, he argues that the topic of race and education is made more difficult for teachers and prospective teachers because society has been so contradictory about the issues, what they mean, and what society is prepared to do about the issues.

A very good resource dealing with the various perspectives that have influenced how different countries frame and attack questions associated with race and education is Ranjit Arora's (2005) *Race and Ethnicity in Education*. Aldershot: Ashgate. Arora focuses on teacher education in England, indicating how contradictions undermine the nation's stated goal of preparing teachers to achieve a more inclusive and just education for the various ethnic minorities.

The third theme taken up in this chapter also pertains to teacher preparation as an intricate aspect of race and education. An excellent article dealing with the complex implications of race and education for the prospective teacher is Linda Valli's (2000) "The Dilemma of Race: Learning to Be Color Blind and Color Conscious." *Journal of Teacher*

Education, 16(3), 120–129. I have used Valli's essay in my race and education courses and detail some of my prospective teachers' reactions to the issues of color blindness and color consciousness in Aaron D. Gresson III's (2004) *America's Atonement: Racial Pain, Recovery Rhetoric and the Pedagogy of Healing.* New York: Peter Lang.

One of the most comprehensive, recent overviews of race in education scholarship is Brayboy, Bryan Mckinley Jones, Castagno, Angelina E. & Maughan, Emma (2007) "Equality and Justice For All? Examining Race in Education Scholarship." *Review of Research in Education* 31, 159–194. This journal chapter, in one of the premier education research journals, makes clear the interplay of research, policy, and practice issues that currently dominate the discourse of race and education. The reference list is both selective and comprehensive.

Suggested Readings for Chapter Two

All discussions of race and education rely on certain core concepts that may vary in definition, importance, and emphasis. These concepts, constructed within different specialties or disciplines, provide nuanced or slightly different but important views of what is real, important, and occurring with respect to race-related educational matters. These concepts include race, ethnicity, education, schooling, equality, domination, assimilation, acculturation, and culture. These terms, and others derived from them, are the main tools used to talk about race relations generally. One very helpful discussion of these and related concepts is James Banks's (2003) *Teaching Strategies for Ethnic Studies,* 7th edition. Boston: Allyn & Bacon. Banks provides both definitions for some of these concepts and illustrations of their applications, especially for a multicultural approach to education.

Over the years, scholars have changed or refined one term or another in an attempt to better present reality and the changes taking place in society as well as in the fields concerned with race and ethnic relations in general, and with race and education in particular. For example, there is educational historian Clarence Karier's (1975) *The Shaping of the American Educational State.* New York: Free Press. In this volume, Karier attempts to show how the guiding concerns within education shaped what we understood about minority education. As noted throughout the primer, however, there are always competing perspectives on race and education. A useful review of Karier's book is Harvey Neufeldt's (1976, Spring) "Textbooks in American Educational History—A Review." *History of Education Quarterly,* 16(1) (1976, Spring), 93–100.

Many scholars, public officials, and laypersons have contributed to the overall picture of race and ethnicity in American education. One of the most useful introductions to some of these thinkers and how they have come to their positions on the topic is found in the work of James Banks, one of the founding scholars in multicultural education. Two very useful essays by him are: Banks, James (1995), "The Historical Reconstruction of Knowledge about Race: Implications for Transformative Teaching." *Educational Researcher,* 24(2), 15–25; and Banks, James (2002), "Race, Knowledge Construction, and Education in the USA: Lessons from History." *Race, Ethnicity and Education,* 5(1), 7–27. James Anderson,

Professor of History and Educational Policy Studies and Head of the Department of Educational Policy Studies, at University of Illinois, Urbana-Champaign, is another important source. Anderson's (1988) award-winning book is *The Education of Blacks in the South: 1860–1935*. Chapel Hill: University of North Carolina Press. In it he gives a minority feel for the guiding concerns that shaped race and schooling just after the Civil War. In addition to this source, one might also see William Watkins's (2001) *The White Architects of Black Education: Ideology and Power in America, 1865–1954*. New York: Teachers College Press. Watkins gives a powerful argument, supplemented by primary sources, of how important it was for the giants of American business to shape the education received by minorities.

An excellent review of Watkins's and other recent histories of minority education is Christopher M. Span's (2002, April) "New and Important Contributions to the Educational History of African Americans, Latino/as, and Native Americans." *Educational Researcher,* 31(3), 33–36. This review essay also offers an excellent model for developing a critical attitude toward scholarship on race and education.

Vernellia R. Randall, professor of law at Dayton University has a Web site (http://academic.udayton.edu/Race/04needs/education06.htm) with a number of useful resources including difficult-to-get journals. One such resource is an excellent article on the law, race, and education by Monique Langhorne entitled "The African American Community: Circumventing the Compulsory Education System." *Beverly Hills Bar Association Journal,* 33 (2000, Summer/Fall), 12–31, 13–17. In addition to coverage of the law and education with respect to minorities, this essay is a very useful introduction to minorities and schooling. It goes into much more detail than is typically found in introductory education textbooks.

The issue of public policy is implicit in the guiding concerns identified in Chapter Two. All of the various minorities have had to fight for inclusion in schooling and the larger society. The guiding concerns or values have been met with counter or alternative values and concerns. The dialectical nature of these competing interests can be seen in the recurring quality of many education issues such as intelligence and social justice. A recent discussion of some of these dynamics is Beverly Tatum's (2006) *Can We Talk about Race? And Other Conversations in an Era of School Resegregation*. Boston: Beacon Press. Tatum, psychologist and researcher, is a recent president of the HBCU Spelman College. This book is especially important because Tatum addresses how a refusal to discuss "race" empowers it over humans.

Suggested Readings for Chapter Three

The material dealing with the achievement gap is wide-ranging. As indicated in the chapter, opinions vary considerably regarding the causes and cures for the observed achievement gap. Perhaps it would be useful to begin with Abigail and Stephan Thernstrom's (2003) *No Excuses: Closing the Racial Gap in Learning*. New York: Simon & Schuster. This volume takes a particular slant on the gap, but it also provides a broad-ranging discussion of the issues. An excellent source of counterarguments to the volume is provided at the Amazon.com site http://www.amazon.ca/

No-Excuses-Closing-Racial-Learning/dp/customer-reviews/0743204468
?ie=UTF8&customer-reviews.start=11.

Another important source to begin further study is Christopher
Jencks and Meredith Phillips's (Eds.) (1998) *The Black-White Test Score
Gap.* Washington, DC: Brookings Institution. In this edited volume, these
scholars have included work by several leading thinkers who review a
broad range of research and scholarship on the education gap.

An important Web source is Danielle Lavin-Loucks's (2006) "The
Academic Achievement Gap," http://www.thewilliamsinstitute.org/. This
report surveys test score data from the National Assessment of Educational
Progress (NAEP) and relates it to previous research findings. This document takes the position that families and schools can make a difference
in narrowing the gap.

Other reports largely parallel the findings and conclusions of the
above scholars. By and large, differences in findings and interpretations
are due to the sources of the data collected. The different definitions of
the achievement gap are another source of variance. The article "The
Black-White Achievement Gap, Family-School Links, and the Importance
of Place." *Sociological Inquiry* 69 (2), 159–186, by Vincent J. Roscigno
(1999), uses data from two national surveys to show how "family and
school influences are themselves embedded in, and partially a function
of, broader structures and spatial variations in class- and race-based
opportunity." Using data from National Educational Longitudinal Survey
and the 1990 Census data, he shows how educational resources and family background influence the gap in academic achievement.

Another worthy work is Ronald Ferguson's essay (1998) "Teachers'
Perceptions and Expectations and the Black-White Test Score Gap," from
the C. Jencks and M. Phillips volume (273–317). Washington, DC:
Brookings Institution. Ferguson offers a useful review of the literature
up to the late 1990s regarding African American student academic performance and its relation to teacher perceptions, expectations, and
classroom behavior. Material presented in Chapter Four on cultural
competence and teachers provide more recent and practical insights into
this topic; still, it is important to know about earlier work such as
Ferguson's.

Suggested Readings for Chapter Four

There is a vast body of scholarship on race and education; work has been
carried out by a number of scholars writing within specific disciplines
such as sociology, psychology, political science, history, and anthropology. In addition, many scholars have written from a multi- or interdisciplinary perspective. Perhaps the best way of gaining a fuller feel for the
specific orientations of these different approaches to this vast topic is to
peruse some of the main journals associated with these disciplines and
their interest in education and schooling for minorities. You can begin
this process by identifying some guiding issues and reading recent journal works on the topic. For instance,

- **Education and Social Inequalities:**

Farkas, George. (2003). Racial Disparities and Discrimination in Education: What Do We Know, How Do We Know It, and What Do We Need To Know. *Teachers College Record,* 105, 1119–1146.

■ **Curriculum and Pedagogy**:
Pescosolido, B. A., Grauerholtz, E., & Milkie, M. A. (1996). Culture and Conflict: The Portrayal of Blacks in U.S. Children's Picture Books Through the Mid- and Late-Twentieth Century. *American Sociological Review,* 62, 443–464.

Generals, D. (2000). Booker T. Washington and Progressive Education: An Experimentalist Approach to Curriculum Development and Reform. *Journal of Negro Education,* 69, 215–234.

■ **Language and Policy**:
Myhill, W. N. (2004). The State of Public Education and the Needs of English Language Learners in the Era of "No Child Left Behind." *Journal of Gender, Race, and Justice,* 8, 93–152.

■ **Pluralism and Equity in Schooling**:
Olneck, M. R. (1990, February). The Recurring Dream: Symbolism and Ideology in Intercultural and Multicultural Education. *American Journal of Education,* 98(2), 147–174.

Another way of seeing how different scholarly trends have evolved with respect to the study of race in education is to begin with some of the historical works on race and education. For instance, consider the special issue of *The Journal of Negro Education:* Carroll, G., & Allen, W. R. (Eds.) (2000). "Knocking at Freedom's Door: Race, Equity, and Affirmative Action in U.S. Higher Education." *Journal of Negro Education,* 69(1/2), 1–149. This issue provides a broad-ranging overview of many of the issues and leading researchers who have addressed minority higher education.

Because "race" and "ethnicity" are concepts that have changing meanings, scholarship has increasingly addressed the need to adjust as well. In doing this, more recent scholars also critique previous work on race and education. This newer work can be a useful introduction to previous work. Consider, for example, Y. Gunaratnam's (2003) *Researching "Race" and Ethnicity: Methods, Knowledge and Power.* London: Sage Publications. Although intended for the advanced student of research, this volume addresses the problem of using race as a category by critiquing (thus reviewing) some of the important earlier scholarship on race and ethnicity.

Finally, there are several excellent encyclopedic resources. These not only provide broad, updated overviews of specific topics in race and education, they also serve as guides to the scholarship in education as it evolves over time. A good starting point is the four-volume series by Praeger/Greenwood: Wayne, R. E., & Ooka, V. (Eds.). (2006). *Race, Ethnicity, and Education.* Westport, CT: Greenwood. Each of the four volumes has different editors and authors, but together they deal with the guiding ideas or issues that have guided policy and practice in race/ethnic education.

Suggested Readings for Chapter Five

Three themes are taken up in the chapter on race and pedagogy. These include the broad areas of culturally sensitive teaching, school reforms, and higher education and minorities. Much of the literature presented in the chapter is the best starting place for further reading on these themes. But a few additional sources might be mentioned here. First, you might start with T. C. Howard's (2003, Summer) "Culturally Relevant Pedagogy: Ingredients for Critical Teacher Reflection." *Theory into Practice*, 42(3), 195–202. In this piece, Tyrone Caldwell focuses on the role of reflection in preparing teachers for culturally relevant teaching.

Another useful resource deals with teacher expectations and responsibility. Diamond, J. B., Randolph, A., & Spillane, J. P. (2004, March). "Teachers' Expectations and Sense of Responsibility for Student Learning: The Importance of Race, Class, and Organizational Habitus." *Anthropology & Education Quarterly*, 35(1), No. 1, 75–98. This article focuses on the educational needs of African American students; particular emphasis is placed on showing how school leaders can help teachers to assume greater responsibility for student learning. Because of the emphasis on school administrator leadership, the article contributes to the clarification of the relation between student learning and effective building level leadership. One useful review of the influence of "school culture"—values, beliefs, and relationships—on success is at the Southwest Educational Development Laboratory Web site: Victoria Boyd, School Context: Bridge or Barrier to Change, http://www.sedl.org/change/school/culture.html.

Racial identity as a construct or theory has been long acknowledged when thinking of African Americans or "Blacks." It is a less well thought about idea with respect to "Whites." But since the 1970s, a growing number of scholars and researchers have turned their attention to the complex dimensions that constitute "racial identity" for everyone who has been racialized. How people understand themselves as a racial being is related to what some scholars refer to as "resolutions." This term refers to the successive steps people go through as they solve or resolve previous ways of seeing themselves and others. An excellent illustration of this orientation is Mark M. Leach, John T. Behrens, & N. Kenneth La Fleur's (2002, April) "White Racial Identity and White Racial Consciousness: Similarities, Differences, and Recommendations." *Journal of Multicultural Counseling and Development*, 30, 66–80.

Postcolonial studies are a new field that addresses many of the issues and themes discussed throughout the primer. What kinds of research ought to be conducted and the methods to be followed are two such themes. In addition, shifting identity—as student, teacher, and researcher—is another related theme. A recent special issue of the very important journal *Race Ethnicity and Education* brings these themes together in several essays. A good starting point here is S. L. Daza's (2008, March) "Decolonizing Researcher Authenticity." *Race Ethnicity and Education*, 11(1) (2008, March), 71–85. Daza's article is concerned with the researcher's relationship to her or his focus of inquiry and asks how this relationship is affected and negotiated in terms of three axes of difference: ethnolinguistic affiliation, sexual orientation, and race/skin color.

Another related article in this issue of the journal is C. Dillard's (2008, March). "Re-membering Culture: Bearing Witness to the Spirit of Identity in Research." *Race Ethnicity and Education,* 11(1), 87–93. Dillard's essay is very interesting because it tries to show how a postcolonial agenda invites, even forces, us to shift from using race as a way of identifying ourselves in the search for a more inclusive and socially healing identity, perhaps in spiritual terms.

Much confusion exists around the nature of minority parents' and students' thinking and behaviors with respect to higher education. Do they think about it at all? How do they participate in thinking about funding college, school selection, and successful completion of college?

A very useful way of entering this area of minority higher education is through a study aimed at revealing families in action: Knight, M. G., Norton, N. E. L., Bentley, C. C., & Dixon, I. R. (2004, March). "The Power of Black and Latina/o Counterstories: Urban Families and College-Going Processes." *Anthropology & Education Quarterly,* 35(1), 99–120. These scholars examined the college-related experiences of 27 African American and Latina/o families in order to understand the diversity of practices utilized by working-class and poor families to support their children's college-going processes. Using ethnographical methods they were able to expand the typically reported understanding of what positive efforts these families made to see that their children might get into college.

Suggested Readings for Chapter Six

An excellent initial resource for a general overview of globalization can be found at the Web site for the Center for Economic and Policy Research: Weisbrot, M. (1999, October). "Globalization: A Primer." http://www.cepr.net/index.php/globalization-a-primer/. Focusing specifically on globalization and education, there is M. Gibbons's (2002, September) "Globalisation and the Future of Higher Education." http://www.bi.ulaval.ca/Globalisation- Universities/pages/actes/GibbonsMichael.pdf. Michael Gibbons, at the time, secretary general of the Association of Commonwealth Universities, provides a perspective from the Canadian context.

Finally, a comprehensive, multinational perspective is provided in Nicholas C. Burbules's (Ed.) (2000) *Globalization and Education: Critical Perspectives.* New York: Routledge. Both educational policy and practice are examined through articles focused on such issues as feminism, multiculturalism, and new technology.

Index

Peter Lang PRIMERS
in Education

Peter Lang Primers are designed to provide a brief and concise introduction or supplement to specific topics in education. Although sophisticated in content, these primers are written in an accessible style, making them perfect for undergraduate and graduate classroom use. Each volume includes a glossary of key terms and a References and Resources section.

Other published and forthcoming volumes cover such topics as:

- Standards
- Popular Culture
- Critical Pedagogy
- Literacy
- Higher Education
- John Dewey
- Feminist Theory and Education

- Studying Urban Youth Culture
- Multiculturalism through Postformalism
- Creative Problem Solving
- Teaching the Holocaust
- Piaget and Education
- Deleuze and Education
- Foucault and Education

Look for more Peter Lang Primers to be published soon. To order other volumes, please contact our Customer Service Department:

800-770-LANG (within the US)
212-647-7706 (outside the US)
212-647-7707 (fax)

To find out more about this and other Peter Lang book series, or to browse a full list of education titles, please visit our website:

www.peterlang.com